D1715909

# Handgun Hunting

# HANDGUN HUNTING

*by Major George C. Nonte, Jr.*
*and Lee E. Jurras*

*Winchester Press*

Library of Congress Catalog Card Number: 75-9267
ISBN: 0-87691-211-0

Library of Congress Cataloging in Publication Data

Nonte, George C
  Handgun hunting.

  Includes index.
    1. Hunting. 2. Pistols. I. Jurras, Lee E., joint author. II. Title.
  SK36.9.N66       799.2'13       75-9267
  ISBN 0-87691-211-0

Published by Winchester Press
205 E. 42nd St., New York 10017

Printed in the United States of America

# Contents

# Author's Preface

I've been a handgun buff ever since I can remember. The men in the Nonte family were shooters, and I was introduced to the sport at an early age. My first recollections of shooting a one-hand firearm date back to the early '30s on the ancestral homestead down in southern Indiana. There, one Sunday afternoon, my lean and gangling Uncle Ray dug his two 1900-vintage Iver Johnsons out of a closet in the big two-story, chestnut-log house on the bluff, and announced that the *men* would all go shooting—and "Junior can come and watch."

I watched, with uncommon attention, and persuaded Uncle Ray to let me pop off a few .22 Shorts. The experience was indescribable, even though I'd shot rifles occasionally since I was four or five years old. But what really frosted the cake was listening to my uncle tell how he'd knocked scores of squirrels out of the river-bottom beeches with those same battered Iver Johnsons, and how he often managed to keep rabbit in the stewpot by walking the fields in winter. And, of course, he also mentioned the dozens of cottonmouths he had decapitated with .22 Shorts along the boundaries of the riverbank corn and peanut fields below the bluff. *Cottonmouths*—the very sound of the word added the essential elements of danger and prickling near-fear.

I was hooked. Right then I resolved that some day I'd own good handguns and take them after all imaginable game. In the ensuing 40-odd years, I've done just that. My first very own "shortgun" was an unidentifiable (as to maker) spur-trigger five-shooter chambered in .32 rimfire. It cost me the impressive sum of $1.50, and it looked big and powerful enough to handle anything. In those days, no one cared if a 10- or 12-year-old boy scraped up a few coins and bought himself a belt gun, as long as he had sense enough not to shoot himself, the livestock, or some innocent bystander. I somehow avoided those pitfalls in spite of tender years, and have never since been without a fair array of handguns.

Since those distant times my guns have given me tremendous pleasure and no small amount of toothsome meals, beginning with cottontails and squirrels as a lad, and progressing gradually up the ladder through all manner of quarry. I've used a handgun to hunt various predators, deer, black bear, wild hogs ranging from the feral Florida variety to 500-pound genuine Russians in Azerbaidzhan, and I've taken various kinds of African game as well. In the process, I've used everything from .22 Shorts in an old H&R Breaktop up through the biggest Magnum sixguns and the recently developed, fabulous Auto Mags.

Handguns have made me technically a better hunter, and mentally a better conservationist. I've learned that there is more satisfaction in stalking a single animal to 40 or 50 yards and dispatching him neatly with one sixgun bullet than there is in a whole season of easier "wait-and-shoot" hunting. On four continents, in countless foreign countries, the handgun has been my constant hunting companion.

Today, anti-gun interests and anti-hunting bigots appear determined to eliminate from the public not only handguns but hunting as well. They may eventually succeed unless we sportsmen make ourselves heard in Congress.

With this in mind, and with many memories of exciting and pleasant experiences hunting with a handgun, I have written this book in the fervent hope that by so doing I can open an entirely new field of pleasant and productive activities to countless thousands of men and women. And, of course, it is also my fervent hope that by swelling the ranks of today's handgun hunters, I can help to counteract the misguided efforts to eliminate this most ancient and honorable occupation and recreation of man.

Now, before discussing all the guns and techniques, I must comment briefly on one other matter. You've probably already noticed that this book has a double by-line—by Major George C. Nonte, Jr., and Lee E. Jurras—yet the word "I" keeps cropping up. I (George

Nonte, that is) find it natural to write in the first person singular. Most writers do. Besides, much of the advice in these pages is based on my own experiences, which I'll be sharing with you. The hands at the typewriter are George Nonte's, but two brains are at work here, Lee's as well as mine. Lee has accompanied me on many of my hunts, and you'll be reading about our combined experiences with guns, loads, and techniques. He helped to prepare much of the material presented here, and some of that material is based on his ballistic testing, his field testing, his work in developing high-performance handgun loads for big game. So this book really is by both of us. And a third man has to get some of the credit for helping us put it all together. My old friend Bob Elman, a hunting editor who has worked with me before, volunteered to do so again because he felt that reading the manuscript might make him a better handgun hunter. I hope it helped him as much as he helped us. And I hope this book will help you, too.

GEORGE C. NONTE, JR.

A photo like this, recording a fine springbok trophy and the gun that took him, will be treasured by any handgun hunter for life.

# 1

## Why Hunt with Handguns?

"Why under the sun would anyone want to go out and hunt a deer or a bear with a revolver or automatic?"

"You must be out of your mind. Nobody can count on killing winter meat with a sixgun."

"You're gonna do *what* in Africa? Better pay up your insurance before you go messin' after a lion with that puny sixgun . . ."

Those are just a few of the typical reactions I've heard after mentioning casually that I had done, or was planning to do, a particular type of hunting with a handgun. And those remarks didn't always come from non-hunters or from people who knew nothing about handguns. They came from ardent hunters and shooters, including some who make their living with handguns. Many a policeman who accepts the idea of using a piddling little .38 Special revolver to defend his own or other lives against dangerous criminals will shudder at the notion of coming along into the swamps with that same revolver to help kill a wild hog for a barbecue. Conventional rifle and scattergun hunters have heard and read so much about the difficulties and supposed ineffectiveness of handgunning that it is almost impossible for them to visualize a sixgun or auto as a practical hunting instrument for anything bigger than a field mouse. And so they ask, "Why?"

"Sportsmanship" is a much overworked word, but I can't think of any word that describes one aspect of handgun hunting more accurately. When we think of sportsmanship, we think of achieving a particular goal by fair means within a framework of legal and moral rules and in such a manner as to give us a personal sense of satisfaction and accomplishment, along with the pleasure of knowing we are developing a skill to a high degree. Sportsmanship is playing a game to win, developing and sharpening our skills and abilities toward that end. And the demonstrable fact that a handgun *is* a most inefficient hunting arm and a difficult one to use makes it that much more sporting if used safely and with regard for the game. A good hunter holds his fire if he doesn't think he can make a clean kill, which means that a good handgun hunter holds his fire even more often than a conscientious rifle hunter. In short, the more difficult the accomplishment, the more "sporting" we consider it to be. There are those who hunt squirrels and rabbits only with .22 rifles, sneering at others who go after the same game with shotguns—insisting that the rifle with its single projectile is more sporting than a basket-size spread of pellets hurled in the general direction of the target. The shotgunner's answer is that his method is just as sporting because he shoots at moving targets. True! He could probably save ammunition while putting more squirrels in the pot if he restricted himself to stationary targets, but that would be too easy, not challenging enough, not "sporting" enough. The sporting content of a particular endeavor is generally conceded to connect directly with the difficulty of accomplishment. And if you think hunting with a handgun is not more difficult than with rifles and shotguns, then, friend, you just haven't tried it yet.

Let's take a look at the relative difficulty of handgun hunting. Where small game is concerned, let's compare the handgun with the shotgun most commonly used on rabbits and squirrels. A typical setup will be with the hunter moving slowly in a known game area, gun loaded and at the ready, eyes and ears alert for a target. Suddenly, out of the brush at his feet or out of a leafy clump up in a tree, a furry animal bursts from cover and attempts to escape at full speed. In the very short time the quarry remains in sight, the hunter quickly unsafeties his scattergun, swings on target, and pulls the trigger—and a charge of shot 18 or 20 inches (or more, depending on range) in diameter and containing a couple hundred or more pellets is hurled at the animal. So long as the gun is aligned well enough on target for any portion of that circular shot pattern to hit it, the animal will most likely be bagged. This isn't to say that shots won't be missed, for they will, but no particularly precise alignment of gun on target is required to achieve a hit. Now place a hunter armed with a handgun in the same circumstances, and let's see what he must do to avoid being skunked.

First of all, he must move much more quietly and covertly, and be much more alert. If he simply walks in until an animal is spooked, he may never be able to even fire a reasonably well-aligned shot before it disappears. He must locate his quarry *before* it attempts to flee, then freeze and avoid giving alarm; then wait and watch or stalk until the animal gives him a reasonably good chance for a killing shot. He must wait until the animal is still and presents a certain target, and then must bring his gun into alignment and squeeze off the shot without frightening his quarry. He must align the sights and squeeze the trigger to deliver the single, tiny bullet precisely to a target area less than two inches in diameter—and that is a hell of a lot more precise operation than blanketing the target with a cluster of pellets. In short, the successful use of a handgun on small game often requires a higher degree of concentration, marksmanship, observation, and woodcraft than the use of shoulder arms.

When it comes to larger game, let's say deer and black bear, we can compare the use of a handgun with the rifle. The typical rifle hunter will cruise the timber where he has reason to expect game, alert for tracks and other signs, and will eventually hope to locate his quarry in a reasonably clear area, unalarmed and offering a standing shot. He'll then get his rifle into position, aim carefully, and squeeze off the shot. His rifle and cartridge will usually be capable of placing all shots within at least a three- or four-inch group at 100 yards, and at that range the bullet's trajectory will be so flat that he needs simply hold or aim on the point he wishes to hit. In addition, the cartridge will possess at least as much energy as the old .30–30 Winchester, and most likely will be even more powerful. In short, there will be no doubt whatsoever about the bullet's ability to penetrate and kill the animal with any reasonably well-placed shot.

The handgun hunter possesses nowhere near that many advantages of accuracy, power, and flatness of trajectory. While his actions until he spots his quarry will be nearly the same as the rifle hunter's, at that point things change. First of all, the combination of hunter/gun/cartridge is probably capable of delivering no better than 10- to 12-inch groups at best at 100 yards, and with any conventional sixgun or auto, the 100-yard trajectory height will be several inches. This combination makes it essential that the hunter not shoot at 100 yards or more, but that he revert to careful stalking until he's within

If anyone questions the "why" of handgun hunting, he's never experienced the throat-drying thrill of Indianing up within range of an elusive trophy like one of these pronghorn bucks and then making a clean shot.

*certain* hitting range without alarming the animal. While a reasonably good rifle shot with a modern high-velocity rifle may take his deer wherever he sees it up to as much as 300 yards, the handgunner must close to within 50 to 75 yards at the outside, and closer is even better. Any woodsman will tell you that the closer you get to an animal the more likely you are to alarm it by your scent, sound, or sight. If the wind is right and there is even a little concealment, a rifleman can sit back at 300 yards, smoke a cigarette and eat his lunch without alarming a feeding deer. That means he has plenty of time to get into a good solid position and take the deer with little effort other than the concentration of the shot. But if you are a handgunner, you must begin a slow and laborious stalk that might take hours, and you run a high risk that by the time you get close enough for a sure shot, the animal will move on or become alarmed and take off, leaving you with nothing to show for your efforts but bruised knees and sweat.

To top it off, the handgun is far less powerful than the rifle, and unless the shot is very precisely placed you stand a good chance of only wounding the animal. I'm well aware that much ado is made about the power of Magnum handguns. However, in the final analysis, even the much-vaunted .44 Magnum possesses a good deal less power than the .30–30 Winchester. And it possesses less than half the power of the popular .30–06 and comparable cartridges so much in use today.

So, handgun hunting for large or small game *is* difficult, more difficult under normal conditions than taking the same game with a scattergun or high-power rifle. Handgun hunting therefore presents a greater challenge to the skill of the hunter, and it is this challenge that many sportsmen seek.

Danger, too, enters into handgun hunting of at least some species. Virtually any potentially dangerous animal can be shot at 100 yards or so with a modern rifle in a caliber suitable for the purpose— without any danger to the shooter under normal circumstances. Even if a poor shot is made and the animal charges, the time it takes it to cover the distance allows for careful follow-up shots. But with even the most powerful handguns, one must approach game much more closely, and if a poor shot is made, far less time is required for the quarry to reach the hunter in the event of a charge. The reduction in time is not all that increases the danger. The fact that even the .44 Magnum possesses so little power in comparison to modern big-game rifle cartridges makes it far more likely that any really big animal will be able to charge after the first shot. It also makes it far more likely that in the event of a charge even several follow-up shots may be insufficient to stop the animal before he reaches the hunter.

Therefore, when one takes a handgun after any potentially dangerous species—bear, boar, big cats, and some of the larger hoofed and horned species—there is a certain anticipation of danger. The *actual* danger is probably a good deal less than it looms in our mind, but danger there is, raising the hunt to a new level of adventure. Perhaps the element of danger has been exaggerated occasionally by self-glorifying writers, but even a 15-pound dik-dik has been known to kill a man with its diminutive needle-pointed horns when he didn't finish it off properly. And I've had a wounded 275-pound wild boar charge and fall so close at the last shot that I could reach out and touch his snout with my hand without moving from the spot where I fired.

Game conservation must also be considered. Pseudo-"environmentalists" have accused hunters of being ravagers of nature. *True* conservationists, those properly educated and experienced in game behavior, biology, habitat, etc., know and can prove that sport hunting has not ever seriously threatened *any* North American species. Yet the common claim of the sidewalk conservationist is that hunters "kill too much." These self-appointed critics generally believe that if hunting were completely prohibited no species would ever again become extinct (defying irrefutable historical evidence) and all wild animals would live happily ever after in an idyllic Bambi-filled woodland devoid of any hazard. Hunters are constantly under pressure to show evidence of their conservation activities. Actually, they are the most productive true conservationists in that *their money* pays for almost all worthwhile conservation efforts.

When a hunter takes to the field with a handgun, he becomes a game conservationist not only in terms of this financial support but in terms of a self-imposed restraint on his harvesting of game: That is, because he chooses to use a handgun, under identical conditions he will be able to kill less game than a rifleman. An area reporting, say, 70 percent hunter success on whitetail deer among riflemen will probably show a handgun-hunter success rate of 25 percent or less.

What we've already discussed are fairly tangible reasons why people hunt with handguns. But while they are the most obvious, there are many, many more which are not so easily identified or explained. For instance, I feel that some of handgun hunting's appeal has its roots in the legendary days of the self-reliant, woods-wise, pistol-carrying frontiersman, whose handgun was kept ready for any emergency, including Indian attack, unexpected meetings with bears, encounters with road agents, stock raids by predators, or maybe just an occasional opportunity to collect extra meat for the table.

Another intangible reason for hunting with a handgun is merely an extension of one of the basic motivations for all hunting. In distant times, man lived by hunting and gathering. To provide food, he faced the dangers of the wilderness, fought for meat, and carried it home in triumph that his family might survive. The urge to do so is still strongly present, though in these times man's traditional "hunting" for food to support his family ends at the supermarket.

This primeval—perhaps instinctive—urge to capture one's own food is surely felt by *all* hunters and fishermen alike. The young lad, such as my own, who visits the river bank daily to bring home a string of bullheads and an occasional bass is satisfying the same yearning as the wealthy attorney on a pack trip after elk in the Rockies. Even the fly-fishing purist who returns most of his catch to the water is satisfying that primeval urge. The handgun hunter is no different, except that he wants the stalking and the killing to be more difficult and more dangerous so that he can satisfy the urge more fully and feel a deeper sense of accomplishment. I, for one, would hate to see this primeval urge bred out of man. If the day comes when it disappears entirely—when men no longer sally forth to the wilds—that day will mark the beginning of man's decline.

# 2

---

# *History of Handguns in Hunting*

I don't suppose it would ever be possible to pin down a particular point in time or geography when and where some pistolero drew down with a flintlock horse pistol—or perhaps a wheel lock or a matchlock in an even earlier period—and slew some animal for food, sport, or protection. Whenever it was, it's extremely doubtful that he was engaged in serious hunting. He was probably simply confronted with an opportunity to bag the main course of a meal, or found himself suddenly threatened by an animal, and dispatched it with his firearm from belt or saddle holster.

Certainly firearms were used for various sorts of hunting soon after their appearance on the scene. Contemporary writings often refer to *any* firearms other than cannon or artillery as "handguns." In the context of the day, I suppose then that we might even say handguns have been used for hunting from the very beginning. But of course the handgun we speak of today is capable of being aimed and fired by means of only one hand, in spite of the fact that the second hand is often used to steady it. Even though those earliest cannon-lock guns may have been called handguns, and were held and aimed ("directed" would be a better word) with only one hand, they don't really qualify. The only reason they were held and aimed with one hand was that the other hand was occupied in introducing a slow-

8

match or other glowing or hot instrument to the touch hole to fire the piece.

Be all that as it may, it's certain that at some point in time some pistol-armed gentleman drew down upon an animal and dispatched it. We can only speculate, but it seems most likely that some cold and hungry soldier, far from his rations, probably even separated from his comrades, resolved that the pistol in his belt or saddle holster would provide him with fresh meat. Perhaps his target wasn't even wild game, but some unfortunate farmer's goat or sheep. Considering the quality of our hungry soldier's firearm, he probably faced no more difficulty at a few paces than we do today at long range on the wildest of game. Actually, if our hungry trooper had the foresight to load his shortgun with "swan drops," some form of shot, or even gravel, that first kill might not have been difficult at all.

Hunting with any pistol loaded with a single ball could not have become practical until the advent of the rifled barrel. Not until then could one reasonably expect to hit a target even the size of deer at more than a handful of yards. Hunting also did not become practical until the introduction of the wheel lock with its reasonably certain ignition.

Even long before practical firearms existed, hunting in Europe was the right of the privileged aristocracy, and anyone else caught taking game was likely to be summarily executed to reduce possible future transgressions by his peers. All game belonged to the landowners or landholders, the aristocracy, who treated it as a *crop* which served the dual purpose of filling the larder and providing sport. Considering that the aristocracy took great pride in their sporting accomplishments, it is quite likely that at some time they used pistols for hunting, probably from horseback on game that could be run down, simply stepping upward from the practice of killing it with the lance which had been in vogue for centuries.

In North America, the New World, game was plentiful, easily approached, and firearms were often held dear. While legend has it that the frontiersman never stepped out the door without his long Kentucky rifle, there is evidence that some carried pistols of similar type as a matter of greater convenience. There are also references to the use of these pistols in killing predators or bears and other dangerous animals that might come along when the rifle was not in reach. I've seen a casual reference in old writings to killing alligators with flintlock pistols in Louisiana, indicating it was considered quite sporting. And when Washington Irving wrote about his tour of the Western prairies in the 1830s, he mentioned the use of pistols in hunting buffalo from horseback.

Probably, though, deliberate hunting with the handgun received its greatest impetus among foraging soldiers during the American Civil War, and among those mustered-out soldiers who trekked homeward or west to the frontier after that bloodiest of conflicts. The cavalry trooper, trained to kill the enemy from the back of a galloping horse with a pistol or revolver, would logically have applied the same tactics to game or stock if he got hungry.

A good friend of mine tells of the ordeal undergone by an ancestor who left central Texas to fight for the Confederacy, mounted on the finest horse in the county, sitting the best saddle money could buy, and carrying a pair of brand-new Colt .36 Navy revolvers. The end of the war found this gentleman battered but not beaten, facing a 1500-mile journey home, much of the way across a devastated land. Without money, but with powder, lead, caps, the pair of Colt Navies, and the horse to ride, he headed west. Months later, barefoot, clad in tattered rags, and retaining only one other important possession —a single Navy Colt—this indomitable Texan returned home afoot. During at least half of the journey every bite of meat that sustained him was brought down by a round leaden ball from that Navy Colt. He never claimed it was all *wild* game, and it seems likely that an occasional shoat or calf might well have collapsed to the bark of the revolver. Being a thrifty man, though, unless forced into it he wouldn't have shot anything too big to eat or carry. That's the story of one man who was forced to hunt with a handgun to survive, over 11 decades ago. Quite a few other Texas families can tell the same kind of tale about a scarred veteran who survived the long walk home—or perhaps to a new land—only by using a pistol to defend and feed himself.

From that point onward, the mid-19th Century, we see frequent references to handgun hunting. The outlaw who feared to enter the towns took with his revolver whatever livestock or game was handy; the out-of-work cowboy riding the grub line welcomed a jackrabbit, javelina, or deer to complement the beans, flour, and sowbelly that might be in his saddlebags; and certainly the homesteader with a raft of hungry kids would carry a pistol in preference to a rifle when working in the fields, and hope for a shot at something suitable for the pot before the day was out. And there's plenty of evidence that game was taken with revolvers purely for fun.

Some of the best-documented *sport* hunting with handguns occurred late in the third quarter of the last century. Artists and authors of the day have depicted several well-known figures galloping across the vast plains, sixgun in hand, overtaking a stampeding buffalo and

TOP Though surely game was killed with handguns before the era of the flintlock, guns such as this rifled Harpers Ferry service pistol were the first sidearms capable of sufficient accuracy for reasonable expectation of a kill.

MIDDLE The so-called Kentucky pistol represented a step upward from military sidearms. With its grace, lightness, and superior accuracy, it made a far better hunting arm.

ABOVE In the percussion era, we find written references to taking game with revolvers such as this .36 Colt Navy. Though lacking in power, the repeating capability of such guns made them superior to their single-shot predecessors.

TOP At one of the popular muzzle-loading jamborees, a handgunner in Confederate uniform gets off some informal practice shots, just as one of his ancestors might have done over a century ago. Foraging Civil War soldiers added new impetus to handgun hunting.

ABOVE LEFT The coming of the big-bore, metallic cartridge in guns such as this Colt Single Action Army gave the handgun aficionado his first really effective hunting sidearm. Elmer Keith and others have written much about big-game hunting with the venerable .44 and .45 Colt SAA.

ABOVE RIGHT In wartime and peacetime alike, U.S. soldiers throughout the world have hunted with the Colt GM .45 auto since its adoption in 1911. Much of their hunting was of necessity in order to survive behind enemy lines. Special ammunition was even issued for the purpose.

TOP The first genuinely hunting-oriented revolver cartridge was the S&W .357 Magnum of 1935. Since then, a multitude of heavy-frame guns have been chambered for it; typical of the current array is this Colt Python, introduced in the 1950s.

ABOVE LEFT S&W introduced its big-frame Magnum revolver in the mid-1930s as a major advance in handguns both for hunting and law enforcement. Since that time it has probably been the most widely used gun for the purpose, though since the 1950s its .44 Magnum chambering has been preferred over the original .357.

ABOVE RIGHT Bill Ruger designed this Super Blackhawk .44 Magnum single-action revolver mainly for hunting and it has been eminently successful in that role.

planting several bullets in his ribcage. The .44 and .45 revolvers of the time didn't have the power to put a bull buff down quickly—except by a spinal hit—but bullets into the lungs were certain if not instant killers. The equestrian sportsman could then veer off to reload safely, knowing the buffalo would run on a way, then drop, and there would be hump meat and tongue for supper.

General Custer hunted this way, along with other frontier figures. The Grand Duke Alexis of Russia made a special trip west to hunt buffalo in this fashion while visiting this country to procure arms for his government. Other foreigners, intrigued with the buffalo, came and did the same.

The other side of the World was not without its handgun hunters. British officers and dignitaries of the "Inja Service" were often avid sportsmen, devoted to "tent-pegging," taking game with a lance at full gallop, and also with revolvers from horseback. Even tigers are reported to have been killed in this manner. Cavalry officers of the day were accustomed to pistoling enemies from their saddles, so the transition to tiger, bear, or boar wouldn't have been considered difficult.

Other printed records of the exploits of the early handgun hunters are rare. Not until the 1920s did such matters begin to see print in periodicals to any significant extent. In the middle 1920s a young cowpoke from Montana began writing letters to the National Rifle Association about his experiences with sixguns in the game fields. The by-line that appeared thus in *The American Rifleman* even before I was born is still seen regularly. Its owner no longer punches cows or runs packstrings for a living; he has become one of our best-known proponents of handgun hunting. That cowpoke in the broad-brimmed, high-crowned Stetson was named Elmer Keith, and today he expounds his theories and recommendations from Salmon, Idaho.

Keith's writings for over half a century have probably done more to encourage the use of the sixgun (he loaths autoloaders for such activities) than any other single factor. Most of the other writers who today deal with the subject were unknown a couple of decades ago and until then, anyone who wanted to read about handgun hunting hied himself to the newsstand and bought whatever magazine was publishing Keith's current work.

Some pistoleros may have killed game the size of elk and moose before Keith did in the 1920s, but they never told the world about it. Keith told the world, not only about *what* he did, but *how* and *why*. Others followed in his footsteps, and a decade later, Colonel D. B. Wesson (of Smith & Wesson) toured North America taking numerous big-game trophies as part of his development and promotion program for the then-new .357 Magnum revolver and cartridge. Others took heart and tried the same, and Elmer Keith's old correspondence files are filled with letters from men (and a few women) from all walks of life who ventured into the timber with the most potent sixgun cartridges of the day.

Still, not until the mid-1950s did we begin to see repeated references to this great gunning sport. Since then, it has increased rapidly and today it is difficult *not* to find a handful of handgun hunters in any town of reasonable size. Handgun hunting now seems to be entering its golden era, with special guns, cartridges, and equipment of all sorts.

# 3

## The Possibilities Today

A great many people seem to have the impression that hunting with a handgun is a sport reserved for just a few lucky outdoorsmen—a sport available only in wilderness areas of the West. "Why learn to hunt with a handgun," they ask, "if most states don't allow it?" It is a common misconception that handgun hunting is difficult to do legally and is often flatly prohibited. The fact is, most of our states do allow some form of handgun hunting. Of course, in some instances, there are restrictions on calibers or cartridge size or energy, but in general such regulations are reasonable. Even some states that place severe restrictions on possession and use of handguns still allow them to be used for hunting if lawfully owned.

To simplify determining where you may hunt with sixgun or auto, I've screened the state regulations and prepared here the basic information. It has been boiled down to the essentials. Obviously, I can't present all the relevant details for each state in this space, so you should investigate further before committing yourself to a hunt. If I indicate that handgun hunting is lawful in a certain state and you wish to hunt there, write to that state's game department for a copy of its hunting regulations and study the parts governing the firearms that may be lawfully used in taking game. Also bear in mind that—apart from the hunting regulations—local laws and ordinances apply

There is a lot more handgun game available than one might expect. For example, armadillos are considered pests in some parts of the Southwest, and can be taken in large numbers. Almost any gun may be used, from .22 rimfires like the Beretta Sable that Dick Eades is holding in this photo to the biggest of the Magnums.

to the possession, carrying, and use of handguns. To avoid problems, always familiarize yourself with handgun laws in the state where you plan to hunt. Now here's a state-by-state listing to show where, if you conform to all applicable regulations, you can enjoy some form of handgun hunting.

LEFT Squirrels, rabbits, and the like abound throughout the nation. In most states they may be lawfully taken with handguns, and in some areas big game may also be hunted with sidearms.

BELOW The woodchuck, gopher, prairie dog, or other small varmints are found throughout the country. They make ideal handgun-hunting targets and may be lawfully hunted by pistoleros in most states.

ABOVE Though the shooter in this picture isn't about to bust that doe running across his front, whitetail deer are our most common big-game animal and are legal handgun quarry in many states.

BELOW In some regions where little or no native handgun game is available, private hunting preserves offer year-round handgun hunting for a wide variety of animals such as these feral goats.

ALABAMA: Permit required to carry handgun; legal for hunting, subject to area restrictions.

ALASKA: Center-fire handgun legal for use on big game and marine mammals; any handgun legal for small game.

ARIZONA: Big game—.357, .41, and .44 Magnums only. Small game —other handguns.

ARKANSAS: Handgun legal for big game, small game, and unprotected wildlife.

CALIFORNIA: Prohibited for waterfowl and upland game. Permitted for small game except in Los Angeles County. The .357, .41, and .44 Magnums only for bear and wild boar.

COLORADO: Permitted only for predators and rabbits.

CONNECTICUT: Permitted for small game and unprotected wildlife. Not legal for deer. Permit required to carry sidearm.

DELAWARE: Permitted for unprotected wildlife and predators. Not legal for game species.

FLORIDA: Legal for game, non-game animals. The .22 rimfire prohibited for game animals.

GEORGIA: Permitted for small game; illegal for deer.

HAWAII: Legal for predators and unprotected wildlife.

IDAHO: Legal for forest grouse and game and non-game animals.

ILLINOIS: Prohibited for deer; legal for small game and unprotected wildlife.

INDIANA: Prohibited for deer; legal for small game and unprotected wildlife.

IOWA: Legal for small game, predators, and unprotected wildlife.

KANSAS: Prohibited for deer; legal for small game and unprotected wildlife.

KENTUCKY: Legal for small game, predators, and unprotected wildlife.

LOUISIANA: Legal for deer, small game, and unprotected wildlife.

MAINE: Legal for big and small game, unprotected wildlife, and predators.

MARYLAND: Legal for small game, predators, and unprotected wildlife.

MASSACHUSETTS: Prohibited for big game. No caliber larger than .38 is permitted for night species.

MICHIGAN: Legal for deer and small game, but prohibited in southern Michigan during deer season.

MINNESOTA: Prohibited for game, but legal for predators and unprotected wildlife.

MISSISSIPPI: Legal for big and small game, unprotected wildlife, and predators.

MISSOURI: Prohibited if under .357 Magnum for deer.

MONTANA: Legal for big and small game and unprotected wildlife.

NEBRASKA: Legal for deer but only .357 Magnum or .44 Special may be used; Keith Magnum handloads are required.

NEVADA: Prohibited for game birds and for all game animals except rabbits.

NEW HAMPSHIRE: Legal wherever rifle hunting is permitted.

NEW JERSEY: Prohibited for game species.

NEW MEXICO: Prohibited except for .357, .41, and .44 Magnums. Soft-nosed Magnum ammunition must be used.

NEW YORK: Legal for deer and bear where rifles are permitted; center-fire handguns only.

NORTH CAROLINA: Legal for unprotected wildlife. Prohibited for big or small game.

NORTH DAKOTA: Prohibited for big or small game; legal for predators and unprotected wildlife.

OHIO: Legal for small game, predators, and unprotected wildlife, but with restrictions on wildlife areas.

OKLAHOMA: Legal for deer—minimum of 75-grain bullet with 500 foot-pounds of energy (.357, .41, and .44 Magnums): permitted for rabbits, squirrels, and unprotected wildlife.

OREGON: Prohibited for big game or game birds; legal for predators, unprotected wildlife, and various small-game species.

PENNSYLVANIA: Manually operated arms legal for game. Prohibited —semi-autos, auto, air pistols, and autoloaders.

RHODE ISLAND: Not technically prohibited but outlawed for practical purposes by restrictive handgun-carrying policy.

SOUTH CAROLINA: Legal for big game, small-game predators, small game, and unprotected wildlife.

SOUTH DAKOTA: Prohibited for big game and small game; legal for unprotected wildlife.

TENNESSEE: Legal for small game, predators, and unprotected wildlife, but prohibited on wildlife areas.

TEXAS: Not prohibited, but laws governing the carrying are not clear.

UTAH: Legal for predators and unprotected wildlife.

VERMONT: Permitted where rifle hunting is allowed.

VIRGINIA: Legal for predatory or undesirable birds and animals; also legal for game animals if .23 caliber or larger.

WASHINGTON: Prohibited for deer, elk, mountain sheep, goat, bear, and most game birds.

WEST VIRGINIA: Not technically illegal but outlawed by restrictive policy in issuing handgun-carrying licenses.

WISCONSIN: The .22 rimfire legal but may be used only for same purposes that are legal with .22 rimfire rifles.

WYOMING: Prohibited for game animals or game birds; legal for predators and unprotected wildlife.

# 4

## The Hunter's Handgun vs. the Hunting Handgun

The title of this chapter isn't meant to be mysterious or confusing; in fact, it's intended to clarify a poorly understood aspect of the handgun's place in all sorts of hunting activities. It's all a matter of definition. A *hunting handgun* is carried and used afield as one's *primary* hunting arm. It is the gun with which you *intend* to take all your major shots. If a rifle or shotgun is also carried, it's supplemental to the handgun—for finishing off a cripple or potting camp meat or predators. On the other hand, a *hunter's handgun* may be a *secondary* arm, carried only to supplement a rifle or shotgun which is to be used for most shots.

The two types of handguns may or may not differ. Depending upon the game and circumstances, a hunting handgun may be anything from a lightweight .22 rimfire auto, revolver, or single-shot on up to a .44 Magnum sixgun or Auto Mag autoloader. If you're hunting squirrels, rabbits, or small varmints close up, the .22 rimfire may very well be all you need. But if you are out to pistol a grizzly or elk, then nothing but the biggest and most potent cannon will do.

Again, depending upon the use to which it will be put, the hunter's handgun may come from just as wide a spread. If it's being carried to kill rattlesnakes or take grouse and squirrels for the pot, most likely it will be a small, light .22. On the other hand, if you feel you need a spare gun in case your rifle packs up or isn't handy when something mean and hungry comes at you, the bigger the better.

The hunting handgun is covered throughout this book in great detail, so we needn't belabor that subject here—but the *hunter's handgun* is a different kettle of stew, so we'll elaborate a bit.

Since the scattergun or rifle hunter is already burdened with a seven- to nine-pound gun, heavy cartridges, binoculars, compass, knife, lunch, and maybe even canteen and camera, anything added to his load should be as light as possible. This means a small gun of small caliber, as much so as possible without sacrificing reliability and accuracy. It also needs to be compact (meaning short), for a 10-inch barrel dangling along your leg can snag on brush and generally be a distracting nuisance. Its ammunition also must be as compact and light as possible.

The most common (perhaps 95 percent) use of the hunter's handgun is potting small game (squirrels, grouse, turtles, etc.) for the camp larder; thus, the .22 LR is the ideal cartridge. Probably the second most important use—at least in anticipation, if not in actuality—is dispatching dangerous or obnoxious varmints around camp. Venomous snakes, predatory birds, small scavengers, and the like fall into this category and succumb with equal ease to the .22 LR cartridge.

The several ammunition makers supply the .22 LR in 40-grain solid lead-bullet loads at standard (1,060 feet per second) and high velocity (1,125 fps) loadings, and with a 37-grain lead hollow-point at about 1,200 fps; these are standard velocities published for six-inch test barrels. (There is also a "match" load of superior quality and accuracy, but it costs more and isn't needed for this kind of shooting.) All this makes the .22 LR the most versatile cartridge for the hunter's handgun.

Type makes little difference in such a handgun, except that single shots of suitable accuracy and quality are generally too big and heavy. Between revolvers and autos, I'd say the revolver has the better of it, even in single-action form. Great rapidity of fire or reloading won't be needed, and the revolver is inherently safer to carry and easier to manipulate than most .22 autos. Further, should the occasion arise, the revolver can be used quite successfully with .22 Shorts, CB caps or BB caps, and even shot loads, whereas autos cannot, as a general rule. You'll find a greater variety in price, quality, and size of .22 revolvers than any other handguns. You may have a cheap revolver, a tiny but high-quality five-shooter, a three-pound target gun, or anything in between.

Best of the lot as a hunter's handgun is the class generally desig-

ABOVE LEFT The S&W Kit Gun, Model 34, is my idea of a first-class hunter's gun—.22 caliber, light, compact, accurate, reliable.

ABOVE RIGHT A big Magnum such as this S&W .44 may qualify as hunter's handgun or a *hunting* handgun, but the latter is more likely.

nated "Kit Gun" (after the Smith & Wesson model of that name). These .22s are built on relatively small (originally .32 caliber) frames, have barrels three to four inches long, and are equipped with adjustable sights. They range in weight (in the all-steel models) from 17 to 26 ounces. Even less weight is possible in the S&W line, with its aluminum-framed Kit Gun tipping the scale at a mere 14 ounces without any loss of accuracy or reliability.

In the modern double-action, solid-frame, swing-out-cylinder designs we have the Smith & Wesson Kit Gun, the Colt Diamondback, the Charter Arms Pathfinder, and the High Standard Sentinel. In single-action, frontier-style guns, we have the Ruger Bearcat and Single-Six and the Colt Frontier Scout. There are also similar guns of foreign make. All do the job very nicely.

Most of those same guns are also available with spare cylinders or separate chamberings for the much more powerful (and costly) .22 WMR cartridge. This cartridge does have advantages for some uses, but generally not for our main use. The .22 LR is all you really need.

With most of these models, you can carry the gun, a light holster, and at least 50 cartridges without adding more than a mere couple of pounds to the weight of your gear. On the other hand, a big auto or Magnum sixgun and 50 rounds will weigh five to seven pounds— nearly as much as your rifle or scattergun. At that weight, the handgun can cease to be an enjoyable convenience and become an energy-draining burden.

This isn't to say that autos and calibers larger and more powerful than the .22 rimfire don't have a place as hunters' handguns. If you feel you really need more power, then many of the same guns may be obtained in .32 S&W (Long) caliber, driving a 98-grain bullet at 705 fps, and when properly handloaded this performance can be

The hunting handgun may well be used on big game such as this fine pronghorn.

exceeded by a considerable margin. Some of the same-size guns are also available in the ubiquitous .38 Special.

Both of these larger calibers *do* have a good deal more power, but they are more difficult to shoot with *good* accuracy, and their ammunition is heavier, bulkier, and more costly. The added power alone is not of real value to the uses we've described for the typical hunter's handgun.

If, however, the handgun is carried to back up or substitute for the rifle, then the picture is entirely different. Under those conditions, nothing less than the bigger Magnum guns and cartridges possess sufficient power to be considered—and even then, the longest barrels available are necessary if maximum power is to be obtained.

In any case, the desire for a spare gun should be tempered with horse sense. Your rifle won't let you down if it is properly chosen and maintained, so a backup handgun will seldom if ever be required. Then, too, considering that the most potent handgun will have far less power than a rifle, it seems ridiculous to expect a Magnum sixgun to bail you out of something the rifle couldn't handle.

Best of all hunter's handguns is the ubiquitous .22. Shown here is a .22 Beretta Sable used by Dick Eades to bag armadillos for the pot.

Also, by carrying a big handgun, you're automatically ruling out much of the fun that can be had in the field with a small, light, .22 sixgun or auto and a few boxes of cartridges. In the end, the ideal *hunter's handgun* is the .22 rimfire of your choice. The *hunting handgun* can be the same, or it may be the most potent Magnum to be had.

# 5

---

# Revolver or Auto
# or Single-Shot

"Sure, I'd like to do a little handgun hunting, but I don't think I've got a gun that's made for the job."

I've heard that comment many, many times from people who owned handguns ranging all the way from .22 rimfires to the big-bore sixguns and autos. Actually, *some* handgun hunting can be done with virtually any shortgun that produces reasonable accuracy, even with the lowly .22 RF Short or .25 ACP cartridge. As with any other endeavor, if one has the *wish* to do something, he simply structures his activities around the available equipment.

The basic characteristics and specifications of purely hunting handguns are discussed extensively in another chapter. We are more concerned here with the selection of a particular *type* of handgun—a revolver, an autoloader, or a single-shot—one of the three principal forms of action which have been with us since before the turn of the century.

Each of the three possesses capabilities that the others do not, and each possesses particular characteristics that adapt it better to *some* form of hunting and some species of game than the others. Thus, in choosing your equipment, it is essential to study the three types. Quite often, the problem isn't to select a purely hunting arm, but rather a gun that will possess the maximum suitability for a certain type of hunting and yet retain substantial utility for target shooting, personal defense, etc. Let's examine each of the types, considering first their capabilities purely for hunting, and second their utility in other roles.

REVOLVER: The traditional American sidearm, the gun that rightly or wrongly gets credit for taming the Western frontier, and a type with a remarkable traditional and historical appeal.

First, let's look at the good aspects of the revolver. In standard forms, and in various centerfire calibers, it normally offers six rapid shots without reloading, and in the event of an ammunition malfunction, can *usually* bypass the defective round and still produce a subsequent shot with hardly a perceptible delay. Second, being entirely manually operated, it is not dependent upon certain levels of ammunition power or quality for proper functioning. Third, it is available in a very wide range of cartridge size and power, stretching from the .22 rimfire (which may be used with five different loadings, the BB and CB caps, Short, Long, and Long Rifle) where minimal power is acceptable, up to the powerhouse .44 Magnum with its 240-grain bullet at nearly 1400 fps. There is a revolver cartridge available for every purpose from potting mice in the basement up to taking on a cantankerous grizzly in his own territory. Fourth, the revolver has long been noted for its inherent safety in carrying (when properly loaded). And for what it is worth (really a good deal more than most people give it credit for) most of the better-grade revolvers possess a unique esthetic appeal which generates great pride in ownership. Admittedly, this doesn't improve the gun's performance in the game field, but it produces intangible benefits in better handling, a greater likelihood that an individual will practice and develop a higher degree of skill, etc. Additionally, the better modern revolvers are superbly accurate and are fitted with excellent sights. Not only are revolvers chambered for the most powerful modern cartridges, but there is no mechanical or functional limit upon the length of barrel they may use. Therefore, the performance level of the cartridge may be exploited to the maximum.

Now let's take a look at the minus side of the revolver. It's a complex mechanical device containing (in most instances) a large number of small, closely fitted, highly stressed parts which are not only subject to wear and failure, but which normally require the services of a skilled gunsmith (I don't mean a kitchen-table parts-replacer) when anything goes awry. Further, the frame/crane/cylinder arrangement of a modern revolver is relatively weak and can be

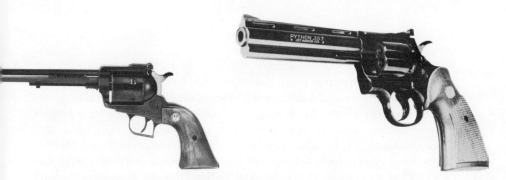

ABOVE LEFT Single-action revolvers are entirely satisfactory for most hunting—even though slow to reload—and they come in the most potent sixgun calibers.

ABOVE RIGHT Modern double-action revolvers offer maximum versatility and sixgun speed of operation. This Colt Python is excellent example of the type, but only S&W models are available in calibers over .357 Magnum.

damaged (bent, alignment spoiled) by relatively mild impact or mistreatment. Further, the frame itself is a very complex, costly, and relatively weak structure. The revolver is the slowest of all repeating types of firearms to reload. When fouling and dirt accumulate in the chambers and mechanisms, extraction of fired cases preparatory to reloading becomes difficult, and sometimes impossible without outside help.

Furthermore, the revolver is a rabbit warren of gaps, spaces, and holes into which dirt, moisture, and foreign material may enter to interfere with functioning. Even a few grains of sand or a bit of leaf or bark can easily render a revolver out-of-service—totally incapable of firing—until the problem is identified and solved. In most instances, revolvers of substantial power (and, therefore, size) place the centerline of the bore well above the upper edge of the gun hand, thus creating a relative severity of *apparent* or *felt* recoil, and muzzle jump is greater than with autos. And, generally speaking, the standard stocks or grips on revolvers are poorly suited not only to accurate shooting but to the absorption and distribution and control of recoil. If compactness is of importance in hunting, and I think it is, the long-barreled revolver makes a most ungainly package. For a given length of barrel and cartridge capacity, it forms a much thicker, longer, and more cumbersome package than a comparable autoloader. It is also more difficult to obtain a first-class holster fit on a revolver.

There are two basic types of revolver. One is the double-action or *trigger-cocking* type in which a shot may be fired by simply pulling the trigger, even though the hammer be at rest in the fired position.

This type normally also allows manual cocking of the hammer prior to the shot, to permit more deliberate fire with a lighter trigger pull. In most instances (at least in guns of good quality) this type also allows you to eject all the fired cases at once and will allow, with proper accessories, simultaneous loading of all chambers. Opposite this double-action type, we have the traditional single-action or *thumb-cocking* type which originated, for all practical purposes, with the 1836 Paterson Colt. This type may be fired only by manually cocking the hammer prior to the shot, and allows fired-case ejection and reloading only by individual chambers, with a number of operations required for each chamber. Further, the ejection system on single-action revolvers is generally weak and can be easily damaged when a fired case requires more than normal effort to dislodge it from the chamber.

For more or less normal use, where the gun is kept assiduously clean and undamaged, where ammunition of known quality is used, and where no dire emergencies arise, it would be difficult to make a choice between double-action and single-action revolvers. On the other hand, where one might expect to be forced to make very rapid repeat shots or a very rapid first shot from draw, the double-action gun seems a bit more desirable. Likewise, if rapid reloading is anticipated, or if conditions might be such that fired cases stick a bit, then the DA gun is also superior. Though it's not of great significance, you might also keep in mind that in an emergency (as in the case of an injury) the DA gun may be drawn, fired accurately, emptied, reloaded, and placed back in action with only one hand—while this is not normally possible with the SA sixgun. For other purposes, aside from hunting, the DA revolver is more versatile and useful.

AUTOLOADER: Over 60 years younger than the revolver, the autoloader is considered by many to be a relative late-comer on the handgun scene. As with the revolver, let's first take a look at the advantages the autoloader has to offer.

It's available for a wide variety of cartridges ranging from the .22 Short up to .45 caliber; and, if we examine the complete spread of makes and models, continues in power up to the .44 Auto Mag, which has greater velocity and energy than any revolver cartridge. It possesses a large magazine capacity, up to 16 rounds in some models—not usually that many but invariably more than a revolver of comparable caliber. It may be reloaded in the merest fraction of the time required to recharge a revolver cylinder. At its present state of development, the autoloader is functionally as reliable as the best revolver, and under many circumstances may even exceed the revolver's probable reliability. The auto, by being fitted with a solid barrel, eliminates the cylinder/barrel misalignment common to most revolvers, and also eliminates the loss in internal ballistic efficiency brought about by the barrel/cylinder gap.

Mechanically, the frame and other major components of the auto are stronger and less liable to damage from outside influences than the revolver. Most modern big-bore autos have a butt frame and standard grips which are readily adaptable to the average individual and which absorb recoil well. In the auto, the barrel inherently sits lower in relation to the hand, and thus causes felt recoil and muzzle jump to be substantially milder. Generally, for a given length of barrel and cartridge capacity, the auto is shorter than a revolver and much less thick, producing a more compact and easily handled package. The autoloader, when loaded, presents very few orifices through which foreign material may enter to interfere with the mechanism. Most (but not all) autos may be carried "cocked and locked"—that is, with the hammer cocked and the manual safety applied, in complete safety, whereas revolvers cannot. This makes it possible for a hurried first shot to be taken from the cocked position without any preliminary effort or time expended in cocking the hammer.

Generally speaking, autoloaders are of relatively modern design, using strong and comparatively few parts which are not easily damaged or worn; also, these parts can generally be replaced by an owner with little training, thus reducing the need for a much-experienced gunsmith. For example, replacement of an auto's firing pin is a one-minute job for the owner, usually without tools, while the same operation in a revolver requires special tools and skills. The barrel of

**BELOW LEFT** Big-bore autoloaders such as this Llama version of the Colt Government Model are the best of the conventional autos, but all fall short of Magnum revolvers in power and long-range performance.

**BELOW RIGHT** Massive Auto Mag autoloader offers maximum power and accuracy of all self-loaders, and even exceeds the most powerful revolvers.

many autos can be replaced in a moment or two without tools, while the proper replacement of a revolver barrel requires the skills and facilities of a well-equipped gun shop.

However, all is not roses where hunting is concerned. There are disadvantages, probably the best-known of which is the auto's utter dependability upon high-quality ammunition loaded to within fairly narrow performance limits. Thus, an auto will not normally function properly with a wide variety of ammunition. Older autos, at least those of single-action type, require both hands and several seconds of time to clear ammunition malfunctions before firing can be resumed. Because of their basic layout, autos are placed under fairly strict limitations of barrel length. Small-caliber, rimfire autos are not bound by these limitations, nor are the more recent developments such as the Auto Mag—but the more common big-bore guns are made in one or, at best, two barrel lengths, not exceeding five or six inches. These barrel restrictions often preclude developing the maximum ballistic potential from a particular cartridge.

While the effect in hunting is not great, many shooters also consider it a disadvantage that the autoloader hurls its empty cases clear of the gun, and recovery for handloading becomes difficult. Some autos also damage the cases slightly during ejection.

Again, as with revolvers, we have a choice of single-action or double-action. Here the distinction is far less clear, for all other functions and characteristics of the two types are virtually identical, the only difference being in the capability of the DA auto to be drawn and fired with the hammer down. That is, your first shot can be fired fast by simply pulling the trigger. While this may be considered a distinct advantage for *combat* use, seldom if ever would one encounter a hunting condition where the presence or absence of a double-action first-shot capability would be significant. Rapidity of repeat fire, reloading, and all other functions remain the same in both types after the first shot.

SINGLE-SHOT: The single-shot pistol has been with us far longer than any other type of one-hand gun—ever since the development of the first muzzleloaders intended to be fired with one hand. However, owing to the superiority of the revolver and autoloader for general use, the *modern* single-shot did not receive particularly great acceptance until the past few years. Now there are several available, but the only make and model widely encountered is the Thompson/Center Contender. Thus, our discussion here becomes oriented more to a single make and model than to a general class of arms.

The principal advantage of the single-shot is that it offers the least complex mechanism and is therefore generally the most durable under field conditions. Beyond that, it offers almost unlimited choice of barrel length and weight, it may be fitted with a wide variety of "iron" or optical sights without regard to its functioning, and it may be chambered for a cartridge of any length, even including some designed primarily for rifles and completely incapable of use in any other conventional handgun. For example, the Contender may be chambered for the .30–30 Winchester and other bottle-neck rifle cartridges which are totally beyond the capabilities of any other one-hand gun design.

Of particular value to the individual who must make one gun serve as a battery, or who simply prefers to use a wide variety of cartridges and barrel lengths, is the fact that the single-shot generally accepts interchangeable barrels. Thus, with a single action, you might acquire a dozen or more barrels of different calibers, weights, configurations, and lengths, then exchange them on the gun to suit it to any particular wish or circumstance.

The single-shot also generally allows lighter and finer trigger regulation inasmuch as it must be opened, reloaded, and recocked manually for each shot, and the mechanism is not subject to the jars of automatic functioning after the shot. And, of course, as has already been touched upon lightly, the properly designed and manufactured single-shot pistol may be chambered for cartridges that vastly exceed the ballistic performance of any revolver or autoloader caliber. Velocities well in excess of 3000 fps may be obtained, and muzzle energies nearly doubling what's practical in other types of handguns can be had with little difficulty.

In regard to accuracy, the single-shot pistol is mechanically capable of shooting tighter groups (other conditions being equal) than

Single-shot pistols, especially this interchangeable-barrel Thompson/Center Contender, offer fine accuracy and versatility of caliber and power. But they are bulky and slow for certain types of hunting.

either the revolver or autoloader. For all practical purposes, the single-shot pistol behaves like a rifle—it is not saddled with the barrel/cylinder alignment or barrel/cylinder gap problems of the revolver, nor is it hamstrung by the mobile barrel concept of many autoloader designs. In fact, one other single-shot pistol, the Remington XP-100, is in reality a standard bolt-type rifle action fitted with a short barrel and pistol-style stock.

Obviously, the single-shot pistol does have numerous disadvantages, the greatest being that it can only fire a single shot, after which it must be opened, the empty case extracted, a fresh cartridge chambered, the gun closed and recocked, before another shot can be fired. Under normal conditions without gloves, these operations may be performed in a few seconds, but often they take substantially longer.

So, having examined the good and bad characteristics of all three basic types of handguns, how do you determine which suits you best? Let's outline those circumstances under which the single-shot would be a good choice. Suppose that you wish to shoot at maximum ranges, that your targets are small, that the game is not dangerous, that it is relatively easy to kill, and that it is not likely to escape wounded. Actually, we've just described the sport known as varmint hunting —shooting chucks and such. For that type of hunting, where shooting is deliberate, at long range, at small targets, the single-shot pistol (sometimes with a telescopic sight) chambered for a high-velocity, small-bore cartridge is unquestionably superior to any other type. But if your hunting is less specialized, more the general-purpose type, the single-shot pistol becomes less and less appealing.

There is one other condition under which the single-shot pistol is a superior, if not the only, choice. Thompson/Center makes its Contender with (among other barrels) a special shot barrel and removable choke tube, and supplies a special plastic-encapsulated shot loading of the .44 Magnum cartridge for use in it. With this combination, taking running small game on the ground and feathered game flying becomes entirely practical. This sort of thing may also be done with revolvers that have been extensively modified, but we're concerned here with standard factory guns, not custom modifications. Under those conditions, then, if you wish to use shot on small game and birds, the *only* practical choice is a single-shot, preferably the Thompson/Center Contender. It is much superior, with its special ammunition, to even the most extensively modified revolver utilizing specially handloaded ammunition.

At the opposite end of the scale, let's say you wish to hunt mainly large game and therefore need maximum power, maximum reliability of gun/ammunition, and the best possible accuracy compatible with those first two requirements. Let's say further that the game might occasionally be dangerous, and that ranges might vary from as little as a few feet to a couple of hundred yards. Under those conditions, you'll want maximum rapidity of fire and reloading, plenty of gun weight to hold it down under recoil and other unfavorable conditions, and a relatively long barrel for ballistic efficiency and recoil reduction. Consequently, substantial size and weight will be desirable rather than objectionable. Then you'll look first at the autoloaders, and as this is written there is only one make and model which fully satisfies all the requirements—the big recoil-operated Auto Mag pistol chambered for the .357 to .45 AMP cartridges. Much like the single-shot pistol, the Auto Mag is a highly specialized design with relatively little overall utility or versatility outside of big-game hunting. There are other specialized hunting areas in which it serves very well, but those capabilities are secondary to the big-game mission.

In between those two extremes, we have the entire range of small-game and medium-game hunting, for which nearly all requirements may be met equally well by the revolver or autoloader. For the smaller, non-dangerous species that require cartridges no more powerful than the .357 Magnum, a choice between the revolver and auto is purely academic, based upon personal preference and prejudice. When getting into the larger non-dangerous species such as deer, the .38 and .45 auto pistols are adequate in killing power and range but offer less safety margin in the form of additional power than the .41 and .44 Magnum revolvers. Therefore, as the size of the game increases, the conventional autoloader (except for the Auto Mag) becomes less desirable. With the larger non-dangerous species such as elk and moose, as well as "semi-dangerous" animals such as boar and bear, the revolver becomes more desirable than the auto— though the preference is based not upon the mechanical system but simply the fact that the sixgun is chambered for the .44 Magnum, which is far more powerful than any cartridge available in conventional autoloaders.

So, as you can see, there isn't really any single best handgun for hunting in general. If your bag is conventional hunting of routine small and medium game, then either the revolver or auto will serve you admirably when chambered for the most appropriate cartridge. For big game, dangerous game, or long-range varmint shooting, you'll want one of the specialized guns I've described if you expect to achieve the ultimate in performance.

# 6

## Specialized Hunting Handguns

Although you can use almost any handgun for a certain amount of hunting under some conditions, the serious pistolero will seek all of the advantages possible, and in so doing must eventually gravitate toward highly specialized guns that are best suited to his particular purpose. Actually, we have two categories of such specialized handguns for hunting. The first includes those guns which were not necessarily developed with hunting mainly in mind, but whose characteristics and cartridges have evolved to the point where they may be considered specialized hunting arms. The second category consists of those guns designed and manufactured with the primary goal of producing maximum hunting effectiveness. Both categories contain single shots, both double-action and single-action revolvers, and autoloading pistols. Further, some of these guns are chambered for cartridges specifically developed to meet certain hunting requirements, and even for some cartridges (like the .30–30) originally developed for rifles.

Let's begin with a look at guns developed mainly for other purposes but, through coincidence or subsequent modification and chambering for special cartridges, now ideally suited for hunting. First on the list is the famed Smith & Wesson N-frame "Magnum" revolver series derived from the original Smith & Wesson .357 Mag-

Smith & Wesson N-frame Magnums, introduced in the 1930s, were the first really suitable hunting handguns by today's standards.

num introduced in 1935. Actually, hunting did play a large part in the development of both the gun and cartridge, though it would appear that Colonel D. B. Wesson used hunting primarily as a promotional vehicle for the gun and cartridge.

The gun was intended to be the epitome of modern double-action revolvers, with major emphasis upon suitability for law-enforcement use. Its .357 Magnum cartridge was a logical development of the earlier .38 Special, intended to be the most powerful handgun cartridge in the world. That Smith & Wesson succeeded in producing a superb double-action revolver is readily confirmed by anyone who has ever handled and used a .357 Magnum revolver of pre-World War II vintage. In more recent years the quality of fit and finish of the .357 Magnum (and its larger-caliber brethren) has deteriorated somewhat, but the basic excellence of the design and its admirable characteristics remain undiminished.

Colonel Wesson, assisted by the late Philip B. Sharp and other independent ballistic experimenters, also achieved the desired goal in development of the cartridge. In its 1930s form, the .357 Magnum utilized a 158-grain bullet of semi-wadcutter form at 1550 fps—by far the highest velocity achieved to that date by any production handgun cartridge, not excluding the high-velocity, bottle-neck, autoloading-pistol, military cartridges developed in Europe. This was achieved with a lubricated lead-alloy bullet, a special propellant powder (a variation of Hercules 2400), and chamber pressures of a level considered until then vastly beyond the capabilities of the basic revolver design. These pressures, which would have ruptured most previous sixguns, were contained safely by using a cylinder and frame of massive dimensions, the finest in material and heat treatment, and by meticulous workmanship. Chamber pressures of that early ammunition (since reduced substantially) often averaged (within a particular lot) well over 40,000 psi.

All this power and quality were aimed at producing a gun superior to everything else for law enforcement. However, in order to promote this rather costly development and achieve sufficient sales to make it worthwhile at a time when the country was in a severe economic slump, Colonel Wesson launched a big-game hunting program throughout North America during the development phase. Using the .357 Magnum with an 8¾-inch (yes, that's the correct length) barrel in order to develop the announced cartridge performance, he successfully took most major North American species. These hunting achievements received wide national recognition, and served not only to bring the new gun to the attention of the shooting public, but to give pure handgun hunting its first really worthwhile public exposure. Many a budding handgunner took his cue from Colonel Wesson, procured the new .357 Magnum, and for the first time seriously sought big game with a sidearm.

Today, the 8⅜-inch barrel is the longest standard barrel offered in the S&W Magnum revolvers. Apparently, that original 8¾-inch barrel was chosen partly because it allowed production of maximum velocities with the cartridge and partly because it was the longest that could be produced without extensive (costly) retooling. However, shortly after the gun was introduced with this barrel length, it was brought to the attention of S&W that the sight radius with the 8¾-inch barrel was greater than the 10-inch maximum allowed by the National Rifle Association rules governing formal competitive target shooting. So, in order not to sacrifice any potential sales, S&W shortened the long barrel to 8⅜ inches, thus complying with that rule. Today, when very few shooters use a revolver in formal competition, this may seem a bit unusual, but in those days the revolver was the universal choice for competitive shooting except in matches that required the use of .45-caliber service autoloader. And, considering that the .357 Magnum was the finest and most accurate revolver of the time, it was logical that serious shooters would want to use it in matches.

For those who are unfamiliar with guns of this type, a .357 Magnum revolver can be loaded with .38 Specials, though a gun chambered only for .38 Specials can't handle .357 Magnum cartridges. The target-shooting popularity of the S&W .357 revolver was boosted by the fact that it shot with superb accuracy when loaded with the then-new .38 Special wadcutter bullets in both "mid-range" and full-charge loads.

Since the introduction of the original .357 Magnum, S&W has continuously produced this big N-frame revolver. In 1955, it introduced the same gun chambered for the new .44 Magnum cartridge, and again in 1964, chambered for the even newer .41 Magnum. Both cartridges were developed by Remington for use specifically in the S&W revolvers. For nearly 40 years, then, these Magnum revolvers —when fitted with six-inch or longer barrels—have been considered the epitome of double-action hunting handguns.

In the late 1950s, Sturm, Ruger & Co. introduced a new frontier-style single-action revolver chambered for the new .44 Magnum cartridge. This evolved from the Ruger .22 rimfire single-action revolver of a few years earlier and a subsequent adaptation of that design in a larger size to the .357 Magnum cartridge. William Ruger,

The Ruger Blackhawk, introduced in the 1950's, was the first SA revolver really designed for hunting—that is, featuring adjustable sights and offered in proper calibers.

founder and president of the company, immediately recognized the hunting potential of the .44 Magnum cartridge when it was introduced. He enlarged and adapted his basic single-action design to this most potent of all cartridges. Initially called the "Blackhawk," this revolver was of larger size and weight than its .357 Magnum predecessor. To achieve maximum cartridge performance for hunting, it was offered with a 7½-inch barrel. In this form, it was and is eminently successful as a hunting handgun.

Since the .44 Magnum Blackhawk's introduction, it has been further modified to better adapt it to hunting. It has been given greater weight by utilizing an unfluted cylinder, the trigger guard profile has been changed to protect the shooter's index finger, and the butt shape has been modified somewhat for better control. Internally, it has been modified in the interests of carrying safety. And since 1973, guns are fitted with a completely new lockwork whereby the hammer operates the firing pin only through a transfer lever or bar which absolutely prevents inadvertent firing except when the trigger is deliberately held to the rear.

If one prefers autoloading pistols for hunting, then there is only one conventional model and caliber which approaches the desired characteristics—the Colt .38 Super Auto introduced in 1929. Originally, this gun/cartridge combination was an effort to boost flagging sales of the old 1900 Model .38 Auto and at the same time to reduce tooling and the number of models being produced. Colt's technicians simply took the old .38 ACP cartridge with its 130-grain bullet at 1150 fps and increased the speed to 1300 fps, case and bullet remaining unchanged. Then, to eliminate the undesirable characteristics of the earlier .38 pistol's design (and also to eliminate the need for producing it), they adapted the standard .45 ACP Government Model pistol to the new .38 loading.

The Colt Government Model, preferably in .38 Super, is best of the conventional autos though it needs target-type sights installed for best results.

As with Colonel Wesson's efforts later, it is doubtful that hunting potential played any significant part in the development of this combination other than to provide a promotional vehicle. With the introduction of the .38 Super Auto, there appeared numerous magazine articles extolling its efficacy on big game, and advertisements of the period depict it being used to halt a charging grizzly. In spite of all this, the original .38 Super loading with its full-metal-jacketed bullet was not at all suitable for hunting by today's standards. It possessed great penetration but little tissue damage and shock, which we now consider essential for quick, sure kills. Attempts were made to improve its performance by offering hollow-point and soft-point versions of the same bullet weight. But little was understood about handgun expanding-bullet design in those days, and the bullets invariably failed to show any significant advantage in performance over the jacketed load. Today, however, we have superb JHP and JSP high-performance loadings of the .38 Super cartridge, making it and the guns chambered for it the best *conventional* combination of all the autoloaders for hunting.

In the early 1960s there was a rash of interest in ultra-high velocity, small-bore, varmint-type cartridges adapted to revolvers. Most likely this interest had been spurred by the development of the .22 K-Chuck Wildcat (based on the .22 Hornet case slightly shortened) by the late Jim Harvey of Lakeville Arms. Remington developed a necked-down version of the .357 Magnum case, utilizing a .22-caliber bullet weighing 40 grains at a *claimed* velocity in excess of 2100 fps. This number was known as the .22 Remington Jet. It was introduced by Smith & Wesson in its K-frame revolver series, simply fitting an appropriately chambered cylinder and a .22-caliber barrel to the standard K-frame Masterpiece target revolver.

This gun and ammunition became available in 1961. The gun was offered with steel chamber inserts and a unique, movable center-fire/rimfire hammer/firing-pin combination to allow the use of .22 rimfire cartridges when desired. Problems were immediately reported from the field, with the sharply tapered cartridge case jamming tightly against the recoil shield when fired and thus preventing cylinder rotation. Attempts were made to eliminate this problem, but even to this day it is still encountered. The combination of a rotating cylinder and sharply tapered cartridge case caused the shell to jam rearward upon firing.

In spite of these problems, the S&W .22 Jet revolver has maintained a fair degree of popularity because it offers an excellent combination of high velocity and flat trajectory for varmint hunting. This is in spite of the fact that factory ammunition and factory guns normally produce only about 1700 fps, as opposed to the 2100 fps velocity claimed.

At the same time, Winchester-Western developed its own .256 Winchester Magnum revolver cartridge by necking the .357 Magnum case down to .25 caliber. Both Colt and Ruger chambered existing revolver models for this cartridge, but encountered the same difficulties described in regard to the .22 Remington Jet, and so no production revolvers were offered in this caliber. Instead, to cater to the varmint-hunting market, Sturm, Ruger adapted a single-shot variation of its Blackhawk revolver to the .256 Winchester Magnum cartridge. This was accomplished by replacing the conventional cylinder with a flat breechblock, pivoting about the original cylinder axis. This breechblock contained a long, slender firing pin reminiscent of that found in the old Trapdoor Springfield rifle, and the cartridge was chambered in the rear portion of a conventional revolver barrel. The existing side-rod ejector was modified to function with this chamber location. Though odd in appearance, and more so in function, this adaptation of the Blackhawk performed quite well as a single-shot pistol, and many shooters found it ideal for use on varmints. The .256 Winchester Magnum, like the .22 Remington Jet, failed to produce its claimed velocity—in this case 2350 fps. Nevertheless, its 60-grain thin-jacketed bullet did very well on varmints at long range.

This Ruger Blackhawk adaptation, known as the "Hawkeye," represents the maximum modification that has been applied to an existing standard-model handgun in the interest of hunting.

So much for guns developed for other purposes but well-suited to hunting. Now let's take a look at those guns which from the beginning were developed primarily to provide the handgun hunter with maximum efficiency and performance. First on the list we must place the Remington XP-100 pistol and its accompanying .221 Remington Fireball cartridge. At the same time the handgun makers were attempting to develop high-velocity, small-bore combinations, Remington sought to gain the same market by producing a unique single-shot pistol with a rifle-type turnbolt action. This was a very short and compact bolt-action based on the existing Model 721/722 rifle series and also destined to become the action of the M600 carbine. The action was fitted with a 10½-inch barrel carrying a ventilated plastic rib and conventional open sights, and the entire assembly was let into a molded plastic futuristic-looking stock. To achieve proper balance, the pistol grip was placed forward under the receiver ring, and a remote trigger also placed appropriately forward was connected to the fire-control mechanism by rods inside the stock.

The accompanying .221 Fireball cartridge was simply the .222 Remington case shortened, with its shoulder set back, and loaded with a 50-grain pointed bullet driven at a velocity of 2650 fps. This cartridge did (and does) produce its claimed velocity, and in the XP-100 pistol it achieved superb accuracy. My files contain many reports of 100-yard groups hovering around 1¼ to 1½ inches when shot with a 1.5X scope sight.

The Remington XP-100 may look weird but it does provide a degree of performance that is unobtainable in other types of one-hand firearms. The devoted varmint shooter will find that this

The Remington XP-100 is the most specialized of all pistols. It incorporates a rifle action and rifle cartridge into a handgun package. It is best of all for long-range varminting.

gun/cartridge combination will produce long-range kills that cannot be approached by any other model. Never tremendously popular, it nevertheless continues in production, and may be considered the most unusual of all domestic hunting handguns.

In the late 1960s, an investment-casting firm took an entirely different approach to developing a specialized hunting handgun. Under the name Thompson/Center Arms, this firm designed a break-open, single-shot mechanism with exposed hammer, quick-change barrel, and trigger-guard release for opening it. Because of the company's expertise in precision investment castings, Thompson/Center designed this gun for maximum use of this manufacturing method. Somewhat ungainly in appearance and handling in its original form, this gun was designated the "Contender." Because of its very sturdy construction and generous dimensions, it was adaptable to a wider range of cartridges and calibers than any other handgun before or since. Its interchangeable-barrel feature and barrel-mounted sights allow the shooter to possess as many barrels as he likes, in different calibers, lengths, and weights, and to shift them around to suit his

Possessing all the other virtues of the single-shot, the T/C Contender's greatest advantage to the hunter is its quick-change barrels in calibers from .22 RF to .308 or larger.

mood or needs. To date, Contender barrels have been produced for more than 30 different cartridges, ranging from the lowly .22 rimfire up through all of the handgun numbers and a variety of rifle cartridges, including the .30–30 and .308 Winchester. The design of the Contender is quite simple and sturdy and produces superb rifle-type accuracy.

If an individual were restricted to a single hunting handgun and wished to take a variety of game under a variety of conditions, his ideal choice would be the Contender, accompanied by a handful of barrels in different calibers.

To the surprise of many, a unique specialized autoloading handgun appeared on the scene in the mid-1960s. Designated "Auto Mag" and produced by the Auto Mag Corporation, it was lavishly advertised in advance of production and did not appear in the form of production guns (and then even only to a very limited extent) for several years. A great deal of difficulty occurred in achieving series production with this gun, most of those difficulties being financial and organizational rather than technical. Eventually, though, a standard model entered production in .44 AMP (Auto Mag Pistol) caliber, followed somewhat later by an additional chambering in .357 AMP.

The gun is unusually massive, weighing 57 ounces with a 6½-inch barrel, and is fabricated entirely from stainless steel. It is of short-recoil operation, utilizing a barrel and barrel extension joined rigidly together and mounted "slideably" upon the main frame. Inside the barrel extension is a short, light, rotating bolt fitted with multiple locking lugs at its head. Upon firing, the barrel, extension, and bolt

Among the autoloaders, the Auto Mag is outstanding in power, velocity, and long-range accuracy.

recoil rearward a short distance upon the frame, during which time a pin passing through the bolt and affixed to the frame rotates the bolt to unlock through helical cam grooves. After unlocking, the barrel and extension are halted, and the bolt continues rearward under its own momentum to extract, eject, cock, compress driving springs, and then be driven forward by those springs to strip a cartridge from the magazine, feed, chamber, and finally to be rotated into the locked position by the pin already mentioned. Because of the relatively great weight of its recoiling parts, the Auto Mag incorporates an accelerator which gives the bolt additional rearward velocity and energy when unlocking is completed. Only one other modern pistol, the Finnish Lahti, has been so fitted, accelerators generally being reserved for machine guns and automatic cannon. The barrel of the Auto Mag is fitted with a ventilated rib, and it features an exposed hammer, manual safety, automatic slide stop, and seven-shot magazine.

The .44 AMP originally was loaded to drive a 240-grain bullet at approximately 1800 fps at rifle-level chamber pressures of around 45,000 psi. Early factory loads, produced by the CDM plant in Mexico, fell far short of these specifications. Because of reduced velocity and chamber pressure, this ammunition could not be relied upon to cycle the Auto Mag action. The massiveness of the gun required the recoil impulse of the 240-grain bullet at 1400 fps or more for proper functioning. Today, only Super Vel loads the .44 AMP, and its 180-grain bullet at 1800 fps produces quite positive functioning with a substantial safety margin. The current .44 AMP factory load is the most powerful of all *production* big-bore handgun cartridges. The

later .357 AMP employs the same case necked down to use .355–
.356-inch-diameter bullets of 125-grains weight and upward. The Super Vel loading of this cartridge produces approximately 1900 fps
with a 125-grain bullet, giving it the flattest trajectory of any handgun
cartridge.

From the beginning, the Auto Mag pistol, a joint development of
Harry Sanford and Max Gera, was intended purely as a hunting gun.
Its size and weight alone—advantages for hunting—are disadvantages for any other purpose. Likewise, the AMP cartridges were
developed purely with hunting in mind, the goals being maximum
velocity, energy, and flatness of trajectory. In order to achieve these
goals, the gun was designed to safely withstand normal working
pressures in excess of 50,000 psi. This is why it has to be so heavy and
massive.

In the few years it has been in service, the Auto Mag has emerged
as a highly sophisticated, specialized hunting handgun superior in
performance on big game to any other—and virtually all species of
North American big game have been taken successfully with it. In
addition, it has been used extensively in Africa, mainly by Lee E.
Jurras, of Shelbyville, Indiana, on everything except the very largest
and most dangerous game.

There is a tendency to think of handgun hunting only in terms of
single-bullet ammunition—that is, the conventional bulleted cartridge combined with a rifled barrel. Seldom is any thought given to
serious use of shot cartridges in handguns, though there is one commercially available gun offered with modifications specifically for the
use of special shot ammunition.

This gun is the Thompson/Center "Hotshot" single-shot pistol
chambered for the .44 Magnum Hotshot cartridge. It's really the
standard Contender pistol fitted with a special barrel. The barrel, of
course, may be put on *any* Contender action. This barrel is chambered for the standard .44 Magnum case but is deeply throated for
an extended plastic shot capsule protruding .825-inch beyond the
case mouth. The barrel is rifled in conventional fashion, and is fitted
with a unique choke tube threaded to the muzzle. This tube provides
choke constriction, but its interior is not smooth. Instead, it contains
straight rifling-like lands and grooves which increase in depth from
rear to front. The grooves are not for choking action on the shot
charge, but instead serve to ensure that the tough plastic shot capsule
breaks up as it exits the muzzle, falls away in fragments, and allows
the shot charge to continue unimpeded. The sharp edges of the lands

cut through the capsule walls. It has been found that a plastic shot capsule of sufficient strength to withstand the stresses placed upon it by firing in a rifled bore simply will not break up consistently as it leaves the muzzle without additional help; and the grooved choke tube provides that assistance.

The question doubtless arises as to why the barrel is fully rifled if it is intended primarily for shot cartridges. The answer is simple: federal government regulations.

The Alcohol, Tobacco, and Firearms Division of the U.S. Treasury Department killed smoothbore revolvers by classifying them as sawed-off shotguns. A companion ruling at the same time allowed the use of shotshells in handguns, *provided* that the barrel remained rifled. Thus, in order to legally produce and sell a shotshell handgun, Thompson/Center was forced to rifle the barrel. This offers the sec-

Nonte isn't just shooting up a tree in this photo. He's using cylinder-length shot loads in his modified New Service Colt to peg a branch-running squirrel for the pot.

ondary advantage of being able to use standard bulleted .44 Magnum or .44 Special ammunition in the Hotshot pistol if one wishes. The extended throat does not appear to have any significant effect on accuracy with bulleted ammunition.

The Hotshot cartridge was developed and is currently loaded in the standard .44 Magnum cartridge case. From the beginning, it was obvious that the case alone could not contain a sufficient quantity of shot to make an effective load. In order to increase the shot capacity, Thompson/Center went to a longer molded plastic shot capsule which is seated and crimped in the case just as one would seat and crimp a conventional bullet.

The efficiency of the Hotshot barrel and ammunition has been well established in the field. I've seen skeet shot with them, and I've seen a good deal of upland game taken at reasonable ranges. It makes an ideal combination for helping to feed a camp full of hungry hunters whenever birds and other small game are available.

Probably the best-known handgun/shotshell combination was for a number of years the converted revolver turned out by the late Jim Harvey of Lakeville Arms. Harvey took S&W .44 and .45 revolvers and modified them extensively for use with specially concocted shot loads which provided adequate shot charges and patterns for consistent small game and bird kills out to 25 yards or so. No factory-loaded ammunition was ever produced for these guns, but Harvey provided instructions, dies, and components for customers to load their own, and also supplied custom-loaded ammunition on occasion.

Essentially, Harvey reamed out the rifling to produce a shotgun-style smoothbore barrel, either with conventional choking or with a removable choke tube threaded to the muzzle. Then the chambers were bored straight through to cylindrical form, and special cylinder-length cartridge cases were made up from appropriate rifle brass. Harvey's load for these cases consisted of a moderate charge of pistol powder (usually Unique), an over-powder wad, and a thin felt or composition filler wad, topped off with the amount of #9 shot that the remaining portion of the case would hold. A thin zinc disc was used as an over-shot wad and was secured by a heavy roll crimp applied to the case mouth. So loaded, some calibers would accommodate a full half-ounce of shot, an amount equal to the standard 2½-inch .410 shotshell load. When these loads were paired with a properly choked barrel of adequate length, they were nearly as effective as a .410 shotgun.

Unfortunately, before the Harvey conversions became very widely distributed, the U.S. Treasury Department ruled that smoothbored handguns were to be classified the same as sawed-off shotguns and, thereby, subject to special federal tax and registration. This was done in spite of the fact that there had not been any reported instances of a shot revolver involved in the commission of a crime. For all practical purposes, this governmental interference eliminated the Harvey shot-revolver conversion.

Of course, Harvey was by no means the first man to develop reasonably effective methods of loading and firing shot cartridges from revolvers. At least 50 years ago, one Bud Dalrymple was converting old .45-caliber single-action Colt revolvers by smoothboring and choking the barrels, then handloading shot cartridges in standard .45 Colt cases. Others have done likewise, and from way back in the black-powder days until recent years, factory-loaded shotshells in the various larger revolver calibers have been available. Today, none of those shot loads survive as standard items, and original cartridges are generally priced as collector's items.

It is occasionally possible to stumble onto some of the military .45 ACP shot loads designed for survival use and designated M15. These cartridges differ from the commercial revolver loads in that they are assembled in elongated cases—that is, the case is the same length as

During World War II, the long-case, .45 ACP shot load was issued for jungle-survival use by downed aircrewmen. Shown alongside the standard ball cartridges. These cases work well in either revolver or auto, but are quite difficult to locate in any quantity.

a standard bulleted cartridge, with the forward portion reduced somewhat in diameter to enter the chamber throat. This particular cartridge will not feed through the standard .45 Government Model magazine and must be manually chambered and fired single-shot.

One of the guns in which the author has used shotshells in the field is this four-inch M1950 S&W .44 Special. Typical field loading consists of the three shot loads shown and three Keith-type bulleted cartridges.

I've experimented to a considerable extent with various hand-loaded shotshell cartridges for handguns, as well as modifications of guns to obtain maximum performance from those loads. A fairly detailed treatment of the subject was published in the November-December, 1969, edition of *Handloader* magazine, and it seems appropriate to insert that material here, with the kind permission of editor Neal Knox and the publisher, Wolfe Publishing Company.

"It's great sport to bowl over a bouncing cottontail or a squirrel—even quail, if you're lucky—for the pot. More utilitarian is the use of shot in a sixgun to eliminate a pestiferous rattler or copperhead who

The smallest practical shot load is this standard-length .38 Special. Only a few #9 shot can be accommodated beneath the gas-check over-shot wad. A .38 Special heavy wadcutter load is shown for comparison.

objects to your use of his pet foraging ground. Half an ounce of shot in the bigger bores is sure poison on any flicker-tongued reptile you'll meet.

"The closest to a shot pistol to be commercially offered in recent years is the Thompson/Center Contender [with the Hotshot barrel and choke]. . . . Long before Thompson/Center or its Contender was conceived, and after a great deal of experimenting which led to the loads for standard guns discussed in this article, I decided that I wasn't going to be satisfied until I had a handgun designed specifically for shot loads. Although properly assembled shot loads can give surprisingly good performance in unaltered guns, standard handgun cases lack the capacity needed for effective patterns at longer range. The big-bore revolver we brewed up to handle those heavy shot loads does a very fine job and still does not have to be registered as a sawed-off shotgun, for the barrel remains rifled.

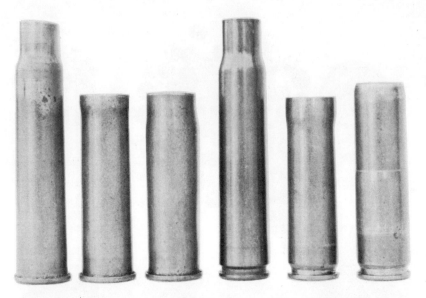

Once a big-bore revolver has been altered, it will handle formed and handloaded cases such as these with up to 1/2-ounce of shot.

"A Colt or Smith & Wesson M-1917 revolver, caliber .45 ACP, is the basis for the conversion job. Either will do nicely, but Colts are somewhat cheaper in this area and are also a wee bit less trouble to alter; we used the old Colt New Service revolver pictured here.

"Ammunition is the first problem. There is no commercially available shot cartridge that will do the job well, nor is there a ready-made case that will hold the needed amount of shot. This is solved by first altering the cylinder to take a straight 1.60-inch-length case, made especially to fit.

"First, remove the crane and cylinder assembly by turning out the crane lock screws on the right of the frame ahead of the trigger guard. Then use tape-wrapped needle-nose pliers to unscrew the ratchet, allowing the cylinder to slide off the crane. The chamber throats must then be opened up to the diameter of the rest of the chamber. Careful hand use of 7/16- to ½-inch expansion or adjustable reamer will do a good job. Should you have a drill press available, the job is easier and simpler. Chuck a 31/64-inch drill, then clamp the cylinder to the press table solidly while the drill is seated inside the chamber. Make certain of correct alignment.

"Once the cylinder is clamped in place, the drill may be easily run

This old handgun, a Colt New Service revolver, becomes doubly utilitarian when its cylinder is loaded with three bulleted cartridges and three clipped cylinder-length shot loads for close-range work on small game. Made from .30–06 brass, the shot cases hold an adequate charge of pellets.

through the throat, cutting it out to the same diameter as the rest of the chamber. This process is repeated for each chamber. Progressively finer grades of abrasive cloth should then be wrapped around a dowel and used to polish all tool marks from the throat as well as any roughness that exists in the original chamber walls. Use a scraper or sharp knife blade to remove the burr that will have been turned up at the front of each chamber. If not removed, this burr could interfere with free rotation of the cylinder.

"The bored-out cylinder will now accept a straight case capable of holding up to slightly over ½-ounce of No. 9 shot, depending on the wad column. Shorten .30–06 cases to a length of 1.60 and chamfer the mouths. Charge these cases with four grains of Bullseye powder, topped with a ¼-inch wad and whatever shot the case will hold. Secure the shot in place with a heavy grease or soap wad. Fire-form these loaded cases, loading them one at a time in the cylinder since the grease wad will not hold the shot in place under force of recoil. Of course, half-moon clips must be used, both to permit extraction of the cases and to support them against the firing pin blow, since the shoulder that supported the original .45 ACP case no longer exists.

"If the idea of using half-moon clips doesn't appeal to you, make up rimmed cases in the same manner, using Norma 8x57JR brass. Krag .30–40 will also work, but is about .010-inch undersize at the head, though perfectly safe. With either, the rim is too thin. Epoxy thin brass washers to the front of the rims to produce a total rim thickness of .080. Any other practical method of increasing rim thickness may be used. Incidentally, if you begin with a .455-caliber cylinder, no rim thickness increase is necessary. Sarco, Inc., 192 Central, Stirling, N.J. 07980, can furnish such cylinders.

"After fire-forming, these cases may be loaded with 7.5 grains of Unique powder; a .44-caliber gas check, open side down (as over-powder wad); a ¼-inch filler wad; and shot of your choice (I use No. 9's) to within 1/16-inch of the case mouth. An inverted .45-caliber gas check serves as an overshot wad. Crimping the wad in place is accomplished in standard .45 Long Colt seating/crimping dies after running the seating screw down far enough to contact the over-shot wad to hold it level and in place. Careful adjustment is required. Too much pressure on the over-shot wad will bulge or dimple the case. Resizing of cases prior to reloading is easily accomplished in .45 Long Colt or .45 ACP sizing dies of any make reamed straight through; that is, without a shoulder the extra long case will encounter before entering full depth.

"Rifling chews up naked shot and produces erratic patterns. Eliminate this by cutting shot wrappers from thin polyethylene or vinyl sheet. The type used in garment bags is thick enough; that used in dry-cleaning bags is not. Cut the wrapper to reach from over-powder wad to mouth of case and to completely encircle the shot charge without overlapping. The wrapper prevents shot from being deformed by the rifling and results in improved patterns. It parts company with the shot charge very soon after exiting the muzzle.

"Alternatively, you may, at greater cost, load with prepared "Shot-Caps" sold by Remco, 1404 Whitesboro St., Utica, N.Y. 13502. They consist of a molded plastic cup into which the shot charge is sealed at the factory. The .45 Colt size works best in the altered .30–06 case and contains roughly ½-ounce of shot. The over-powder and filler wads must be eliminated for Shot-Cap loading.

"With cylinder altered and ammunition available, the gun will give pretty fair short-range results without further work. Maximum effect is obtained, though, when a choke tube is added to the muzzle. This is not particularly difficult to do, though it will require the services of someone with a lathe.

"Remove the crane and cylinder, then carve out a pair of hard-

Barrel removal for lathe work incidental to choke-tube installation is not difficult and the gun will not be damaged if reasonable care is exercised. With the barrel pin removed and barrel securely clamped in a vise, the frame will normally turn off easily by use of any convenient hardwood lever, in this case a hammer handle. Keep the pressure point as far forward as possible on the topstrop to avoid bending it; if the barrel is very tight, use a square-section lever to distribute the stress more widely over the frame.

wood blocks between which the barrel of your gun may be sand-wiched in a vise. A little rosin sprinkled in the grooves will help get a good grip on the barrel. Clamp the barrel tightly in a heavy vise, then shape a hardwood stick so that it may be inserted in the frame opening. Using this (a hammer handle works fine) as a handle, turn the frame off the barrel. Don't forget to drift out the barrel pin first. Now, take the barrel to your friendly neighborhood machinist and have him turn down the muzzle. Some small part of the front sight may be lost in the process, especially on Smith & Wesson guns. This doesn't hurt a thing. Turn a piece of steel stock 2½ inches long. Drill through its length with a 7/16-inch drill, then counterbore to fit the trued-up muzzle. Saw, file, or grind a slot that will pass snugly over the front sight base, then scrape or polish out the rear of the counter-bore (if necessary) so the choke tube will seat solidly over the muzzle without binding and without slippiness. Clamp the tube in place, then drill a lateral hole through the sight base and upper part of the tube. A roll pin, taper pin, or screw then serves to hold the tube tightly in place, yet permits quick removal when you wish.

"Finishing the choke tube up to proper inside dimensions is no great problem. Slot a piece of 7/16-inch rod with your hacksaw, file the flats, then soft-solder or epoxy two pieces of old hacksaw blade in the slot. Carefully grind the pieces of blade to the shape indicated in the drawing of the reamer. Stone the ground edges smooth and square with the sides. Attach a handle of some sort to the rod. Insert this reamer into the rear of the choke tube and twist it. The pieces of saw blade will take scraping cuts off the inside of the tube and go progressively deeper as you keep turning. It will take a while to get the job done, but keep at it until only ⅜-inch of the original 7/16-inch hole is unaltered. Back the tool up frequently and keep chips cleaned out of the hole. A dab of drilling or tapping lubricant will help. Don't try to rush the job by spinning the reamer rapidly in a drill press—the edges will burn up.

"Now polish the remainder of the 7/16-inch hole out to a diameter of .450, using abrasive cloth wrapped around a dowel or metal rod. Polish the tapered portion of the choke as smooth as you can get it in the same way. Spinning the dowel in a portable electric drill or drill press is the fastest way of getting this done, but don't go too fast or you will enlarge the hole too much and spoil the tube.

"Attach the tube to the gun as already outlined and you are ready for a little test shooting. The dimensions shown in the drawing gave excellent results on the gun we made up but you may want to make slight changes in the interest of getting just the pattern that suits

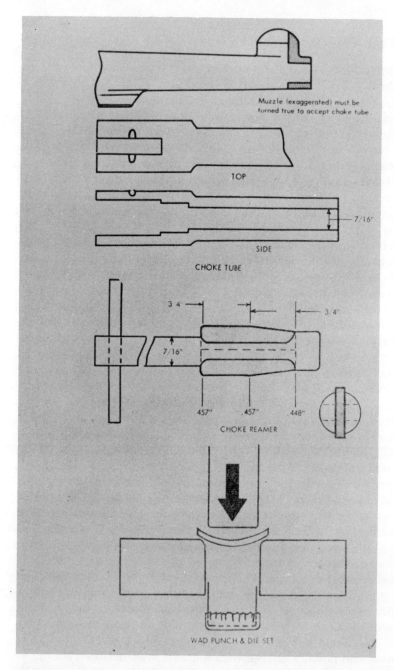

Muzzle (exaggerated) must be
turned true to accept choke tube.

TOP

7/16"

SIDE

CHOKE TUBE

3 4

3/4"

7/16"

.457"  .457"  .448"

CHOKE REAMER

WAD PUNCH & DIE SET

This drawing shows the alterations to a barrel, the basic choke tube for attachment to it, and beneath that a shop-made choke reamer in .45 caliber for shaping the tube to produce best patterns. At bottom is a punch and die set for forming over-powder cup-type wads from cardboard.

your needs best. I have always patterned this type of gun at 15 to 25 feet, feeling that seldom will it be used at any appreciably greater range. Patterns shot at that range are deadly on snakes.

"Incidentally, a similar choke tube can be fitted to some auto pistols. In the case of the Colt .45 Auto, make essentially the same tube, but leave off the slotted counterbore to fit over the barrel. Instead, have the tube carefully welded or brazed to the front of a spare barrel bushing. Installation is then simply a matter of installing the modified bushing. Care must be exercised to ensure that the tube is aligned on the bushing so as to form a straight extension of the barrel.

"To be sure of the legal status of a smoothbore choke tube, we went direct to the horse's mouth for an answer. Telephone queries were made to members of the legal, operations, and enforcement branches of the ATFD in Washington. The opinion received was that the use of a detachable choke tube would not be in violation of the law as long as the rifled bore remained unchanged and the revolver chambers would not accept a commercially available shotgun shell.

"It is entirely practical to use ball ammunition in the altered gun. Standard .45 ACP loads can be used as long as they are placed in half-moon clips. Since the guiding chamber throat has been greatly enlarged, accuracy is nothing to brag about, especially with jacketed bullets. Use of lead-bullet .45 Auto Rim loads produces slightly better results. The slight amount of constriction at the muzzle of the choke tube will not cause any trouble.

"Best results with bulleted ammo are obtained, however, with cartridges loaded especially for the altered chambers. This is done by using your favorite powder charge in the long cases, seating inverted bullets flush with the case mouth. My favorite ball load is the Lyman/Keith No. 454424 bullet seated upside-down, base flush with the case mouth and crimped tightly in place. Accuracy is excellent since the bullet enters directly into the rifling as it leaves the case. I use 7.5 grains of Unique behind it regularly, but up to 10.0 grains can be used with safety, still producing acceptable accuracy out to 50 yards or more. A good short-range defense load consists of 7.5 grains of Unique behind two .454 diameter lead balls seated right down on the powder charge with a grease wad between them.

"Since ex-military .45 and .455 cylinders for both Colt and S&W '17's are readily available, it's worthwhile to use a spare for the shot conversion. Then you can switch cylinders to shoot either shot or standard bulleted ammunition. Best of all is to make up a complete cylinder/crane unit which can be easily exchanged, even in the field.

"It isn't necessary to alter a gun to obtain pretty damn good performance with home-brewed shot loads. Several different approaches may be taken. In the .45 M-1917, alter .30–06 or .308 cases as described earlier, and fire-form them in the unaltered chamber. They can then be resized in dies RCBS makes for ".45 ACP Long Shot." This produces a cylinder-length case with a slight bottleneck and a sharp shoulder to headspace on the chamber shoulder. The bottleneck portion fits into the cylinder throat nicely. A .45-caliber card wad must be used over powder because a .45 gas check cannot be seated through the neck without deformation. The card wad will go through okay, and still expand to fit tight down where it belongs, as will the filler wad. Use a .44 gas check over shot, and crimp in the manner already described. Crimping requires the RCBS special die or a .44 crimp die opened up to accept the rear part of the case.

"Another alternative in the same guns is to use the Remco .45 Long Colt or .45 ACP Shot-Cap in .45 ACP or .45 AR cases. The much longer .45 Colt Shot-Cap is best since it holds the most shot. Length is no problem in revolver cylinders, but is greatly restricted in autos. Shot-Cap loading and performance data is given in the accompanying table.

# HANDGUN SHOTSHELL LOADS

### *.38 Special*

| | | | |
|---|---|---|---|
| Remco Shot-Cap | 3.5 Bullseye | 156 grains shot | 782 fps |
| Gel. Capsule | 4.5 Unique | 140 grains shot | |
| Std. Case | 3.5 Bullseye | 98 grains shot | |

### *.357 Magnum*

| | | | |
|---|---|---|---|
| Remco Shot-Cap | 4.0 Bullseye | 156 grains shot | 874 fps |
| Gel. Capsule | 4.5 Bullseye | 140 grains shot | |
| Std. Case | 5.0 Unique | 120 grains shot | |

### *.44 Special*

| | | |
|---|---|---|
| Remco Shot-Cap | 6.0 Unique | 250 grains shot |
| Long Case | 6.0 Unique | 240 grains shot |

## .44–40

| | | |
|---|---|---|
| Remco Shot-Cap | 6.0 Unique | 250 grains shot |
| Long Case | 6.0 Unique | 240 grains shot |

## .44 Magnum

| | | | |
|---|---|---|---|
| Remco Shot-Cap | 7.0 Bullseye | 250 grains shot | 1125 fps |
| Long Case | 7.5 Unique | 240 grains shot | |
| Std. Case | 7.0 Unique | 175 grains shot | |

## .45 ACP

| | | |
|---|---|---|
| Remco Shot-Cap | 3.5 Bullseye | 150 grains shot |
| Long Case | 3.5 Bullseye | 140 grains shot |
| Long Case | 7.0 Unique | 250 grains shot |

## .45 Colt

| | | | |
|---|---|---|---|
| Remco Shot-Cap | 4.2 Bullseye | 270 grains shot | 827 fps |
| Remco Shot-Cap | 7.5 Unique | 270 grains shot | |
| Long Case | 7.5 Unique | 250 grains shot | |

"The above loads include approximate shot weight, which will vary according to the capacity of the case, since all space above the over-powder wad or wads is filled with shot. Standard-case loads are assembled with an appropriate-sized gas check seated flange-down directly upon the powder, remainder of case space filled with shot (usually No. 9), with another gas check as an over-shot wad, flush with case mouth, moderate crimp. Loads for .44 and .45 are improved by approximately ⅛-inch filler wad between OP wad and shot (a split ¼-inch .410 wad is satisfactory). Gelatin capsule containers are seated against a thin card OP wad and secured in case with waterglass or light crimp. Many odd-diameter card wads are available from Alcan Co. Remco Shot-Caps are seated directly against the powder and secured by a light to moderate crimp.

"Other calibers present different problems. In addition to the more or less standard methods outlined in the load table you can use standard cases and Remco Shot-Caps in .38 Special, .357 Magnum, .44 Special, .44 Magnum, .44–40, .45 ACP, and .45 Long Colt. Alternatively, go to a large pharmacy or veterinary-supply house and obtain gelatin capsules of bullet diameter. Fill them with No. 9 shot and then finger-seat in the case on a card over-shot wad. Secure it in the case with waterglass or a light crimp. The capsule protects the shot from bore damage and adds to case capacity.

"Capsules aren't listed by dimensions, but rather by capacity and/or arbitrary numbers in pharmaceutical catalogs. Your best bet is to take an empty case along and ask your pharmacist to let you check his stock. Pick a capsule size that fits snugly in the mouth of the case. If you need some for .44 or .45 caliber, better try a veterinary, rather than a run-of-the-mill pharmacy. The latter won't usually have sizes so large.

Either a Five-In-One blank case (suitably fire-formed) or a plastic shot capsule will greatly increase .45 Colt shot capacity over that of the standard case.

"Recently, I've discovered another solution for shot loads in .38–40, .44–40, and .45 Long Colt. The Remington "5-in-1" blank cartridge is made for film-industry use to fit all three chambers. Unprimed cases can be obtained on special order through your Remington dealer. They are about ¼-inch longer than standard cases, so will hold more shot. In .38–40's, use the case as is, with a .40-caliber gas check for over-shot wad. A special over-powder wad will have to be formed from waxed cardboard.

From left to right are standard bulleted cartridges in .41 Magnum, .44 Special, and .44 Magnum, each alongside its companion cylinder-length shotshell case ready for fire-forming in unaltered chambers.

"For .44–40 expand the neck to the point where the case will just barely chamber easily. Some chambers are loose enough that a .44 gas check may be used over-shot; others will require that you cut a slightly smaller card wad. A .45 card wad may be used over-powder as described for the .45 ACP Long Shot case. This same case may be used in .45 Colt by expanding the neck as above, using a .45-caliber card wad over-powder, a .44 gas check over-shot. Powder charges (I prefer Unique) within those recommended for bullets of weight equal to the shot charge should be used. In all instances, performance will be considerably improved by the use of polyethylene shot wrappers and a choke tube.

"Self-loaders present a problem—but not an insurmountable one —in the use of shotshells. Personally, I consider only the .45 ACP worthwhile. Smaller calibers simply don't hold enough shot to be practical. If it can be found in quantity, the long military .45 ACP shot case is the simplest to use. Unfortunately, it is difficult to find either empty or loaded except as collector's specimens. However, it can be loaded just as the necked revolver cases already described, and RCBS can furnish the dies.

"An alternative is to make similar cases from .308 brass. Cut to 1.224-inch length, then size in the RCBS .45 ACP Long Shot die to form the headspacing shoulder. Expand the neck to .450 outside diameter, then ream neck-wall thickness to no more than .010 with an adjustable expansion reamer. Load as for the necked .45 M-1917 revolver case, using 4.0 grains of Bullseye, card over-powder wad, ⅛-inch filler wad, shot to fill, then .44 gas check over-shot wad. A special die must be made for crimping—a shorter version of the .45 ACP Long Shot die. With careful polishing of the feed ramp, some guns will feed this round okay, but only as the top round in the magazine.

"To obtain normal magazine feeding, the forward half of the necked portion must be given sufficient cone shape to enter the magazine freely to full depth. A simple 60-degree hole in a die blank will serve to accomplish this, then cut card over-shot wads to fit. The coned cases will feed, and with 4.0 to 4.5 grains of Bullseye, will function the action semi-automatically. Incidentally, the coned portion of the case should be carefully annealed. And, even then, such cases are pretty much a one-shot affair, for the coned portion frequently splits on firing.

"The .38 Super may be given similar treatment, making cases from .38 Special brass with the head turned to .38 Super dimensions. I don't think it's worth the effort, but it will work with a relatively small charge of shot. Single-shot .38 Super shot loads can be made from standard cases with Remco .38 Special Shot-Caps, but must be hand-chambered.

"Shot loads can be more than utilitarian. They are great for potting small game for camp meat; and with a choke-fitted gun, you'd be surprised at the fun you can have on the skeet field or shooting over a hand trap. Give it a try."

# 7

---

# *Customized Guns*

We are a nation of individualists, and gun buffs are particularly individualistic. Handgunners like to think they are even more different; and the handgun *hunter* is even less likely to run with the pack than the rest. That makes him a fellow with firm convictions, one who likes what he likes and wants what he wants to the extent that he is seldom entirely satisfied with across-the-counter guns and equipment.

Hunters of all sorts have a proclivity for wanting something just a little bit different, a little bit better, or made or modified to suit certain preferences or foibles which gave rise long, long ago to so-called "custom gunsmithing." Specialized artisans scattered across the country, unfortunately not too great in number, cater to these wants with the ability to take any standard handgun and rebarrel, rechamber, resight, restock, refinish, tune, cut and file, and perform all manner of other operations that will transform a standard gun so that it meets a particular individual's needs or wants.

To quote a good friend of mine who loves modern revolvers and who embarks on a handgun hunt two or three times each year, "Why in hell do people like you want to cut up or change a perfectly good gun?" He wants all of his guns to remain exactly as they were produced at the factory, even if some of their characteristics are by no means ideally suited to the game or shooting involved. My response to his question (and his sometimes profane comments on the customizing I've done on my own guns) is simply, "A gun will do some jobs better when it is changed a bit; the factories make guns for everybody, so they can't be perfect for *each* individual."

Therein lies the basis for customizing. A standard model is a combination of features and characteristics intended to suit the most people the best—this is a simple economic necessity brought about by the realities of the mass market and mass production. It is not economically feasible for the factory to offer more than minor variations in barrel length, caliber, sights, finishes, and stocks. As a result, the gun is acceptable or adequate to a large number of shooters, but ideal for very few, if any. So we customize.

Functionally, there are many desirable results to be obtained by customizing your sixgun or auto. The ultimate goal is to improve the field performance of the gun/ammunition/shooter combination, and here is a fairly extensive list of the operations that may be performed toward that end:

1. Install a longer barrel to improve ballistic performance and lengthen the sight radius.

2. Install a heavier or lighter barrel to improve balance for the individual shooter or to alter recoil and jump characteristics.

3. Change the caliber to one more or less powerful to suit a particular need.

4. Alter the sights (a category that ranges from modifying existing sights or installing a better-designed or adjustable sight to mounting a telescopic sight) to suit the shooter's eyesight or hunting conditions.

5. Fit a muzzle brake or compensator to improve accuracy and follow-up shot efficiency by controlling jump and recoil.

6. Install a sighting rib to improve sighting efficiency and perhaps to change weight and balance.

7. Tune and polish the mechanism for maximum functional reliability (not always offered in standard factory guns).

8. Alter the trigger pull or lockwork (this may include installation of wider or different-shaped trigger and/or hammer) to produce maximum handling ease and speed for a particular individual and to improve accuracy through better gun control.

9. Add weights to improve balance or dampen recoil.

10. Alter the configuration of the trigger guard and/or butt to provide maximum control with a two-hand grip.

11. Install a grip or stocks of special materials and shape to suit the

individual's hands and shooting style.

12. Remove sharp edges and corners to prevent snagging on clothing or brush.

13. Apply special surface finishes to protect against corrosion and to reduce glare that might alarm game when hunting.

14. Modify the gun to adapt it to slings, neck straps, shooting rests, shoulder stocks, and the like, to improve long-range accuracy.

Of course, the foregoing list is not necessarily complete, and in evaluating what you would like to see in *your* ideal hunting handgun you may well come up with several other modifications.

It would be difficult to conceive of a single gun and situation under which all of those 14 listed modifications could be applied as a practical matter. The typical customizing job involves only a few of the operations. To show how they will—when properly chosen—improve the efficiency and game-taking capabilities of a particular gun, let's take a look at a pair of Ruger .44 Magnum Super Blackhawk revolvers which have been customized for Lee E. Jurras, president of Super Vel Cartridge Corp., and well-known international handgun hunter.

The first of these guns is quite a few years old, and has taken about 35 head of big game in the U.S., Canada, and Africa. It has evolved through several trips to the pistolsmith into its present form in order to make it comply with the owner's changing ideas based upon many hunts. It is intended to be as compact as is compatible with acceptable performance from the .44 Magnum cartridge, suitable for all but dangerous game at short to medium ranges, resistant to corrosion and the vicissitudes of field service—and yet it retains a fair degree of utility as a general-purpose sidearm.

Toward this end, the original 7½-inch barrel has been cut and crowned to 5½ inches; the barrel has been Mag-Na-Ported to reduce recoil and jump; the lockwork has been carefully tuned and fitted and then plated to prevent rust; the grips and straps have been slightly reshaped to suit the owner's hand; the hammer spur has been modified for ease of rapid cocking; and the entire gun has been given a velvety matte nickel finish to resišt corrosion and prevent massive sun-glare. I've shot this gun many times, and there is no doubt that all of the alterations have improved its efficiency and utility as a hunting gun under the conditions for which it was intended.

The second of Lee's Rugers also began as a .44 Magnum Super

Blackhawk. It now sports a heavy 10-inch barrel made from a Douglas premium-grade blank, highly refined lockwork and trigger pull, custom-fitted stocks, and a few minor cosmetic modifications, but remains otherwise standard. This gun evolved into its present configuration in order to squeeze the maximum velocity and energy (compatible with safe chamber pressures) from the .44 Magnum cartridge for use on the largest North American game. It was, in fact, made up primarily to be used on Alaskan brown bear on Kodiak Island. It performs superbly, delivering over 2000 fps with a 180-grain JSP bullet and providing rifle-like accuracy on the order of two minutes of angle. The only reason it has not yet put down a substantial brownie is that on its trips to Alaska, weather and other conditions have combined to prevent one big enough from being seen over its sights.

This second Ruger has been customized to suit a narrow set of conditions and for the primary purpose of taking dangerous game at close range where maximum power is demanded; therefore, its handiness and ability to meet some other hunting conditions have been sacrificed. On the other hand, the first gun has been customized to meet a wide variety of other hunting conditions that might be encountered almost anywhere in the world.

Every operation performed on both of those guns has been aimed at functional improvement. There are no fancy frills except a pair of carved ivory grips—made from the tusk of an elephant killed by Jurras in Botswana—which are occasionally installed on the short-barreled gun for display only.

This isn't to imply that cosmetic customizing is not worthwhile. Reshaping of certain parts may be undertaken to improve the lines and appearance of a gun, and special finishes may be used as much for eye appeal as for the protection they offer. Fancy-grained woods may be used for stocks, and they may be combined with decorative carving, artistic inlays, or the owner's monogram; some pistoleros go for ornate gold and silver Mexican-style grips in order to dress up a gun. Of course, the ultimate in handgun decoration is fine hand engraving, combined with precious-metal inlays—the latter usually depicting assorted game animals. Cosmetic customizing is even more costly than functional modification. Even a modest amount of good engraving will cost more than a complete functional alteration job, including a special barrel—and thorough engraving coverage and inlay work can easily exceed $1,000 in cost.

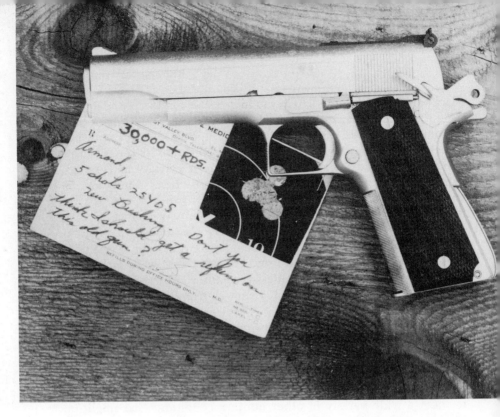

This is a Swenson-customized GıT .45 Auto with special finish, new
sights, an accurizing job, and other modifications. Note the degree of
accuracy produced, as shown on the test target.

   If artistic guns turn you on, and if you can afford them, by all means
carry on in that direction—but keep in mind that these modifications
will contribute nothing whatever to the gun's ability to take game
cleanly. If your fancy gun is to be used in the field as well as displayed
in your den, then add whatever *functional* modifications are needed
*first;* then dress it up to suit.
   I've often heard it said that there simply isn't all that much that can
be done to customize the more popular hunting handguns such as
the Smith & Wesson Magnum revolvers. Actually, any of the modifications I've described can be applied not only to S&W products but
to the products of every other foreign or domestic handgun maker.
There are, of course, operations that can be performed upon revolvers that cannot be performed upon autoloaders, and the reverse is
equally true.

This handwritten note in the image reads:

4/2/72

#T176911
5 SHOTS
25 YDS OFFHAND
1940 ISSUE
MILITARY AMMO
9M.M.
SHOT BY ARMAND
SWENSON APRIL 7, 1972
FOR LEE JURRAS
OF SUPER VEL CO.

This Browning auto was customized by Swenson for Lee Jurras, especially for use with 90-grain JHP 9mm loads. The goals were improved accuracy, reliability, and handling, and all three goals were achieved.

Generally speaking, autoloaders offer easier installation of special sights and ribs, but place severe limitations upon special barrels, permitting only a modest increase in length. On the other hand, sight changes are a bit more difficult on revolvers, but one has almost complete freedom in installing a barrel of any reasonable length, weight, or configuration. Revolvers also offer a great deal of freedom in reshaping the butt and trigger guard, while autoloaders offer very little latitude in these areas. Revolvers allow all manner of recoil- and jump-reducing muzzle devices to be fitted with relative ease, while the inherent characteristics of autoloaders make it extremely difficult to achieve a practical installation of any such device.

Perhaps the simplest way for you to determine the practicality of various customizing operations on both revolvers and autos is to lay one of each out in front of you, then go step-by-step over the list of operations set forth earlier in this chapter. What can and cannot be done to each type should then be readily apparent.

Generally speaking, most hunting-handgun customizing is functional in nature—intended to improve the game-getting capabilities of the gun/ammunition/shooter combination under a given set of conditions. Regardless of what you may have been told, both revolvers and autos of various sorts are adaptable to a wide range of customizing operations. The best way to learn more precisely what is available in this area is to write for catalogs and listings from the custom pistolsmiths listed in the Directory of Supplies & Services in Appendix 5 of this volume.

# 8

## Ammunition

A handgun or any other firearm is merely the vehicle for launching a projectile. The projectile itself is the only part of the entire system —shooter/gun/ammunition—which actually contacts the game and thus achieves the desired result of a quick, humane kill. Therefore, assuming reasonable skill on the part of the shooter, the ammunition actually assumes considerably greater importance than the gun. Obviously, the gun *is* important—but, given identical caliber, a cheap, fixed-sight gun with proper ammunition will be more effective on game than the most costly and sophisticated gun used with an inferior or incorrect load.

The inherent shortcomings of handgun ammunition (compared to that for rifles) must be discussed if one is to understand the full importance of proper load selection for handgun hunting. The principal limitations of *all* handgun ammunition—bar none—are in the area of velocity, energy, penetration, and trajectory height. Spinoff disadvantages due to those factors may be found in poor expansion, excessively high velocity-loss rate, and relatively poor accuracy. (All of these, of course, are "poor" only in comparison with contemporary rifle ammunition.)

Most of the disadvantages may be traced directly to a single factor: the inability of *any* ammunition to produce rifle-class velocities in handguns. And, of course, that inability may be laid directly at the very short barrel length of handguns and their inability to safely withstand rifle-class chamber pressures (with the exception of an Auto Mag pistol, which does function at rifle pressures). To a lesser degree, this lack of velocity is due to the fact that dimensional limitations of handguns do not allow the use of cartridges with sufficient powder capacity. It is interesting to note that the very largest of handgun cartridges, the .44 Magnum, has a capacity of only 25.2 grains of water (see the Case Capacity table in Appendix 1) which is substantially less than the 35.8-grain capacity of the smallest rifle cartridge normally recommended for big-game hunting, the .30–30 Winchester.

In any event, the maximum velocities that can be obtained in conventional handguns (excluding the Auto Mag) range from 1500 to 1800 fps, which is only about 60 to 70 percent of the velocity normally produced by conventional non-Magnum, hunting-rifle ammunition.

This velocity limitation is directly responsible for lack of striking energy. As if the velocity handicap weren't enough, even the velocity levels that *can* be reached are achieved within a rather severe bullet-weight limitation. The .357 Magnum's highest velocities, a bit over 1600 fps, can be obtained only with light bullets weighing about 110 to 125 grains—while a rifle cartridge of the same .36 caliber (the .358 Winchester is a good example) will normally use a bullet weighing *at least* 200 grains. More likely it will be 225 to 250 grains, with a velocity well in excess of 2000 fps.

These two factors, limited velocity and bullet weight, are responsible singly or in concert for all the other shortcomings mentioned. Low velocity means high mid-range trajectory height; light bullet weight (with attendant high velocity-loss rate) also enhances trajectory height, and in addition reduces penetration at target; low velocity reduces bullet expansion in game, no matter how efficient the projectile is.

Therefore, it is impossible for any handgun ammunition to even approach the effectiveness of the most mediocre of modern hunting-rifle cartridges.

Some handgun hunters do apparently run up better kill records than some rifle hunters—but this is due to careful and skillful hunting and shooting, and is achieved in spite of handgun ammunition limitations rather than because of them.

However, the picture isn't nearly as black as I have painted it. Handgun ammunition, bullets in particular, has in recent years undergone a considerable design overhaul. Beginning with the advent

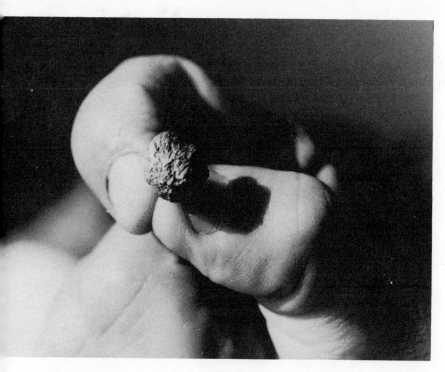

Modern handgun bullets are designed to expand well. This 137-grain .357 bullet expanded to nearly twice its original diameter in a South African blesbok.

of the first Super Vel ammunition (developed and produced by my co-author, Lee E. Jurras), jacketed bullets that will expand reliably and well at handgun velocities have been developed and are currently available in a wide range of calibers and ammunition makes. These same designs have been further refined to achieve higher velocities than were previously available. In addition, bullet profiles and other characteristics have been modified to permit greater transfer of energy to the target. As a result, bullet *lethality* has in some instances been doubled or tripled for given calibers from what was available a bare 15 years ago. With that as a background, we can discuss the selection of factory-loaded handgun-hunting ammunition with better understanding.

First of all, we have two basic types of loadings available, and minor variations within those types. The first is the traditional, lead, heavy-bullet load, producing moderate velocities ranging from a bit over 800 fps in the .38 Special up to about 1500 fps in the Magnum cartridges. Bullets in these loads are generally swaged of a slightly

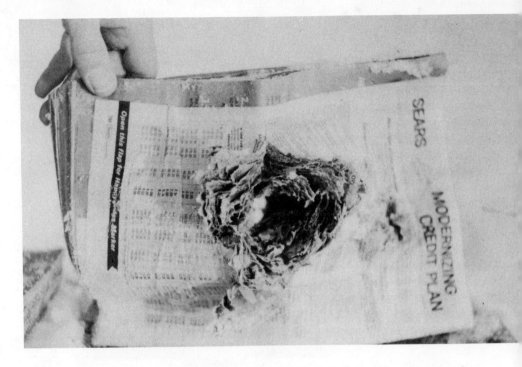

Lacking any more sophisticated test medium, bullet performance can be rated by shooting through wet catalogs, phone directories, or tightly packed newspapers or magazines.

hardened (with antimony) lead alloy, and are lubricated with grease or wax placed in circumferential grooves or cannelures rolled into the bearing surface of the bullet. The bullet may be entirely of lead construction, or it may have a thin copper or brass gas check pressed onto its base. At the higher velocities in this range, a gas check reduces the probability of bore leading, and is, in fact, essential for this purpose with the softer lead alloys used in early .44 Magnum ammunition. The lack of a gas check is responsible for the notorious reputation of the .357 Magnum for leading bores heavily. These lead-bullet loads generally produce good penetration because of their relatively great bullet weight, and at the upper end of the velocity range will produce *some* bullet expansion if the lead alloy is soft enough. Generally speaking, the ammunition manufacturers use a fairly soft alloy, not only to promote expansion but because it is less wearing on swaging equipment and is, therefore, more economical to manufacture. Alloys differ, and it is possible to identify those which produce maximum expansion and those which produce maximum penetration by trying several different makes. Obviously, one cannot have maximum levels of *both* expansion and penetration in the same load, for each of those attributes is present to the detriment of the other. In the past, these lead-bullet loads have all been of solid form and round-nose or semi-wadcutter profile. Other factors being equal, the semi-wadcutter shape produces more tissue damage, a larger wound channel, and somewhat less penetration than the round-nose. Recently, though, at least one maker (Winchester) has added a hollow point in its semi-wadcutter lead-bullet line and has combined this with a relatively soft alloy to produce greater expansion than the solid bullets of the same profile.

ABOVE LEFT These rimfire cartridges are suitable only for small game. The Magnum .22 at right will destroy edible meat but is excellent on varmints.

ABOVE RIGHT The three bullets at left are different types of expanding, jacketed .45s suitable for hunting. At right is lead target bullet that is much less effective, especially at the low velocities of typical target loads.

It should be pointed out that the foregoing discussion of lead bullets applies only to *revolver* ammunition. No lead-bullet factory loads are available in autoloading pistol cartridges with the exception of those very light numbers intended purely for formal paper-punching at ranges of 50 yards and less. They are in no way suitable for hunting anything more than small game or pests at short ranges. It should also be pointed out that the similar light target loads offered for revolvers suffer the same limitations.

The second type of handgun ammunition embraces both revolver and autoloader cartridges and consists of metal-jacketed bullets, the jacket normally being composed of soft copper alloy. Within this category, we have the typical "ball" bullets in which the jacket continues unbroken over the nose, enclosing a lead-alloy core which is exposed only at the base. Nothing more need be said about this type of bullet, for it is totally inadequate for hunting, possessing excellent penetration but generally being incapable of any expansion whatever, though it will sometimes deform or tumble upon impact with heavy bones. This type of bullet is found mainly in auto cartridges, but also to a limited extent in revolver calibers, and generally utilizes heavy bullets at moderate velocities not exceeding 1300 or 1350 fps.

ABOVE Here are four different jacketed-bullet nose shapes. The one at far left has a vast conical cavity that produces massive expansion. The others are arranged in descending order of expansion produced.

BELOW The semi-wadcutter shape produces a maximum combination of penetration and tissue destruction when no great expansion can be counted upon. It is best for lead bullets.

The only jacketed handgun bullets suitable for hunting are those designed to expand as they penetrate animal tissue. These may be lumped in two categories, jacketed soft-point (JSP) and jacketed hollow-point (JHP). The former utilizes a thin, copper-alloy jacket in the form of a cup which encloses the base of the bullet and extends forward over the bearing surface and part-way down over the ogive, leaving a portion of the lead-alloy core exposed at the nose. The exposed core is solid, while in the case of the JHP, the exposed portion of the core is penetrated by a conical (usually) cavity which promotes expansion more rapidly than the solid JSP nose. Generally, both JSP and JHP bullets have the core lead extending beyond the jacket edge, and in profile a substantial portion of lead may be seen protruding beyond the end of the jacket. One variation exists, the truncated-cone form of bullet for autoloading pistols, introduced by Super Vel some years ago. In this bullet, the nose is flattened for a third to half the bullet's major diameter, and the jacket extends fully forward to this flat, and is turned over slightly at the edge. Thus, the flat portion exposes the end of the core, but no core material is visible when the bullet is viewed in profile. When the core fills the jacket flush to form this flat, the bullet is designated JSP, and when a wide, deep conical cavity appears there instead, it is designated JHP.

While various minor variations of expanding-bullet form (shape) will be encountered, the most common is the simple round nose with at most a two- or three-caliber ogive radius. One unusual form introduced fairly recently was developed at the now-defunct Amron small-arms ammunition plant, and is marketed under the Smith & Wesson name. It is called the "Hemi" form. The nose of this bullet is formed by a hemisphere of the same diameter as the bearing surface. A variation of the round nose will also be encountered where the tip is flattened. The other form is the truncated-cone, introduced by Super Vel and now also offered by Sierra bullets, and perhaps other independent bullet makers. This profile did not originate with Super Vel, having first appeared around the turn of the century in

Bullet expansion will vary—that at left struck a less-resistant part of the animal and expanded far less than the other, taken from the same animal. Bullet types and gun were the same.

ammunition designed for the then-new Parabellum (Luger) autoloading pistol.

Regardless of bullet form, the same rules govern expansion and
penetration: You can't have both—for expansion reduces penetration as it increases the frontal area of the bullet and therefore increases the target's resistance to penetration. The two principal factors which govern expansion (and therefore penetration) are core
hardness and jacket ductility. Those handgun bullets which produce
maximum expansion contain a soft core of virtually pure (not hardened by any additional metal) lead enclosed in a *very* thin and very
soft copper jacket. To produce maximum expansion, the jacket must
be just sufficiently strong to resist the forces placed upon it by feeding
and firing, yet remain soft and ductile enough that it will place as
little restriction as possible on the outward flowing of the lead core
as it is deformed by impact with the target.

Because of this, two bullets which appear identical may give totally
different expansion/penetration characteristics under the same conditions. One bullet may be explosively expansive, while the other
barely deforms, penetrating quite deeply without significant expansion. Hardness of core and jacket make the difference, and this cannot be determined by simple examination or thumb-nail scratching
of the bullet. In the absence of factual test data, the only way to make
a selection between two apparently identical bullets is to shoot them
into game or a test medium, such as Duxseal or gelatin, from the
same gun at the same velocities, and then compare their performance.

Generally speaking, other design factors being equal, the JHP bullet will expand more, will expand more rapidly upon penetrating the
target, will produce a larger wound cavity, and will, therefore, penetrate less than the JSP. In some instances, with bullets of identical
core and jacket hardness, weight, and profile, the difference in behavior between JSP and JHP bullets may be almost non-existent. If
too heavily constructed, as were the older 9mm Luger and .38 Super
bullets, they *both* punch right on through tissue without expanding.
At the other end of the scale, when properly designed and constructed, the JHP may produce one-third more tissue destruction and
wound volume than the JSP.

When it comes to selecting a load for your gun and for a particular
species of game and set of shooting circumstances, keep these factors
in mind: The shorter the gun barrel, the less expansion *and* penetration will be produced by any load at any range, and the shorter the
barrel, the shorter the range at which *acceptable* expansion and

penetration will be produced; the longer the range, the less expansion you may expect; as the animal grows larger, you must depend more upon penetration and less upon expansion for a quick, one-shot kill; the smaller and lighter the animal, the less resistance it offers to the bullet, and therefore the less expansion will be produced. Let's boil that down to some basic choices in different calibers for different kinds of hunting.

In 9mm Parabellum, maximum expansion and velocity for small varmints and non-edible game is most likely to be obtained from the 90-grain, JHP loading; and in the same caliber for edible game and species comparable to whitetail deer, a JSP loading such as the Super Vel 112-grain is a more desirable choice. In .38 Super automatic, the JHP 107-grain bullet is best for the small stuff with the 112-grain JSP more suitable for deer and the like. In .45 caliber, of all the factory loads currently available the Super Vel 190-grain JHP is superior for all purposes, keeping in mind that this caliber is strictly a 50-yard (or less) hunting gun.

These typical high-performance hunting loads are, from left, a .45 ACP 190-grain JHP, a .44 Special 250-grain lead SWC, and a .45 Colt 200-grain JHP.

In revolvers, there are so many more individual loads produced by a wide variety of makers that it becomes impractical to give such precise recommendations. However, for varmints and non-edible game, invariably the lightest-bullet load in JHP form will be best—however, one must consider that some bullets of this type are too heavily constructed to produce the explosive expansion for which the type has been noted since its introduction. For larger game, the light-to-medium weight JSP bullets at high test velocities are to be preferred because of their greater penetration combined with good expansion. In this range, we find a number of 125- to 137-grain loadings in .38 Special and .357 Magnum, and 180-grain loadings in .44

Magnum. In some instances, though, lighter-bullet JHP loadings too strongly constructed for proper expansion on small game will perform well on deer, black bear, and the like.

For truly *big* and perhaps dangerous game, the heavier JSP bullets in only the biggest calibers will normally be best. A fast-expanding bullet may produce a large and very deadly looking surface wound without penetrating to the vitals or breaking major bones to bring the animal down. Obviously, then, we need deep penetration combined with as much expansion as can be reasonably expected on game of this sort. At reasonable ranges, this requires substantial bullet weight, a fairly thick and strong bullet jacket, and, for once, a core alloy somewhat harder than pure lead may be desirable. At this time, there is no factory-loaded bullet which is ideal for this type of work in the typical, conventional handguns. The 180-grain JHP is a good choice in .44 Magnum, while the Super Vel .44 JSP is a good choice in .44 Auto Mag. There simply aren't any good bullets for the largest game in .41 Magnum, and the .357 Magnum is too small a caliber. In .41 Magnum, probably the best results I have obtained have been with a 210-grain JSP loading with which I have killed a couple of bears and a variety of the larger African antelope.

Even the finest target gun with poor ammunition is inferior to this old fixed-sight Colt M1917 paired with proper cartridges.

As this book goes to the publisher, I've been notified that the Super Vel Cartridge Corp. is permanently closing the doors of its Shelbyville, Indiana, plant. Consequently, the above recommendations for Super Vel ammunition become of only academic interest, and secondary recommendations are in order, at least for the auto-pistol loads. In 9mm Parabellum, the Remington-Peters 115-grain JHP and the Winchester-Western 100-grain JSP are fine choices. Circumstances for the .38 Super are unfortunate, for no other company offers any expanding-bullet loads for it. Only ball loadings remain. The .45 ACP situation is a bit better, because 185-grain JHP loads are available.

Actually, as has already been pointed out, even at its very best and with the very best in ammunition, the handgun is a marginal arm for hunting *dangerous* game—though I've done it successfully when shots were very carefully chosen and set up.

In any event, as stated at the beginning of this chapter, it is extremely important that the hunter recognize the fact that the choice of ammunition for handgun hunting is *more important* than the choice of the gun.

# 9

## *Handloading for Hunting*

There are at least five major producers who offer an array of loadings, both light and heavy, for both autoloaders and sixguns. All the same, there are two major reasons for handloading for your hunting gun, and lots of little ones. First there's the fact that you can duplicate the performance of many factory loads for a reduced cost; the second reason is that it is often possible either to improve upon factory-load performance or to assemble a load with characteristics not available across the counter. The other reasons are less important. More often than not they simply add variety (rather than performance), usually in the form of non-standard bullet weights, odd bullet designs, unusual combinations of powder and primer, etc.

Let's take a look at the economy angle first. The most expensive hunting handgun ammunition on the market is that made from the .357 and .44 AMP cartridges to suit the big Auto Mag pistol. As this is written, this fodder will set you back $18.50 per carton of 50 rounds; a cost of 37¢ per shot. Next in line is the .44 Magnum, at a per-shot cost of 28¢. The other calibers cost less, but those cartridges and loads suitable for serious hunting seldom fall below 20¢ to 25¢ per round. That sounds like a lot of money, but for anything less than a long run of fast varmint shooting, ammunition is still the least of your costs. If you are hunting deer and are a reasonably good stalker and marksman, you should get the job done with no more than two or three rounds—and even if the cartridges cost $1.00 each, that is still a miniscule amount.

It isn't the ammunition you shoot in hunting that burns the hole in your wallet. It is the hundreds of rounds that any serious handgun hunter must shoot in practice. Anyone really concerned with performing his best during a hunt will fire at least 1000 rounds in practice for each round he fires at hide and hair. If you shoot 1000 rounds during the year with the .44 Magnum in preparation for a fall mule deer or elk hunt, using factory ammunition, it may cost you nearly $400. Handloading will cut that bill down. Assuming you buy 100 rounds of factory ammunition, that leaves you 900 rounds to go, all of which can be loaded in those same original 100 cases if you're careful. Though the price of components may vary, you should be able to buy primers for a penny each, powder charges should cost you in the neighborhood of 2¢ each, and the very best in jacketed bullets will cost you about 6¢. That's a total of 9¢ per round for components, and you may very well be able to whittle that cost by careful shopping. That is less than a quarter of the price of factory ammunition.

You can do even better by using cast, lubricated lead bullets for practice rather than the more costly jacketed, expanding projectiles —without the least loss in practice productivity. In that case, assuming you make the bullets yourself from fresh lead alloy, bullet cost comes down to around 2¢ each, making your cost a mere 5¢ per cartridge.

Of course, those figures don't take into consideration the cost of loading equipment. But even if you are starting from scratch, purchasing everything new at retail prices, the cost isn't terribly great. The RCBS Junior loading set, which contains the press, shell holder, and complete set of dies, costs $52.50 as this is written. To that you must add a powder scale at anywhere from $15 to $20, for a total cost in the range of $70. Amortize that over the first thousand cartridges you load, and it will add less than 1¢ per round to your practice-ammunition cost.

Of course, you'll eventually want to add accessories to the basic outfit. If maximum economy is your aim, then a bullet-casting outfit will come first at about $75 (for one mold, lubricator-sizer, and a melting pot and dipper). Beyond that, you'll most likely want a powder measure for about $20 to $35, because it will allow you to charge cases much faster than the basic powder scale.

At the end of this chapter I've provided a table showing per-round handloading costs for all the popular handgun hunting cartridges

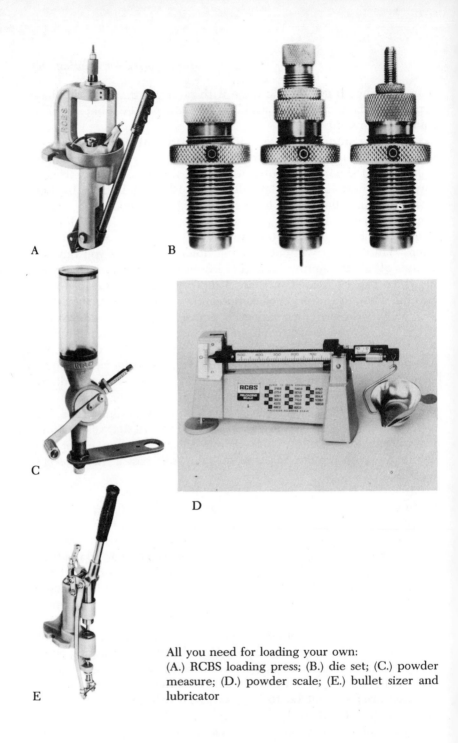

A

B

C

D

E

All you need for loading your own:
(A.) RCBS loading press; (B.) die set; (C.) powder measure; (D.) powder scale; (E.) bullet sizer and lubricator

in both lead-bullet and expanding-bullet loads, as compared with factory-load prices as this book goes to press. A quick glance at that table will give you a picture of the economic merits of handloading any particular caliber.

Now let's look at the second reason mentioned—being able to assemble loads with characteristics not available in the factory product. Again, the .44 Magnum is an excellent example. As loaded by the major ammunition factories, it is offered (with the exception of the Super Vel 180-grain) only in one bullet weight, 240 grains, at the standard full-charge velocity of 1470 fps. Except for the early-type Remington lead, gas-check, semi-wadcutter bullet, all other loads are essentially the same, containing flattened or bluntly rounded-nose jacketed bullets with a goodly amount of lead exposed at the nose.

Cast lead bullets such as these will suffice for many hunting and all practice needs at a fraction of the cost of factory-made bullets.

None of these standard factory loads are particularly good performers on small edible game or varmints, and they usually do not expand well on game the size of whitetail deer. They are generally at their best on much heavier game, where greater resistance is offered to the bullet. By handloading you can assemble much better .44 Magnum loads for varminting, for edible small game, and for the lighter big game such as deer, feral hogs, antelope, and the like. Let's

Several makes of bullet molds are available for an almost infinite variety of bullets. Casting them is simple, easy, and economical.

examine each of those areas and point out what the handloader must do to concoct a top-flight load for each.

VARMINTING: Here you need the flattest-shooting bullet possible, one that is driven at highest velocities, and that will expand violently upon small targets yet will give maximum accuracy at relatively long ranges. This requires a light bullet to achieve maximum velocity, one in the range of 170 to 180 grains. Such bullets are available from several bullet makers, and may also be home-fabricated if you care to invest in bullet-forming dies and press and the necessary supplies. Coupled with such a lightweight bullet, you want a relatively fast-burning powder in large quantities to produce maximum velocity in typical handgun-barrel lengths. This means something on the order of Olin #296 ball powder or Hodgdon H110, the charge usually consisting of all the case will hold beneath the seated bullet with light powder compression. Using the loading-data tables in one of the standard handloading manuals, such a load can be assembled to produce well over 1800 fps from an 8⅜-inch revolver, with much better long-range characteristics and expansion than the typical 240-grain factory load.

SMALL GAME: Here, especially if you intend the small game for food, the requirements are just the opposite of your varminting needs. You do *not* want a violently expanding bullet which would destroy most of a rabbit or grouse; you do not need high velocity or flat trajectory because such game is normally shot at close range; and you do not particularly want the muzzle blast and report of full-charge loads. In my experience, using again the .44 Magnum as an example, the ideal velocity for small game is no more than 1000 fps, and a relatively light lead bullet of wadcutter or semi-wadcutter form gives the best combination of sure kills and minimum meat destruction. No factory loads meet these requirements.

The handloader not only can meet them ideally but can do so at low cost. My favorite small-game load in the .44 Magnum consists of a hard lead bullet (Lyman #429348) weighing about 175 grains, driven at about 950 to 975 fps (from an 8⅜-inch revolver) by 8.0 grains of Hercules Unique powder. Equally good is the 200-grain #429303 bullet and the same powder charge. Both shoot with superb accuracy, don't destroy meat unnecessarily, and kill small game like a lightning bolt. The lead bullet and small powder charge keep the cost of these loads down to less than 4¢ per round.

In addition, this small-game load is quite mild in blast, report, and recoil—and is therefore ideal for training youngsters and ladies, for practice and plinking, and for serious tests of marksmanship between yourself and other bragging pistoleros.

DEER: Most whitetail deer (America's favorite and most common big game) weigh less than 200 pounds, with probably far more than we realize running closer to 100 pounds; and they are shot at relatively short ranges—under 75 yards.

Being a small, lightly constructed animal, the whitetail offers little resistance to the bullet. The heavy-bullet factory loads do not generally expand well. Instead, they tend to punch right on through. I have had most excellent results with a .44 Magnum load driving a 240-grain cast-lead bullet driven by 18.0 grains of 2400 powder at about 1250 to 1300 fps. The best bullet seems to be the Keith/Lyman 429421 weighing 240 grains nominally in solid form, or around 230 grains hollow-pointed, and cast of a relatively hard alloy—about one part tin to 15 or 16 parts lead. The hollow-point is not needed at the shorter ranges, but beyond 50 yards it increases expansion somewhat without causing undesirable meat destruction. Again, this load is quite economical, on the order of 5¢ per round. It is ideal not only for deer but for feral hogs, small bear, and general utility shooting. About the only medium game for which it is *not* ideal is the pronghorn antelope —which because of its fleetness and open habitat requires a load more closely resembling my recommendation for varmints.

So much for *what* handloading can do for the handgun hunter. Now let's take a look at *how*. It isn't my purpose to offer an instruction course on handloading. For that, you should obtain other references such as the various handloading manuals offered by tool and component manufacturers, and the basic references on the subject —not the least of which is my own *Modern Handloading* (Winchester Press, 1972). Here I'll simply cover those aspects of handloading which are uniquely applicable to handgun hunting ammunition and are essential if you are to produce the most efficient loads possible.

First of all, handgun ammunition develops maximum performance only when loaded in fresh, new, unfired cases. I recommend that the cartridges you will fire at game be loaded in new or only once-fired cases. This needn't be an economic burden, for a single batch of 100 new cases should take care of several hunts, after which they will serve you for many practice loadings. Proper ignition and powder combustion depends to a considerable degree upon a factor called "bullet pull." This is the static force, measured in pounds, required to draw the bullet from the case. New cases are formulated to maintain the proper grip on the bullet and to retain the solid, heavy crimp which is applied in revolver cartridges. With each subsequent firing, the case loses some of this ability to hold the bullet securely and to retain its crimp as the brass work-hardens—with the result that bullet pull decreases. As bullet pull decreases, the efficiency of the load drops, as does the velocity and energy which it can produce.

All factors being equal, a case fired six or eight times will produce less velocity (with the same load) than it did at its first loading. Further, the more times a case has been fired, the more likely it is to develop a neck crack after loading. Merely the jar of recoil can cause the neck of a many-times fired case already in the gun to crack and release its secure hold on the bullet. In revolvers, this can allow the bullet to move forward out of the case and chamber mouth to tie up the gun solidly and prevent further firing; in an autoloader it can cause the bullet to move either forward or rearward in the case, to cause a feeding failure or jam the magazine so that no further shots are possible.

Fair weather is great for hunting, but you can't always depend upon it. Factory handgun ammunition is waterproofed so that even when it is totally submerged, moisture cannot normally seep inside the cartridge and damage the primer or powder charge. Conventional handloads lack this advantage, and water can be prevented from entering only by the tight fit of bullet and primer in the case. This will usually prevent moisture from entering during a shower, but should not be relied upon.

To avoid any problems of misfires or substandard performance due to moisture, waterproof your hunting loads by applying a drop of good-quality, thin, clear lacquer at the junction of case head and primer; the lacquer will flow completely around the primer, penetrating between primer and pocket wall, thoroughly sealing any gap. Do the same at the junction of bullet and case mouth. Here the lacquer may be applied after crimping, and it will normally penetrate to provide a tight seal, but a somewhat better and more durable seal can be obtained if the bullet is seated first, then the lacquer applied copiously to fill the narrow gap between flared case mouth and bullet—after which the crimp is formed while the lacquer is about half-hard. This will squeeze the surplus lacquer out upon the bullet where it must be wiped off with a cloth moistened with acetone. This will provide the most reliable case/bullet moisture barrier.

If the areas contacted by lacquer are oily, dirty, or wet, a poor seal will result. This is avoided by wiping the appropriate areas with a cloth moistened with acetone before assembling primer and bullet to the case. However, make certain the acetone has dried thoroughly before seating the primer. Acetone is a solvent for the sealing compound used in most primers, and if traces of it remain, it might easily soften that seal and possibly damage the primer.

Many older references recommend only neck-sizing of cases for reloading handgun ammunition. This practice has fallen into some disrepute in recent years, as well it should. Even when the cases have been fired previously in the same gun—particularly in revolvers with their varying chamber dimensions—a case that is not resized full-length may well fail to enter the chamber after reloading, or at best chamber with difficulty. This can be avoided by full-length resizing in properly dimensioned dies for every loading. Even then, any ammunition to be taken to the field should be manually chambered in the gun in which it is to be used as a form of gauging to ensure that when the time comes it will chamber freely and smoothly.

Also, all handloads to be used afield should be inspected very carefully for any nicks, dents, burrs, bent case rims, deformed bullets or crimps, protruding primers, bulges, or any other surface defects that might interfere with feeding or functioning. This is particularly true in regard to autoloaders, but inspection should not be stinted for sixguns, either.

When loading for auto pistols or revolvers, fit of bullet in case is quite important to bullet pull, already mentioned. With light loads, it is only necessary that the bullet be held tightly enough by the case before crimping so that it cannot be rotated with the fingers. For heavy loads, though, it must be tighter. This is accomplished by using a resizing die that reduces the case mouth so its inside diameter is .006-inch to .010-inch less than bullet diameter. An undersize expander plug is then used to open up case mouths uniformly to a diameter about .004-inch less than bullet diameter. Then, when the bullet is seated the case is stretched over it, and it clings very tightly to the bullet.

This tightness combines with the crimp to produce the desired bullet pull, which amounts to resistance to the initial build-up of powder gases and improves ignition and combustion. Further, this tightness prevents revolver bullets from moving forward out of the case during recoil; and it likewise prevents autoloader bullets from being driven rearward into the case by feeding impact.

In autos, though, mere tightness of bullet/case assembly is sometimes not enough to hold bullets securely in place during feeding and recoil. Added stability can be given the bullet by expanding the case mouth only to a depth about 1/32-inch less than the depth to which the bullet will be seated. Then, when the bullet is seated, its base forms a slight shoulder in the case wall. This shoulder adds support to the bullet.

Alternatively, the case may be cannelured at a point to form an even larger shoulder against which the bullet base may rest. Both SAS and C-H offer simple and economical canneluring tools for this purpose. These tools are quickly and easily operated to roll a neat cannelure into any case. The tools are also useful for forming crimping cannelures in jacketed bullets or lubricant grooves in lead bullets.

As I've already pointed out, handloading serves many useful purposes to the handgun hunter; it saves money, and it provides much greater versatility of ammunition. One hardly needs more recommendation than that for getting into the game. Here's a table of costs to give you a clearer idea of the economics of handloading.

# HANDLOAD COST TABLE
(Price per individual cartridge)

| CALIBER | PRIMER | POWDER | BULLET | TOTAL |
|---------|--------|--------|--------|-------|
| .32–20  | $.01   | $.006  | $.005  | $.021 |
| .38 Spcl. | .01  | .007   | .007   | .024  |

| CALIBER | PRIMER | POWDER | BULLET | TOTAL |
|---------|--------|--------|--------|-------|
| .357 Mag. | .01 | .009 | .007 | .026 |
| 9mm P. | .01 | .007 | .006 | .023 |
| .38 Super | .01 | .007 | .006 | .023 |
| .41 Mag. | .01 | .01 | .012 | .032 |
| .44 Spcl. | .01 | .008 | .012 | .030 |
| .44 Mag. | .01 | .012 | .012 | .034 |
| .45 ACP | .01 | .007 | .012 | .029 |
| .45 Colt | .01 | .008 | .012 | .030 |

The above costs are based upon cast-lead bullets and normally available powder and primer costs with scrap lead at 35¢ per pound. For jacketed bullet loads, add 3¢ per pound in calibers .357 and under; add 4¢ for larger calibers.

# 10

## Handgun-Hunting Techniques for Big Game

To most people, the term "big game" includes just about every North American species from the whitetail up. This is in spite of the fact that whitetails in some parts of the country are smaller than a fairsized German shepherd dog. I've seen thousands and shot quite a few that weighed from 75 to 90 pounds, and mature bucks in parts of the Southwest often weigh less. Probably a better break-down would be to class the various deer, pronghorns, wild boar and feral hogs, and black bear (though not the grizzly or the brown) as medium game, in contrast to our true big game such as those larger bears, elk, and moose.

However, for the purpose of instruction in this chapter, I'll stick to the generally accepted big-game classification and simply insert any additional observations that might be appropriate with regard to truly big species. Dangerous game is something else, not to be lumped together with ordinary big game in terms of hunting procedure even though the actual techniques are comparable. Sure the techniques are comparable, but they involve vital if simple modifications—precautions, that is, to reduce as much as possible the hazard to the hunter and his companions. I'll devote a separate chapter to the precautions needed when handgunning the big bears, cats, and other species that may bite, claw, or otherwise mess up a careless hunter.

I'll also devote separate chapters to some of the individual non-dangerous species that I'm including right here in my general coverage. Deer, for example, are so popular that they merit independent, more detailed treatment, and pronghorns present special problems that I'll touch on later in this chapter and then discuss more thoroughly in another section.

The various hunting methods with a rifle are well known, and I'll just review them here briefly. In most instances the same basic methods are used with a handgun but—ideally—with even greater skill and patience because the range must be shortened; where appropriate, then, I'll compare the techniques as employed by a rifleman with those for bagging the same species with handguns.

*Still-hunting* is a traditional method of timber hunting where you drift slowly through likely game territory, hoping to jump an animal from its bed or feeding, under circumstances that will offer a quick shot or will permit you to follow the animal up with the hope of a standing shot later. Of course, a still-hunting rifleman—particularly if he's an experienced woods-watcher with fine powers of observation—has a good chance of spotting an animal before it becomes alarmed, and making a clean standing shot. This requires caution and good woodsmanship, and an appreciation of the quarry's habits. Later in this chapter I'll show why still-hunting is more difficult with a sidearm and what skills a handgunner must cultivate in order to take game in this manner. Chiefly it's a matter of going slower and often shooting faster.

*Stand-hunting* might be considered the opposite of still-hunting. The hunter parks—in concealment or at least inconspicuously—near a game trail, feeding area, or other avenue used by game, and simply waits for the animal of his choice to drift by, unalarmed and within range. Actually, hunters often pair up, with one still-hunting to push game ahead of him toward another on a strategically located stand. Far less woods skill is required off a stand, provided it's well chosen and the hunter remains silent and alert.

*Drive-hunting* is common in Europe and in some parts of this country. Several hunters position themselves in a line across a likely avenue of game movement, after which other hunters or non-hunting beaters move through an area to push game past the guns. This is probably the most practical method of hunting very densely wooded and brushy areas in daylight and has been used successfully on all non-dangerous game. While it produces more game seen than other methods, running shots predominate, with their attendant high percentage of misses and woundings. In some areas, dogs are used to drive or run animals to the hunter, and the same disadvantages are present. However, when dogs are used to pursue and "tree" bear, cats, boar, or other animals, much easier shots can be had.

*Stalking* represents the epitome of hunting skill, and involves the hunter locating a particular animal, which he has often identified well in advance and studied long before the hunt, and then hunting that animal *only*—for days on end if necessary—until it can be approached closely enough for a reasonably certain shot. Many long-range shots are taken in stalking with a rifle, 300 and even 400 yards being not uncommon among excellent riflemen (or the foolhardy). Stalking requires the highest standards of woodsmanship and game knowledge.

Of course, there are numerous variations of the foregoing rifle-hunting methods brought about by individual temperament, terrain, game habits, etc., and they can all be applied in varying degrees to handgun hunting. However, the relatively low power, short effective range, and lesser accuracy of the handgun make getting within practical range much more difficult. Perhaps the required modification of basic methods for taking big game can best be illustrated by some particular examples I have encountered.

Steve Herrett, founder of Herrett Stocks, favors the single-shot Thompson/Center Contender pistol chambered for his own series of wildcat cartridges. He is shown here (left) with a wild boar bagged with such weaponry, in the company of Bob Gustafson of Thompson/Center Arms.

High-country sheep and goats probably represent the ultimate achievement in handgun hunting. Only a few such animals have been killed with handguns over the years, but some day we expect greater numbers of handgunners to be stalking close enough and shooting straight enough to bring home this type of trophy.

A successful Texas rancher with extremely large land-holdings cruises his range regularly in a pickup truck; he always carries one of his S&W .44 Magnums and keeps a sharp eye out for game. When a worthwhile buck is seen in his regular rounds, he parks the truck and stalks the animal on foot, usually successfully, until he is within range for a certain kill. Of course, being an old-time handgun hunter, sure-kill range for him is two or three times what it might be for the average pistolero. He doesn't consider the actual stalking for a handgun shot any different than with a rifle, except that the last portion of the stalk, say from 200 or 300 yards in, requires greater care and concentration to avoid alarming the animal as the distance shortens.

(Incidentally, the foregoing does not constitute unlawful hunting from a vehicle. So long as the vehicle remains on recognized roads, and shooting does not take place from the vehicle, the law does not prohibit scouting for game in this fashion. It is a fairly common method of hunting in the Southwest, where distances are great and cover is often sparse.)

Long-range handgunning on the open plains is Steve Herrett's forte. For this he favors the Thompson/Center Contender pistol, suitably scoped and chambered for one of his own high-velocity wildcat cartridges. Steve is shown here with a pronghorn antelope taken with the .30 Herrett cartridge at well over 100 yards.

Other handgunners often do the same thing from horseback when working the range, but the stalking method is varied a bit. After game is spotted, the hunter stays aboard his pony so long as it remains practical to do so, moving in as much as possible. Then he ground-reins the pony, dismounts, and leaves the horse there for whatever decoy value it might have. The hunter then takes advantage of cover to move off to the flank and stalk the remaining distance on foot until a satisfactorily close approach has been achieved. One fellow tells me that this method has been particularly effective for him in low brush, even though he uses a relatively low-powered gun/cartridge combination in comparison to the big Magnums so many hunters carry today.

Sitting at a stand or in a wisely concealed and located blind can be especially productive to handgun hunters if well-used game trails or particularly accessible feeding areas are identified. In some parts of the country where second-growth timber is larded with small, grassy clearings, it is often possible to build a blind that will, when the wind is right, allow shots to be taken at as little as 25 or 30 yards. I know of one place up in New England where there's an old orchard and abundant ground feed immediately adjacent to a long-abandoned farmhouse. There a hunter can hide inside the house, making it in effect a blind, and be assured of seeing deer feeding at dusk in the old orchard at under 50 yards.

Similarly, I once hunted an area in Oklahoma where a huge pecan tree offered a comfortable seat about 12 feet off the ground, within 30 yards of a favored watering spot which was also the only practical crossing of a sparkling creek. I needed only to perch in that big pecan for no more than two or three mornings or evenings running to be assured of a close-in chance at a shootable buck. At that range and under those conditions, no Magnum was needed; a good .45 auto or .38 Special revolver was quite adequate. After all, even a *small* whitetail makes a pretty fair-sized target at 30 yards, especially if you're wedged solidly in a tree crotch and resting the gun across a folded jacket on a sturdy limb.

Another use of blinds or stands was encountered in the high veldt of South Africa when Lee Jurras and I hunted private lands there. Our host placed us in small rock outcroppings and brush clumps in otherwise open expanses, situated within reasonable range of game routes. Then, starting perhaps a mile or more away, a couple of farm hands would start drifting across the veldt toward us. The game moved away from them (a visible potential hazard) and toward us (an invisible *genuine* hazard). Eventually, if all went well, the game in question—usually in herds of 20 to 100—moved by at acceptable (if not ideal) handgun range, with plenty of time available to pick the best trophy and let drive.

In one instance, we were able to improve our concealed positions inside a clump of brush by building low barriers of indigenous rock which not only provided further concealment but a good, solid rest for shooting from either the prone or sitting position. At this spot one morning, when I had laid my gun and binoculars a few feet away and switched to a long-lens camera to photograph some distant animals, suddenly a full herd of blesbok appeared not 25 yards away, having circled my hiding place from the rear where I couldn't see them. When they spotted me and the camera gear, they froze, as did I. After a few seconds I couldn't stand it, but when I attempted to reach my Magnum sixgun they galloped madly off and no shot was taken. That herd, incidentally, contained several good heads, one of which I bagged a couple of hours later by moving a quarter-mile or so to another "hide" and waiting for them to drift by.

That deployment of farm hands in South Africa was not truly drive-hunting, but did embody some of its characteristics since the presence of other men was used to move game gently and slowly toward the hunters. It will only work where good concealed gun positions are available, and where there is an ample field of view through which it is reasonably certain the game will move.

Still-hunting in timber can be especially challenging with a handgun. Like the rifleman, the handgunner proceeds slowly and cautiously, ever alert, gun at the ready. To carry the gun in a holster could easily result in the loss of shots in thick brush, for when an animal is spooked from its daytime bed, often only split-second opportunities will be presented, either as it first lunges to its feet and takes off, or as it passes open avenues in the timber which offer some chance of an unobstructed shot. The rifleman under those circumstances must shoot quickly, but he also has the opportunity for a fairly long-range shot if the animal—as often happens—halts after a short run to observe his back trail or take a closer look at the disturber of his slumbers. If the animal does that at 100 to 150 yards and there is a reasonably clear lane through the timber, a rifleman has an excellent opportunity for a shot. Not so the handgunner; that distance is usually too great for adequate shot placement, and a relatively small opening through the trees and brush—sufficient for a rifle—is usually not enough to accommodate the rainbow trajectory of the handgun bullet. Therefore, the pistolero's best chance is the instant the animal arises from its bed and before it builds up a full head of steam and is masked by trees and brush.

Ideally, though, the handgunner will obtain the best results from still-hunting if he trains himself to be observant enough and to move slowly and carefully enough so that he can spot bedded animals before alarming them. Such animals will often lie perfectly still, watching the hunter's approach, for as much as several minutes before finally deciding that an urgent departure is essential to safety. If the pistolero will train himself well enough to spot the animal during this period of time, he will find himself presented with an ideal opportunity for a clean shot at a stationary target. That the animal's head is usually up and toward him is an added advantage in simplifying shot placement.

Again, still-hunting with a handgun differs from that with a rifle only in that greater care and attention is required in order that the shot may be taken within the lesser capabilities of the short gun.

It might be thought that some species simply can't be hunted very successfully with the handgun because of its relatively short effective range and the fact that they inhabit primarily open country, devoid of cover, which might seem to preclude a close stalk. When preparing for my first pronghorn-antelope hunt with a handgun, much was said about this—many friends who'd hunted the wary pronghorn with rifles assuring me that there was no way to get close enough for a sure handgun shot, and insisting that even if by accident an animal was approached closely, only a running shot would be possible. Having rifle-hunted pronghorn before, I had to admit that there was much in their argument, but I'd be damned if I was going to let all that keep me from trying with a handgun.

Eventually, when we began hunting the big Diamond A Ranch in New Mexico (not far from Wagon Mound), I was beginning to think maybe I really would need to break out a rifle if I was going to take a respectable antelope. However, we eventually isolated a small band containing some bucks with horns that would go about 16 inches, and glassed them steadily for some time while they were leisurely feeding on a malpais ridge a good 1½ miles away.

No logical or conventional stalking approach appeared to be usable. After a bit of head-scratching, we decided simply to work directly toward the animals, clear across that 1½ miles of open space, and see what would happen. I had used the same approach on other species, but none as spooky or with eyesight as good as the pronghorn. We walked leisurely, stopping now and then to look around and zig-zagging a bit, spending most of that time and distance within view of the antelope. Periodically our route dropped down into a draw and we were lost from their sight, but in the main they could see us clearly. Frequently they gazed at us with little concern and returned to feeding. In this fashion, we approached to within a couple of hundred yards, at which point the very ridge they were on, being somewhat flattened at the top, masked us completely. The wind continuing in our favor, we simply made a very cautious and silent approach up the side of the ridge, and eventually reached a point just below the first crest where we could see them clearly.

Ray Speer then promptly shot his buck (with a rifle) and the report of that shot riveted the attention of mine, a bare 65 or 70 yards away. My buck stood there just long enough for me to climb a couple feet higher and bust him with the big .357 Auto Mag pistol. He never saw me after I got within range. I've been told that we merely won a long-odds gamble, and that duplicating those tactics another time would probably produce failure. Well, I'm not convinced. On admittedly less spooky animals, I've used that same approach in the past and managed to get within handgun range without difficulty.

Actually, in conventional stalking, the handgun hunter is less encumbered than the rifleman. If he has equipped himself with a good shoulder holster that will carry the gun securely under his jacket, he'll not only have both hands free for climbing, crawling, or parting brush, but will have only his body to force through, around, or over the various obstacles. Think back about how many times your four-foot-long rifle has entangled itself in brush as you've tried to sneak up quietly and you'll realize how advantageous a handgun can be under those conditions.

Inasmuch as the handgun hunter must stalk as close to game as possible, he'll need all the help he can get. In this area, bow-hunters have shown the way. By their demand, they have also caused development and production of a number of valuable items. Camouflage clothing becomes essential and should cover the entire body and include headgear. This leaves hands and face flaring like beacons, with the handgun itself being nearly as obvious. Flat green or olive-drab (or other color to match surroundings) paint may be used (carefully) on the gun to make it less conspicuous. Camouflage grease paint in sticks is available to disguise face and hands and is effective when applied in the proper patterns. (Don't emulate one hunter I know who camouflaged himself completely, then strapped on a blaze-orange backpack carrying his lunch, coffee thermos, and camera gear!)

When moving, not much more can be done, but when hunkered under a bush or rock, a large piece of camouflage netting is most useful. It can be a blind all by itself if draped irregularly over yourself to break up your outline, and propped up a bit by sticks or bushes. As a matter of fact, you can move, albeit slowly, under a net drape, remaining crouched down to resemble just another bush or rock. There are also portable blinds and other accessories which can be extremely useful to the handgun hunter in some situations. The fact remains that handgun hunting for big game differs from rifle hunting only in degree of necessary caution and skill. Successful work with the handgun requires development of a higher degree of skill in *all* aspects of hunting—observation, woodcraft, stalking, camouflage, marksmanship, and anything else that comes to mind.

# 11

## Precautions with Dangerous Game

Most North American big game is not generally considered dangerous to the hunter. When we say "dangerous," we refer not only to size, strength, and agility, but to the kind of temperament that prompts an animal to attack a human. Many animals possess all of those characteristics except the temperament. An adult buck mule deer could be a real threat to a man if he possessed an aggressive temperament. *Any* animal can be dangerous under certain conditions. Even a tiny Texas whitetail doe may take you on if cornered and afraid you'll harm her fawn. Like people, most animals will fight when cornered. But they aren't inherently dangerous. Those that do present a potential danger include a few relatively small animals such as wild and feral hogs and the smaller cats, which *are* sufficiently aggressive to be a menace. Even a 100-pound hog will rip your legs to ribbons under the right circumstances.

In the U.S. and Canada, the species usually considered dangerous include the big bears (grizzly, brown, polar), the big cats, and the more or less pure Russian boar. The smaller feral hogs and razorbacks aren't considered all that bad, though it's foolish to get careless around them. Dropping farther south into Mexico and Central America, we have the fabled *"El Tigre,"* the jaguar, and that about completes the list. In Europe, there are the big boars, and in the

Scandinavian north the polar bear. Africa and India offer leopard, lion, and tiger, along with elephant, buffalo, rhino, and the placid-looking hippo.

There are other species around the world that will no doubt tear you up a bit if you're so careless or unfortunate as to come close when they are irritated, alarmed, or hungry—but they shouldn't be considered dangerous under *normal* hunting conditions.

In any event, there are two conditions under which a dangerous animal may claw or chew a hunter. One is when a wounded animal charges and gets to the hunter before he can be finished off. Less talked-about but probably responsible for more maulings and deaths is the chance encounter, usually under conditions of very limited visibility, when an aggressive species attacks without warning through fear, irritability from old wounds, severe hunger, previous encounters with man, the mating urge, or some other motivation. Most budding hunters tend to think that the charging wounded animal is the one most likely to present a menace, but, in reality, a chance encounter in heavy brush is probably the greatest hazard.

I consider the big Auto Mag best for dangerous game.

A reasonable degree of caution—even if it only amounts to staying alert and ready to take appropriate action—is in order whenever you're hunting *any* species in an area inhabited by dangerous game. If you're hunting deer or elk—not considered dangerous—and happen to disturb a mean-tempered grizzly, it makes no difference to the grizzly what you were really hunting.

As pointed out elsewhere in this volume, even the very best-armed handgunner possesses very little "knock-down" power compared to the rifleman. Successful handgun hunting depends upon precise bullet placement at quite close ranges rather than on raw power. This puts a premium on marksmanship and stalking ability. Terrain permitting, the long-gun hunter can bust a grizzly or lion from 200 yards, knowing that the range may prevent a charge if he shoots poorly, and that if a charge does develop there will probably be plenty of time for him to finish the animal off before it can reach him. The handgun hunter enjoys no such advantages. He must close to within 50 yards or less of his trophy. From that distance, a charge by any animal is far more likely, principally because the hunter is much more likely to be identified as a menace. That same reduced range makes it possible for a charging animal to reach the hunter before it can be stopped by additional shots. A lion or any other big cat can cover 50 yards in the blink of an eye, and even the more ponderous animals can cover it a damn sight quicker than you and I can run it. As if all that didn't increase the hazard enough, an animal charging fast and head-on is not only difficult to hit, but presents little in the way of a vital-area target.

The hunter—whether rifleman or handgunner—who thinks a charge can be easily stopped with a brain shot isn't likely to have tried it. Unless you are thoroughly grounded in the anatomy of the animal in question, the brain probably isn't quite where you think it is, and it is a damn small target, bobbing and weaving. The brains of

This polar bear was not taken with a handgun, but it has been done—by publisher Bob Petersen using a .44 Magnum S&W Revolver.

most animals are well-protected against frontal assault by heavy curved plates of bone which will deflect bullets that do not strike at the ideal angle for penetration.

Add all of those problems to the fact that your most potent handgun doesn't have the power to stop a charging animal in its tracks with anything less than a brain or spine shot, and it becomes evident that any angry animal headed for you stands a pretty fair chance of getting claws and teeth into your tender body. It makes no difference whether it is an animal you have inadvertently irritated or one you have wounded. In fact, you'll be more or less expecting a charge from an animal at which you are shooting, but you may never even know about a chance-encounter animal until he hits you from behind or the side.

The two precautions one must always take become fairly obvious: Use extreme care to make certain your first (and perhaps only) shot will produce an immediate kill or immobilization of the animal; and exercise all possible caution to ensure that there is no other dangerous animal that will be provoked or panicked into an attack by your mere presence. Beyond that, there is the cardinal rule, "Never hunt dangerous game alone," which has applied ever since man began hunting the larger carnivores for food. It's a simple rule but the temptation to violate it is often great. That it must never be violated, particularly by the handgun hunter, is clearly evident in many writ-

This photo, taken at River Ranch Acres in Florida, shows some of the thick cover in which hogs are occasionally taken. This nicely toothed boar exhibits the light coloration often encountered instead of the better-known pure black. Well-known writer and sportsman Bob Zwirz bagged this one with a Dan Wesson .357 Magnum revolver.

ings based upon hunting dangerous game in Africa. The graves of solitary hunters, even the most competent professionals, dot the landscape of East Africa. If a professional hunter of many years' experience, armed with a big-bore double rifle many times more powerful than your handgun, couldn't survive a charge, the chances of your doing it unaided are mighty slim.

Always have a backup gun available. That doesn't mean simply a deer-hunting rifle slung on your back; it means having a competent marksman literally within arm's reach and carrying a heavy-caliber rifle. He must always be present, and he must not be tied down by any ego-serving instructions or conditions such as "Don't shoot unless I ask you to." Instead, he must have complete freedom to shoot at any time he considers you (or anyone else in the hunting party) in danger. Sure, he might on some occasion put what proves *later* to be an unnecessary bullet or three into an animal you've already hit solidly, but that is a far smaller risk than getting yourself chewed up when the backup man could have prevented the mess. If you're with a professional hunter, you won't have any choice. He will demand that he be allowed adequate freedom to protect you with his rifle. If you're simply hunting with a friend as backup man, then it's essential that you give him the same freedom. Better to have an irritated ego than a lion or brown bear chewing on your carcass.

Of course, some unsporting soul will ask, "Why in hell does anybody want to hunt under those circumstances with a handgun in the first place?" It's the thrill of the chase, of course, and the satisfaction of a stalk well done, and the element of personal danger. All are present in any hunt and are essential to the true hunter. As long as there *is* dangerous game, men will hunt it, and at least some of them will certainly do so with a handgun. That is as it should be.

# 12

## *Handgunning Deer*

Carefully concealed in a tangle of brush, you sweat through the damp chill of the grey pre-dawn, waiting for the light that you hope will show you the Christmas-tree buck you know has been frequenting the glade which you now overlook. Slowly, a pinkish glow in the east spreads, and then, suddenly, the sun breaks over the timbered rise to flood the glade with sharply separated brilliant light and deep, dark shadow. As the sun rises, you spot golden-white flashes off the smooth ivory tips of the horns you seek.

No matter how many times it's happened before, you become short of breath and dry of mouth as you ease the big sixgun out of its holster, suspended in time while the line of shadow slowly marches on to give you vision enough of the buck's body for a clean shot.

Almost as if it were acting alone, the big Magnum moves up to rest solidly across the limb you chose earlier, and the sights align themselves on the darkish lump bearing those magnificent antlers. The shadow creeps with nerve-testing slowness until, as if it appeared from nowhere, the dew-glistening tawny hide is there over your sights.

Shift left and up just a hair, breathing deep to calm a racing pulse, and to sooth jangling nerve ends. The sights are rock-steady, forming the perfect picture, and suddenly without conscious effort on your part, the target is blotted out by a seemingly silent orange flame blooming around the muzzle—and the gun rocks back and up in opposite reaction to the invisible speeding bullet that whips out the barrel. There is an instant of shocked woodland silence in reaction to the thunderclap you never heard, and in it drifts back the slap of the bullet striking home.

As the gun comes back down and you see your quarry still and silent, you rise and go forth to collect your harvest; the warmth of the rising sun soothing away the chills and cramps of that long, silent, pre-dawn vigil. The woods again burst into sound and activity as nature, having witnessed the death of one to feed another, resumes its business. That, friends, is the hunting experience in one of its more rewarding forms. That is deer hunting as the handgunner would have it.

The most popular and most plentiful big-game animal in North America is deer—so plentiful and readily accessible to most hunters that probably 90 percent of all big-game shooting revolves around this one animal. Today the deer population in many of the 48 contiguous states is far greater than it was when the Mayflower made her first landfall off that hostile, rock-ribbed coast. That this situation exists is a tribute to the conservation efforts of hunters, who have contributed more in thought, action, and dollars than all of the armchair and ivory-tower preservationist groups combined—over *1½-billion* dollars in license fees and special taxes alone.

Whitetails like these make up the majority of our big-game hunting, and they don't require top power. Find them in this attitude and the buck is yours.

Among deer, the whitetail reigns supreme, outnumbering all the rest, with the Western mule deer lagging as a distant second. After that, we have a wide variety of others, ranging from the tiny and fully protected Key deer off the Florida coast to the blacktail of the Pacific Northwest, plus several foreign, or "exotic," species that have been introduced into this country over the past several decades: the sika, sambur, three varieties of fallow, and others. (Not everyone realizes that the blacktail is really a kind of muley, but scientists agree that this and other native American types, unlike the imports, are subspecies of the two major groups—whitetails and mule deer.)

Deer, particularly whitetails, are especially adaptable. Whitetails thrive even in densely populated areas. They do well in large numbers nearly within sight of the towering skyscrapers of New York City. In the Midwest, where nearly all the ground is devoted to corn, beans, and like crops, deer have adapted so well that farmers have to chase and fence them out of their fields where they otherwise feed prodigiously.

In size, deer range from the little Texas whitetails of 100 pounds or less up to Colorado muleys claimed to grow to 600 pounds. Whitetails have been shot weighing well over 400 pounds in the Midwest, where food is plentiful and climate mild, and in some areas are plentiful in the 200- and 300-pound range.

Since deer are abundant in so many regions, the handgun-hunting question is not so much where as how and with what. Except for the biggest muleys, deer aren't large enough to require great power for clean kills; they are lightly muscled and boned, so they require no great amount of penetration. Further, they are high-strung, nervous

Mule deer are generally bigger than whitetails, but sometimes they're easier game for handgunners because they aren't quite so spooky.

animals that succumb readily to shock and are therefore relatively easy to kill cleanly with reasonably good shot placement. On the other hand, when thoroughly spooked or frightened, deer have the stamina to keep going for a great distance even with several bad wounds. It is not uncommon for a small whitetail to run a mile or so with a badly shot-up leg, to die only from loss of blood. A gut-shot deer will die eventually, but may travel hundreds of yards and be lost. This is especially true when shot with a handgun whose bullet does not have the great velocity and massive expansion to produce extensive tissue destruction.

With this in mind, the deer hunter should give careful thought to shot placement. There are four vital areas you can aim for, because any reasonably good handgun bullet in one of those zones will produce a sure, though not always instantaneous, kill.

The classic neck shot favored by many riflemen is equally effective with handguns, but its success requires a fine degree of marksmanship and a thorough knowledge of the path of the vertebrae through the deep neck. It is a mistake to think of this as simply a "neck" shot, for the bullet must strike the *vertebrae* to produce an instantaneous kill. If it passes above or below, it may produce eventual death but certainly will not stop the animal in its tracks. Therefore, I recommend the neck shot only for the most meticulous marksman and stalker who is capable of hitting the vertebrae with regularity.

A second classic shot is, of course, to the heart. A highly effective shot if not productive of an instantaneous kill, it is nearly as difficult as the neck shot. The average whitetail's heart is hardly bigger than a small man's fist, and if you can't keep your shots in a four-inch group

This fine muley buck was taken on a Montana hunt with the .44 Magnum single-action Ruger Super Blackhawk.

A wide variety of imported "exotic" deer can be hunted on private lands. These spotted fallow deer make fine handgun game.

at the hunting range, not to mention knowing *exactly* the position of the heart, you won't do well with it. As a rule, you're better off trying for the second classic kill area, the lungs; a slight miscalculation there may put the bullet into the heart, anyway, and the target is larger and equally conducive to a clean kill.

In my experience, the lung shot is the safest for the average hand-gunner, and if it does not produce instantaneous death, its record for sure kills is extremely good. A lung-shot deer will usually travel just a short distance, then collapse and die very quickly. The lungs offer the largest vital target available from almost any angle at which a shot may be taken; and a bullet squarely through the lungs will spoil hardly any meat at all, because it passes only through the rib cage and misses all the large and important meat masses. To be sure, if you pull the shot high, you'll spoil a bit of the loin, but in that case, you'll probably strike the spine, to produce an instantaneous kill. Even then, meat spoilage will be minimized, for the main sections are in the clear.

A fourth classic shot to be considered is to the shoulder. On larger animals the shoulder shot is normally used to immobilize rather than kill instantly, with the justification that a broken shoulder will keep the animal stationary if not put it on the ground, leaving sufficient time for a more carefully placed finishing shot. It has much the same effect on deer, but is also often fatal, killing quickly enough so that no follow-up bullet is needed. With reasonably accurate shooting, a bullet in the shoulder will normally break the major bones there. If it's a bit high, there may also be damage to the spine. If it's too low, damage to the heart or lungs will occur, particularly if the bullet is traveling fast enough to throw off secondary pieces of lead. It may also cut major arteries and produce a quick kill by that means. Mainly, though, it is simply an anchoring shot taken when circumstances do not permit more careful placement in a vital area. It is particularly useful on a running animal, especially if crossing at a right angle to the line of fire; if lead is overestimated, the bullet may strike the neck, and if underestimated, has a good chance of going through the lungs.

The main disadvantage of the shoulder shot is that it produces a goodly amount of spoiled meat. The higher the velocity and the more explosive the expansion of the bullet, the greater the amount of meat ruined. I've seen deer hit in the shoulder with the result that the front quarters were completely bloodshot and not fit to eat. In any event, the average handgun hunter will be more likely to put meat in the freezer with a lung shot than any other he might try.

When it comes to a choice of guns and cartridges for deer hunting, one may select from a wider variety than for any other type of hunting. Assuming reasonable stalking ability and limiting shots to no more than 50 yards, preferably not beyond 40 yards, there is an extensive range of calibers quite adequate for deer.

Beginning with autoloaders, the 9mm Parabellum, .38 Super, .45 ACP, and the entire range of AMP (Auto Mag) cartridges are all quite capable so long as proper loads are used. Of course, standard military ball ammunition should *never* be considered for hunting. In 9mm P., several excellent expanding-bullet, high-performance loads are available. Some of the ultra-light 9mm JHP bullets do not perform as well on deer as the JSP variety in the 112- to 125-grain range. In .38 Super there are only the Super Vel high-performance loads, the 107-grain JHP and 112 JSP, both of which do quite well. In .45, factory loads producing velocities in excess of 1000 fps with JSP or JHP bullets perform much better than the slower loads, regardless of bullet weight. This is due to the fact that a minimum of 1000 fps is required to produce adequate expansion. Auto Mag calibers are available only under the Super Vel label, and all are actually *more* powerful than needed for deer.

In revolvers, an even wider range of choices is available. Of the smaller bores, the .32–20 with proper handloads does an excellent job, as does the .30 Carbine, provided an efficient expanding bullet is used. Up the ladder a bit, we find the .38 Special, in which there are at least a dozen high-performance loads that will dispatch a toothsome whitetail quite efficiently. The medium-weight expanding bullets of 110 to 137 grains seem best. Beyond the .38 Special, the .357, .41, and .44 Magnums in any of their full-charge loads are not only quite adequate for deer but in some cases more powerful and destructive than is really necessary. Of the older cartridges, the .38–40, .44–40, .44 Special, and .45 Colt are all quite adequate for deer in standard factory loads and become even more effective when jazzed up a bit by judicious handloading. They are at their best with standard-weight, lubricated lead bullets of semi-wadcutter or hollow-point form, driven at 1000 fps or more.

The gun itself is probably the least important of all the factors, so long as it is finely accurate and fitted with sights adequate to allow you to place your bullets on point of aim out to 50 yards. The refinements of barrel lengths, special sights, extra weight, etc., which are often desirable for larger game and longer ranges might be nice for deer hunting, but they are by no means essential to success. Even the common four-inch, fixed-sight, .38 Special revolver is adequate with the correct ammunition if you do your part.

The actual *hunting* of deer does not differ from any of the other big-game techniques discussed elsewhere in this book. One simply hunts, first locating the game, then stalking or otherwise arriving in sufficiently close proximity to allow a killing shot to be made. Probably the most popular and the most productive method of taking deer with a handgun is from a well-concealed stand located near a game trail, feeding area, watering spot, or stream crossing—or any other point or area where shootable animals may be expected. In parts of the Southwest, tree stands are quite popular, often being placed in the middle of a brushy clearing frequented by deer at dawn and dusk. An elevated position such as this provides a view of animals that would be hidden by brush if the hunter were at ground level. It has the added advantage of reducing the possibility of discovery since deer seldom look above their own level for danger, and there's less chance that a spooky buck will catch a whiff of human scent. I know of numerous instances in central Texas where hunters have remained silent and unmoving in tree stands while nice bucks moved directly under them, offering a vertical shot at a range of only a few feet!

In any event, the same methods used by rifle hunters in a given area will generally be the most productive with handguns; it is simply required that one be more cautious, stalk closer, and shoot more carefully.

# 13

## Tennessee Boar & Bear with a .45 Auto

"Hunt bear with a .45 Automatic? You've got to be kidding." That was typical of the comments made by friends a number of years ago when I mentioned that Lee Jurras and I were planning to go after Smoky Mountain black bear as part of a test and development program for a new, high-performance, expanding-bullet load for the venerable Colt Government Model pistol. Though the big autoloader has a legendary reputation for knock-down power, the majority of shooters and pistol fanciers who are not themselves expert generally consider it to be incapable of any significant degree of accuracy. In short, due to lack of understanding of the big gun's capabilities, all too many people refuse to consider it as a hunting gun. It was our avowed intention, nonetheless, to take both bear and Tennessee wild boar with the .45 Auto.

Some time before, Jurras had begun development of a maximum-lethality load in .45 ACP, primarily for the law-enforcement market. Bullet design had generally been settled on the basis of extensive laboratory tests, but we wanted to see how it would perform on live animal targets of roughly the same weight and vitality as man. The load pushed a 190-grain JHP bullet at 1,050 fps from the standard Government Model five-inch barrel without exceeding safe chamber pressures. The bullet was constructed with a pure-lead core, a very thin copper jacket, and an unusually large conical cavity in the nose. In profile, it presented a truncated cone atop a short cylinder. The bearing surface was deliberately made somewhat undersized for the standard .45 ACP barrel, allowing the bullet to be accelerated more easily out of the case and thus reducing chamber pressures. Yet the combination of soft, thin jacket and soft core caused the bullet to upset quickly under that acceleration to completely fill the rifling grooves. This permitted it to seal the bore properly and to deliver exemplary accuracy.

All possible tests had been run in the laboratory and test range with a wide variety of military and commercial arms chambered for this cartridge, but Colt had just introduced its Mark IV Series 70 variation of the old Government Model—so a pair of these guns was procured for the hunt. They were carefully checked by running about 200 rounds of the new load through each. Feeding and functioning was perfect, so no gun problems were anticipated.

We had used the Tellico Junction Hunting Preserve on several previous occasions for handgun hunts and knew it to have an excellent population of wild boar and black bear. Run by Tabby Brooks and Joe Meeks, Tellico Junction also contained plenty of wild turkey and deer, as well as exotic game—barbary sheep, Spanish goats, and other species imported and stocked for hunters who preferred that. Another factor in our choice was our knowledge that Tabby and Joe are both ardent handgunners who welcome handgun hunters. We flew in, accompanied by John Stafford, in a Piper Cherokee 6/300. It's an aircraft that has lots of room and carries lots of weight, so it was well able to handle all of our cameras, extra ammunition, and assorted other gear that we like to take along on test hunts.

Not a bad looking Tennessee boar, though perhaps a bit shorter in the tooth than some would expect for his nearly 300 pounds of weight. The gun is the Colt .45 MK IV Series 70 that did the job.

Before hunting, Tabby and Joe wanted to see how well the guns and ammunition would perform. Both were new to them—the Colt just announced and not widely available, the ammunition not yet a standard production item. They set out water-filled gallon plastic bleach bottles on the opposite shore of a pond near camp headquarters, just a bit over 100 yards from our shooting positions on an old earth dam. Jurras, a first-class long-range pistol shooter, hit two bleach bottles out of his first three shots, then with a perfectly straight face handed the smoking Mark IV to me. Tabby and Joe were ecstatic over such shooting, though they must have expected it, having witnessed Jurras' performance on earlier hunts. I took a bit longer to get on target but scored a satisfactory number of hits from the two-hand standing position. Stafford was at that time plant superintendent of Super Vel, accustomed to shooting a couple of thousand rounds weekly, so he was also able to get on those gallon bottles with very little trouble.

It's interesting to note that our guns were fitted with standard fixed sights, and the high-velocity load required hardly any hold-over to print on target at 100 yards even though the guns were factory-targeted for the standard 230-grain ball cartridge at 25 yards. This may be accounted for by the vast difference in recoil impulse and barrel time between the two loads. This does not often occur, and switching from a ball service load to a light-bullet, high-velocity load with most autoloaders (regardless of caliber) will usually require drastic retargeting or sight alteration.

The next day we spent the forenoon scouting the area, looking for big boars and bear sign, both of which were in short supply. The terrain at Tellico Junction Hunting Preserve seems to be mostly standing on edge and is heavily covered with second-growth timber and tangled laurel thickets. Fortunately, the leaves were off and visibility was relatively good, but climbing up and down those razor-backed ridges is hard on the leg muscles and lungs.

About mid-afternoon, Jurras and Meeks moved off to work one area while Stafford and I took another. We were in an area where we expected to see shootable boars, there being plenty of sign. At one point, we took a smoke break behind a log and some laurel bushes a few scant feet off a well-used trail. Being the lazy type who loves creature comforts, I stretched out full length in a patch of sunlight and was half asleep when Stafford prodded me and whispered hoarsely, "Hogs coming."

Not really expecting much, I listened for a moment, then rolled over on my belly, wedged against the log, and pulled out the Mark

IV, thinking I just might get a chance to use it. Neither of us moved another inch.

Suddenly three boars came into view around a sharp bend in the trail, hardly 20 yards away, upwind, led by one that would go nearly 300 pounds. He was well worth shooting, but from my position I couldn't get on him and any move would certainly spook the lot. Completely unaware, the trio proceeded sedately (for hogs) up the trail until they passed within the very narrow field of fire my position allowed. At that point, the big boar's tracks (measured later) passed 12 feet from my gun muzzle as I lay belly-down next to the log. He was several degrees uphill from me.

As he cleared the laurel thicket I held the Colt on his neck and touched one off. I pulled it too low (mainly because of the awkward position and inability to track the moving target) and failed to break his neck. Recovering, I planted a follow-up shot in his right shoulder, before he had taken another full step. The boar still hadn't seen me or Stafford, but he turned into the broken right shoulder, headed downhill, and saw me scarcely 10 feet away. By then the other two hogs were long gone up the trail.

I could see the flash of recognition in the wounded hog's eyes as he identified the source of his problem. Crippled in front, he dug in with his hind feet and attempted a lunge toward me. Later we examined his tracks. The powerful thrust of his hindquarters was clearly evident in the depth and distortion of that pair of prints. When he lunged I figured it was too late to run, and I knew I could plant at least one or perhaps two bullets in the right place before he reached me. Holding on the tip of his snout, I touched off a third shot —which unfortunately went a bit high, striking between his eyes, and skimming over the top of the brain. This was determined after the kill, for at that instant the hog dropped, stone dead, and I *thought* my third shot had been properly placed and had done the job.

The hog fell with his tusks about six feet from the gun muzzle. As I extricated myself from alongside the log and stood up, I realized Stafford was already on his feet, and had obviously fired a shot at some point in the melee. His question, "Did you hear me shoot?" explained it all. Seeing the hog turn on me after the second shot, John had jumped to his feet and fired a single shot simultaneously with my third one. His bullet had ranged steeply downward, striking the hog in top of the head just ahead of the ears and penetrating the brain. It was this shot, not my third, that dropped the hog in mid-lunge.

Later, at the meathouse, we traced the paths of all four bullets, and recovered all but the first which had passed completely through the

This is a re-enactment of the kill when a boar charged me and Stafford backed me up. The photo shows the exact positions from which we fired. The boar lies right where he fell.

neck. My second shot had broken the right shoulder and penetrated to the off side where it was recovered just under the hide. My third struck nearly between the eyes, skimmed through the top of the skull above the brain, then followed the curve of the skull and lodged near the top of the spine. Stafford's bullet had gone straight down into the brain and was found at the base of the skull. All three recovered bullets displayed expansion of .80 to .90 caliber. This was exactly the kind of performance we had been obtaining in Duxseal blocks, making it quite clear that from the standpoint of penetration and expansion either of my first two shots would have produced a clean kill had they been better placed. To put it bluntly, all three of my shots were misplaced by a couple of inches, even at a range of only a few feet, and that degree of misplacement spelled the difference between a clean kill and a hurt and angry animal which John had to finish off.

Had Stafford not made a fast decision to give me an unsolicited assist, I still think there would have been time for me to get in a killing shot before the hog reached me, but there's no way of determining whether my too-high head shot would have knocked him down or stoned him enough to divert his charge and give me a bit more time. My bullet didn't strike the brain, but it played hell with the skull, and was certainly close enough to have done considerable brain damage. It simply wasn't possible to tell, John's bullet having smashed through the brain from above at the same instant. There was nothing for me to say but "Thanks," because he did exactly what he should have done upon seeing a dangerous animal charge a com-

When Stafford located a good boar, Lee Jurras was fortunately behind him with camera in hand. It was a classic shot, and it produced the impressive one-shot kill described in the text.

panion. Anyway, granting that I'd had an assist, I'd still collected a very fine Tennessee boar which subsequently weighed out just a bit less than I had guessed, 275 pounds.

Later, when Tabby and Joe had brought up the International Scout and hauled my boar away to the meathouse, Stafford got a good unimpeded shot at about 40 to 50 yards at a smaller boar crossing a small valley. It was one of those neat, storybook kills, Stafford standing spraddle-legged with the gun locked in both fists, waiting for the unsuspecting boar to clear the brush that partially masked him. As he came clear, the Colt roared and the 190-grain JHP slug took him through the heart, penetrating completely and howling off the semi-frozen ground into the distance. In typical heart-shot behavior, the hog lunged forward a few steps, then tripped over a slight ledge, and rolled end-for-end, dead hardly 10 yards from where he had been hit.

Incidentally, these were by no means the first Tennessee boars we had taken with handguns. They were the first on which we'd used the .45 Auto, but we had all taken at least one at Tellico Junction with assorted sixguns and cartridges. And I had pistoled my first boar in Bavaria nearly 20 years earlier with an old SAA Colt converted to .401 Special by Pop Imer of Joplin, Missouri. I had also taken big, pure Russian boars just south of the Russian border in northwestern Iran in 1960. However, the object of this particular Tellico Junction hunt was not just to kill a couple more boars but to do it with a .45 Auto and to field-test what was to be the new Super Vel police load in that caliber.

Earlier, Tabby had promised, "I'm 99 percent sure we'll get you a bear, too, if you let us use the dogs." Lee and I aren't particularly fond of using dogs on four-footed game. We prefer still-hunting wherever possible. We had asked what the odds might be without dogs. Tabby's response to that was an unequivocal "Maybe." On that basis, we decided to still-hunt for a few days, and if no bear turned up, we'd spend the last day we could afford to be away with the dogs. For two days Tabby's "maybe" turned into a flat "no." We walked and we climbed; we huffed and we puffed. Tracks and sign we saw in sufficient quantity to assure us there were bears to be had, but Mr. Bruin remained out of sight as he is wont to do whenever possible in the presence of man.

The last day dawned wet, cold, foggy, and drizzly and it was with great reluctance we shuffled out of our warm and commodious quarters. Tabby had the bearhounds out, and was bemoaning the fact that one of the best had been killed by a bear only a few weeks earlier and he'd be shorthanded as a result. He had been out earlier to check the lay of the land, and now he led us to a ridge overlooking a steep draw through which he allowed the dogs would push a bear if the one he had in mind hadn't shifted his location. The field of fire wasn't too good, and Jurras, Stafford, and I spread out about 50 yards apart to cover the draw. It was probably fortunate that no bear did come through, for shooting would have been quite difficult. Any possible shot would have to be taken through brush of one sort or another. Those short, stubby .45 bullets don't take kindly to having their progress impeded in the least and will tumble and veer aside upon

This is what a good-sized Tennessee wild boar looks like after he has been pistoled.

striking very little resistance. We could have seen a bear well enough and could have put the guns on him without any trouble, but the odds would have been about even whether the best-aimed bullet could have reached him.

So it was with relief that we heard Tabby charging up the road yelling at us to hurry and come with him. As we bucketed down the old logging trail, he explained between explosive grunts that the dogs had jumped a good bear, well enough, but the inconsiderate beast had gotten around them and headed in almost the opposite direction he had planned, into an area beyond the ridge backing our original position.

After what seemed about a mile in the bouncing Scout, we heard the dogs singing "treed" (for the second time, as it turned out). Tabby stopped and switched off the noisy engine. We bailed out of the Scout and charged up a thickly pined slope toward the music of an unseen dog. A hundred yards off the trail, we saw the bear before the dogs, perched 15 or 20 feet up a pine tree. By prior arrangement, Stafford was elected to do the shooting, while I backed him up and Lee worked the cameras.

Tabby was in a hurry to see the bear shot before he became sufficiently irritated to come down and do battle with the dogs. He wanted neither to lose more dogs nor to run another mile until the bear treed again.

John and I managed to find a clear lane through the trees and limbs, about 20 yards out, making the angle of fire about 30 degrees above horizontal. Catching the bear momentarily unmoving with foreleg raised, John planted his first 190-grain JHP "underarm," so to speak, and through the lungs. It was a spectacular shot in one respect —in that the temperature and humidity caused a big cloud of white steam to jet out of the bear's chest as the bullet struck. Concerned about what a not-quite-dead bear might do to Tabby's dogs, John didn't wait to see the results of his shot. As the bear loosened his hold and started to slide down the tree, the Colt Mark IV spoke twice again in rapid succession, both bullets smashing into the chest area. Knocking off branches and bark on the way, the bear struck the ground and expired. We used up a lot of cussing and swatting to get the dogs off the carcass because a chewed-up bear hide doesn't make a very good rug. John was jubilant because this was his first bear with a handgun, and the first bear among the three of us with a .45 Auto.

Again, bullet performance was Jurras' primary concern, so we got out our well-honed knives for a careful postmortem. As it turned out, John's first bullet entered the chest cavity without striking bone,

A black bear, treed by dogs in Tennessee pines, presents an imposing handgun target.

This black bear is not of the size or temperament usually considered dangerous. All the same, the hunter, who has just put him down with two .45 bullets through the lungs, is wisely holding a bead on his neck until certain that the animal is dead. To walk up on any downed big game without being absolutely sure it is dead is to court disaster—especially when you are armed with a handgun.

punched through both lungs and part of the off-shoulder, coming to rest just under the hide. It expanded to .90 caliber. We couldn't have asked for better performance. Of the other two bullets, one was lost, having penetrated completely, while the other clipped a couple of ribs, traversed the chest cavity at an angle, and came to rest just under the hide at the base of the neck, also expanded to nearly .90 caliber. Both recovered bullets showed classic "mushroom" expansion, fairly concentric with the base. There was no question about the adequacy of this particular .45 ACP load under those conditions. Actual slant range was about 25 yards, and while we never weighed the bear, he felt heavy enough as we loaded him into the Scout for the trip back to the meathouse to have weighed somewhere between 250 and 300 pounds.

All three of the kills described in this chapter show clearly the importance of careful first-shot placement. Stafford's boar was a classic example of a clean one-shot kill. My boar, on the other hand, was a classic example of what can happen when the first shot isn't properly placed. The boar didn't get away, nor did I get chewed up, and only a few seconds elapsed from the first shot to the last and the animal's death. Nevertheless, being poorly hit the first time, the boar could have gotten away to die a lingering death, or he could have reached me and marked up my tender body (which I prize highly in its unmodified condition) with his razor-sharp tusks. Stafford's bear falls into a slightly different category, for even though the first shot

A man's first bear with a handgun is bound to produce an expression like this; John Stafford (left) is more than pleased with his Tennessee bear.

was placed with near-perfection and would have certainly been fatal within seconds, it might have resulted in the death or crippling of valuable dogs had the bear hit the ground with enough life left to fight. In this case, the additional shots were not required to ensure a kill or to protect the hunter or bystanders. But they *were* essential to protect the dogs. Had John not planted the second and third shots in time, the bear might have messed up a dog or two before expiring.

The foregoing also demonstrates the efficacy of the .45 ACP Government Model for taking big game at fairly close range. And, come to think of it, the account also shows where some unusual and excellent handgun hunting can be had. Tellico Junction Hunting Preserve caters to handgun hunters and offers a wide variety of both native and imported game admirably suited to the use of handguns in that terrain. It is not the only preserve in that general area of the South, either. Properly regulated preserve hunting of this type is by no means "fake" sport or easy. It's real hunting in the camps like Tellico Junction, and one never need apologize for a trophy taken on such a preserve.

# 14

---

*Pronghorns the Hard Way*

Traditionally, as I've emphasized, handguns are for short-range hunting, whether by means of stalking, waiting on stand, calling, or whatever. Consequently, one hears about handgunning deer, boar, black bear, and the like, as well as some predators that can be pursued with hounds or lured in with a device such as a dying-rabbit call. But the fleet, open-country-dwelling pronghorn antelope and similar species aren't considered often in that context. While doubtless other people *have* killed pronghorns with a handgun, the only one I know who discusses it much is Steve Herrett. His have been busted with a fast-stepping .30-caliber wildcat cartridge used in a special Contender single-shot pistol with a scope.

The fact is, fleet-footed game inhabiting the vast, wide-open spaces *can* be hunted successfully with handguns—though it does take the very best in gun/ammunition performance, very careful shooting, and a bit of Dame Fortune's grace.

To demonstrate that handguns aren't purely short-range instruments when handled by those thoroughly familiar with them, Lee Jurras and I embarked on a New Mexico pronghorn hunt in 1973. It was to be our premier big-game hunt with Auto Mag pistols. We were not unprepared for the difficult hunting that was expected. We'd spent much time in the ballistic laboratory and on the test range and had also shot varmints as a warm-up exercise all the way west from St. Louis to Las Vegas. The hunt was a unique experience, and was reported in the September, 1974, issue of *Petersen's Hunting* magazine, with whose kind permission we pick up here the major portion of that story.

"Possessed of an often-fatal curiosity, the pronghorn antelope of the Western plains is noted for being missed by more riflemen seeking him than virtually any other North American big game. He has magnificent eyesight, legs that churn like the wheels of a Formula I racer, and dwells in the flat and rolling areas where the hunter is normally in sight long before he's in range.

"As a result, the typical antelope shot is long—more often than not over 200 yards—and if he's spooked at all, the target is usually running flat-out. In addition to all that, the areas in which he is usually found are generally rather featureless and devoid of cover, leading one to underestimate range and target speed. It's very easy to swing on a running antelope's nose, as you would on a galloping whitetail or muley, and expect to plunk him in the rib cage only to find your bullet raising dust well behind him. Their speed is deceptive, and while the statement that 'Nobody ever shoots in front of an antelope' may not be entirely true, the first-time hunter is well advised to lead twice as much as he thinks is right in order to make a solid hit.

"For all these reasons, many people consider the pronghorn antelope one of the most difficult of all species to hit. I've missed my share of them, and am inclined to concur. If it's that way for riflemen with their modern gun/ammunition combinations . . . what would it be like with a handgun?

"So, when John Goodwin (Wildlife Information Officer, State of New Mexico) phoned and told us a long-closed ranch would open up its superb pronghorn pasture for hunting in '73, the stage was set for us to find out. John is also an ardent handgun buff—as are many of the New Mexico Game and Fish officers—and was most receptive to our request for a handgun hunt.

"Preparation had been hectic, and Lee had been stuck with most of the work, especially since his well-equipped ballistic laboratory (outside of Waldron, Ind.) makes valid testing and load development relatively easy. From the beginning, we had decided to use a pair of .357 AMP Auto Mag self-loading pistols. One with ventilated rib, six-inch barrel, the other with a slick eight-inch tube.

"The Auto Mag was at that time highly controversial. We chose the .357 AMP caliber over the .44 AMP for several reasons: It is free of the occasional feeding problems that plagued the early .44; it is inherently quite accurate; it produces a flatter trajectory than the .44; and antelope really don't require the smashing power of the big .44.

"With caliber selection made, we began handloading because .357 AMP factory ammunition wasn't yet available. Cases were formed from factory-fresh, unprimed, .44 AMP brass by simply necking them down in a full-length sizing die. After extensive pressure and velocity testing of several powders, Hodgdon's H110 powder was chosen, paired with the 137-grain JSP Super Vel bullet designed for the .357 Magnum. Cases were fire-formed and a load developed which produced 2,000 fps with a charge of 25.0 grains of H110 from the eight-inch gun. Velocity in the six-inch gun was about 100 fps less, but no measurable difference could be noted during test firing in the trajectory or effect on target. Both guns were zeroed with their original-equipment adjustable open sights at 100 yards, and displayed their ability to place this load in five inches or less at that range when the shooter did his part. Functioning of the guns was flawless.

"Now rifle shooters will doubtless consider a five-inch group at 100 yards a pretty poor substitute for the accuracy to which you are accustomed. Don't knock it, though, unless you can do better. Probably 99.9 percent of all the handgunners I've ever observed in action cannot shoot groups that small with *any* handgun. I've witnessed Jurras do substantially better on many occasions with a variety of guns, but I'll readily acknowledge that he is a superior long-range pistolero. I can do that well occasionally, but not always, and I need all the help I can get from gun and ammunition.

"With all that work done and with guns and ammunition aboard, we drove westward through Missouri and Kansas, and even into the Panhandle of Oklahoma before crossing into New Mexico. En route we kept a sharp eye peeled for likely varmint country and periodically pulled off to warm up both ourselves and the guns for the anticipated pronghorns. We had brushed up on state regulations in view of the fact that some species classed as varmints or predators in one state may be protected completely or classed as fur-bearers or game in neighboring states. Anyone planning on varminting across several states will be well advised to do the same. It would be a shame to move a mile across a state line, hunting the same species, and suddenly discover that you've broken the law and are standing in front of a judge attempting to explain it as a simple mistake.

"We found ample legitimate targets as we moved westward— jackrabbits, crows, and an occasional fox or coyote. The big impressive .357 AMP pistols took all in stride at ranges from 40 to 100 yards,

En route to a New Mexico antelope hunt, Lee Jurras and I warmed up on assorted varmints all the way west from Kansas City. Lee bagged this badger while the animal was moving at a strong 140 yards—a nice clean one-shot kill that demonstrated the efficiency of the flat-shooting .357 Auto Mag cartridge.

and as we warmed up, the gun/shooter combinations were quite clearly doing better than the five-inch groups produced back on the home range. To hit a crow at 70 to 80 yards requires a hell of a lot more accuracy than is indicated by a five-inch group at 100 yards. Take off the feathers, and there is damn little crow left to hit. If groups grow beyond three inches at 100 yards, you'll miss far more than you hit. No, we didn't hit all we shot at, and in fact experienced some embarrassing short-range misses. Handgunning on small live targets calls for the utmost in concentration, and if you let it slip for a moment, you've blown the shot.

"Though other successful shots followed, Lee climaxed his 'warmup' with a superb 140-yard shot on a running badger. Mr. Badger wasn't running full-out, but he was moving quickly, left to right at a right angle to the line of fire. After putting the first bullet over the target, Jurras held amidship just under his backline, and the second speedy 137-grain slug struck within an inch of point of aim— an instantaneous kill, accompanied by excellent bullet expansion as indicated by the exit hole.

"Having depleted our .357 AMP ammunition by half and knocked off a goodly portion of crop- and stock-raiding predators, we felt well prepared for the vastly bigger pronghorn targets as we rolled into Las Vegas to meet John Goodwin and find out where we'd be hunting. He had done us proud and spotted us in a 13,000-acre 'pasture' on the Diamond A Ranch just west of the little town of Wagon Mound. Pronghorn hunting had been closed for the preceding three years there, and we were advised we'd almost be overrun with long-horned antelope. Lee and I took that with a grain of salt because our circuitous route in from the Oklahoma Panhandle had taken us through a section of this very ranch, and we had been impressed by its paucity of pronghorn.

"Nothing ventured, nothing gained, so the next morning we hitched a ride with New Mexico Game and Fish officer Pete Nylander (another handgun buff I had met on a '72 hunt up around Cimarron) to avoid gutting Lee's T-Bird on the rocky ranch roads we knew we'd encounter. Pete happened to be living in Las Vegas, and unknown to us had been assigned to the Diamond A Ranch for the three-day season, along with a couple of other control officers. Pete also assured us that parts of the Diamond A Ranch were knee-deep in big-horned antelope.

"Ray Speer, honcho of Speer bullets, and Lee's long-time hunting buddy, had also been invited and joined us at Las Vegas. Not being a handgun aficionado, he carried along his Ruger M77 chambered for the .257 Roberts cartridge. We all agreed that he could take the long shots, and Lee and I would try to improve the odds for our Auto Mags by getting in as close as possible.

"We saw antelope all over the place while approaching our designated area, and just inside the pasture, Pete dropped us off to go after a small group containing a nice 15-inch buck, and went to check the area. The buck was feeding on one side of the knob in a shallow saddle, and we elected to come up the opposite side to catch him unaware from above. My lungs being unaccustomed to 7500 feet of altitude, the approach was slow, and if not entirely as we planned, effective. The buck and his harem moved sideward by the time we came above the saddle, so Ray moved around to the left while I stayed up on top and Lee dropped down to move around from the right. Moving forward a bit I could see just the tips of the buck's horns over the intervening rock and waited anxiously for Ray to get into position. Unfortunately, something spooked the animals and by the time Ray got the buck in his scope, they were running flat-out and his shots fell behind.

"As they ran with the buck, the buck trailing, the animals came into Lee's view, and at about 120 yards he leveled down on the streaking buck with the big Auto Mag. I could see the buck, but not Lee. With the first report, the buck somersaulted as if he had hit a knee-high trip wire. Exultation died aborning, though, for in an instant he was on his feet and running as if nothing had happened.

"For the next 30 to 45 minutes we sat atop the knob and glassed that buck as he described a wide half-circle across the plain and up onto a long malpais ridge a good 1500–2000 yards away. Try as we could, we could not see any evidence of a hit on him, nor in his gait or actions when halted. In fact, he seemed totally unconcerned, feeding with his harem on yonder ridge. The only conclusion we could reach was that Lee's bullet had nicked him on a horn or hoof and rolled the surprised buck without actually harming him. It wouldn't be the first time a chance hit of that sort had rolled an unsuspecting animal who continued on unhurt. (I hit a blesbok through the horns with the same effect in South Africa during 1974.)

"We walked back out to the nearest ranch road where again a passing Game and Fish pickup (they were checking this newly opened area and its opening-day hunters meticulously) gave us a lift around a roadloop of several miles and dropped us about 1½ miles off the flank of the malpais ridge where our lucky but accident-prone buck had apparently bedded down while his girlfriends fed.

"From this new vantage point, we glassed the ridge and determined that there were at least two quite respectable bucks—15 inches or better. They were looking directly at us, curious but not alarmed, and paid us little mind as in a long line abreast we began nonchalantly strolling in their general direction. As we moved, Lee drifted off to the right, while Ray and I ambled directly toward the ridge, a couple of hundred yards apart. At least half the time during the approach we were out of the animals' sight, masked by lower intervening ridges and valleys.

"By the time we reached the base of the ridge, having taken an hour to get there in leisurely fashion, the animals only glanced curiously at us before we were masked by the ridge itself. By then, they'd become accustomed to our presence and apparently didn't consider us a threat. Ray took the right and I the left, and we moved cautiously up to the rocky rib that was hiding us.

"As Ray eased up out of my sight, I heard his rifle speak once with final authority. At the same instant, I spotted a pair of horns protruding above the rocks. My buck was standing there, head doubled back behind the shoulder, looking behind him to ascertain the source of the noise. Two of his does were fidgeting 50 yards away, eager to be off.

"With the big Auto Mag charged and cocked, I eased up until I could lay the yellow front sight squarely on the junction of neck and shoulder at 60 to 70 yards. I dallied a bit too long, enjoying the view, and the buck decided to move on to a healthier climate. The big Auto Mag thundered, and he rolled over to fetch up against a rock outcropping.

"As I clambered up, Ray came into view, as did his kill, a nearly identical buck down hardly more than 100 yards away. Both were clean one-shot kills, Ray's .257 bullet quartering into the rib cage from the rear, and continuing on up the neck and exiting through the head. Fortunately, it didn't shatter the skull, so the 15½-inch horns were intact. Mine was another matter, for the shot was fired with too much lead, and the speeding bullet shattered the skull and left one horn flopping loose—no spread measurement could be made. A shame, for his horns went 16 inches and were unusually massive. If spread could have been measured accurately, he would have amassed quite a point score and may well have made the book.

"Lee eventually showed up to investigate the noise, having encountered nothing but does fleeing the sound of shots, off the nose of the ridge to the right.

"Next morning we were out early—all three of us—even though only Lee now needed an antelope—and headed down the same road just inside our pasture. We expected the antelope to be more spooky, having been shot at the day before—we weren't the only hunters in the area—but off to the left and up ahead a nice lone representative buck stood watching us. 'Let me see how close I can get,' spoke Lee, and he bailed out of the pickup, then moved nonchalantly on down parallel to the road, masking himself partway with a single rise while

Here I am with a fine 16-inch pronghorn antelope, taken with my 8 1/2-inch-barreled .357 Auto Mag pistol during a 1973 hunt in New Mexico.

we stood in the road and watched the solitary buck who was eyeing us curiously. When he first spotted Lee, the buck fidgeted a few yards farther, then switched his attention back to us. I guess we were bigger and more attractive than the lone man trying to get into position for a shot. Lee had reached a point where there was absolutely no cover between him and the antelope and the animal knew he was there. Every time he attempted to move closer, the buck fidgeted away about the same distance, maintaining a Mexican stand-off.

"Partly out of frustration at being unable to reduce the range, but largely because the conditions were good for a long-range handgun shot, Lee finally settled down into a prone, two-hand position, up slightly on his elbows so as to be able to see over the fairly short grass and scattered rocks. We watched with considerable interest and mentally made book on the shot. Pete's only comment was 'I hope he misses, he'll get a bigger one farther along.'

"At the flat bark of the .357 Auto Mag, the buck remained on his feet, but gave unmistakable evidence of a solid hit as he began trotting away. The next shot kicked up dust under him, and at the next he folded. Total distance traveled from first shot to last was less than 40 yards, angling slightly away from the shooter.

"We went down to congratulate Lee on what were obviously fine long-range shots, and then I carefully paced a direct line from his position to where the animal lay—217 full, long strides that the years have shown me measure an accurate 36 inches—one yard each. That isn't just a *good* shot; with *any* handgun it's *superb*.

"There were two hits, right enough, one in the flank, angling forward through liver and kidneys to completely wreck one lung.

This pronghorn, though not especially long of horn, is highly prized as a trophy by Lee Jurras. It was taken on the Diamond-A Ranch near Wagon Mound, New Mexico, with the 6 1/2-inch .357 Auto Mag pistol shown at a measured range of 217 yards. Some shooting!

Considering the buck's actions at the first shot, this is the one that did it. Certainly a fatal shot, and if he'd been left alone he probably wouldn't have traveled farther than the 40 yards he made before the second one caught him. The other and apparently second hit was in the neck, just a bit too low to strike the vertebrae, but also ultimately fatal since the damage it did would have bled him out in very short order.

"Though both bullets punched clear through and we weren't able to recover them, carefully checking the wound channels clearly indicated quite substantial expansion of the 137-grain JSP Super Vel projectile. From a handgun, mind you, at a range of 217 yards—and if you want to be finicky about the range, just call it 200-plus yards in case my legs didn't quite stretch the full three feet. Neither of the other two who witnessed the shot disagreed in the least with the range figure, and Lee modestly declined comment. 'How high did you hold?' was the first question of Lee after the initial excitement had died down a bit. 'Right even with his back.' A quick check on the defunct antelope and approximate measurement down to the entrance holes disclosed both about the same distance down—roughly eight inches. That's a mere eight-inch drop from a 100-yard zero at over 200 yards.

"Quite impressive—I'm sure we all know a few .30–30 carbines that won't shoot that flat with standard factory loads claiming a lot more velocity than the 2000 fps the .357 AMP produced in our laboratory tests. Frankly, I can't think of anything more suitable to climax a short hunt than an over-200-yard kill with a handgun. Lee's grin made it obvious he didn't give a damn that his buck's horns wouldn't quite measure up to the ones Ray and I had taken. Considering the fact that his kill was made at over three times the range of mine, and over twice the range of Ray's, I can't blame him a bit. The size of the horns doesn't make a bit of difference on a shot like that.

"In retrospect, we can say that we were vindicated in our belief that the .357 Auto Mag pistols were quite adequate for antelope under those conditions. My shot of 60 to 70 yards was an easy one with such a heavy and flat-shooting gun. I don't feel it would have been a bit easier if I had been carrying a scope-sighted single-shot pistol chambered for a rifle or quasi-rifle cartridge as has become rather popular with many pistoleros these days. Lee's shot showed that the .357 AMP trajectory is plenty flat for shots up to 200 yards and that the accuracy in the hands of a superior pistol shot is certainly equal to the task. One hit we might have crossed off to luck, but two prove amply that Dame Fortune had a hell of a lot less to do with it than the combination of gun, load, and shooter. Likewise, bullet performance was all that could be desired. From visual examination of the kill, I am convinced that the 137-grain JSP did as much damage as a .30–30 or .300 Savage would have done at the same range.

"Now, if you think this means that I recommend hunting antelope (or anything else) at 200 yards with a handgun, you're out of your tree. The average handgunner owes it to himself and his game to limit his shots to 50 yards on medium or big game, regardless of the armament he's carrying. It isn't a question of the gun's ability to kill a properly hit animal (even much larger than antelope) beyond 50 yards, but a question of placing the bullet properly. If you can shoot good, tight 50- to 75-yard groups, you can certainly hit a deer or antelope at that range provided your field shooting is as good as your range shooting—a situation that often doesn't exist. But simply hitting isn't enough. Many a sixgun buff I know can crank out three- or four-inch groups at 50 yards on neat paper targets, even under competitive pressure. But a good many of those same shooters undergo a bit of transformation when the target is hide, hair, and horns moving against a natural background. I've seen the same fellows who shoot 99/7X 50-yard slow-fire scores miss standing foxes and jackrabbits at half that range. Game targets and paper targets just ain't the same, and this is just one of the many reasons we feel 50 yards is the practical limit for handgunning big game.

"I took my shot because I was absolutely certain that with the gun and cartridge and conditions at hand I could put my bullet within two inches of point of aim—I didn't *hope* I could do it, I *knew* I could. I still could have missed, but the odds were in favor of a clean hit. Had I been using a lesser gun, I wouldn't have taken it unless I could have gotten within 50 yards. Jurras knew he had a fifty-fifty chance of a clean hit on his first shot from the solid prone position. The target was immobile, as was the shooter. Had he been forced to take the shot standing, he'd have passed. Further, the animal was in the open and would have had to run at least a couple hundred yards before reaching any cover. With seven rounds in the magazine, this would have given Lee ample time to correct from bullet strike if his first shot had been off. That he has the ability to do this is clearly evident by his second hit.

"Further, we have both killed a good many head of big game with handguns of various sorts, ranging from .380 up through the .44 Magnum. We had just proved to ourselves (nobody else was watching, so we had only ourselves to satisfy) on the trip out that we could hit much smaller targets at long range with those same guns and ammunition. And, mind you, our en-route practice was on *live* targets, not paper."

Since then, we've hunted other antelope species elsewhere in the world under similar circumstances—and quite successfully, I might say. To ourselves, at least, we've proven that the *properly trained* and *equipped* handgun hunter need not limit himself entirely to close-in game. Taking the spooky ones at far-out ranges ain't easy, but it can be done.

# 15

## Long-Range Handgun Work

Traditionally the handgun—whether auto or revolver—is considered a very short-range weapon. To be sure, some handguns have no potential for any significant long-range accuracy. Generally speaking, though, handguns and cartridges that are suitable for hunting— that possess the accuracy, power, and velocity needed—will produce surprising accuracy at long range if you equip and train yourself to extract it. You must learn to develop the full accuracy potential of the gun/ammunition combination.

When I speak of hunting guns in this context, I don't mean varminting pistols. Shortguns designed for varminting will be covered in the next chapter. Such guns are intended specifically for hitting small targets at ultra-long distances, whereas conventional revolvers and autoloaders are intended primarily for short to medium range and yet can be made to perform adequately at what are normally considered rifle-shooting distances. Scopes are sometimes used, but they're most commonly mounted on varmint guns so they, too, will be discussed in the next chapter. What I plan to deal with here is how to stretch the effective range of your conventional, open-sighted handgun.

The first question is, why bother? Under ideal conditions and with just the right equipment, a really good pistolero can hit fairly consistently at 200 yards, but in the chapter on hunting pronghorns I made an important statement about that, and it bears repeating here: "If you think this means that I recommend hunting antelope (or anything else) at 200 yards with a handgun, you're out of your tree. The average handgunner owes it to himself and his game to limit his shots to 50 yards on medium or big game, regardless of the armament he's carrying. . . . 50 yards is the practical limit for handgunning big game." Then why go through the immense amount of practice needed to hit a target at the unheard-of pistol range of 200 yards?

There are three answers. First, it will will help you to judge range at shorter distances and will simply make you a much better handgunner. Second, it's great fun to test the limits of your gun's ability and your own—to find out just what you, your gun, and your cartridges can do. And third, there are exceptions—admittedly rare exceptions but exceptions all the same—to the 50-yard rule. In that chapter on pronghorns, you'll recall, I explained that I took an antelope at about 70 yards because "I was absolutely certain that with the gun and cartridge and conditions at hand I could put my bullet within two inches of point of aim—I didn't *hope* I could do it, I *knew* I could." I also described a shot Lee Jurras made at more than 200 yards. In his case, half a dozen elements in the situation made it an exception to the rule. First, Lee is a superb pistol marksman; second, he was using the ideal pistol and load; third, he knew what the range was with fair precision, so there wasn't much chance of making a mistake about bullet drop; fourth, the terrain was open and flat, and there wasn't any wind; fifth, the target was perfectly stationary and standing broadside; and sixth, Lee was able to fire from a rock-solid prone position.

You'll also recall that he was testing long-range gun/ammo performance on live game or he'd have passed up the shot—but that's not the point. The point is that a special set of circumstances made the shot possible. Most handgunners would love to be able to make such a shot, just in case they're ever lucky enough to find themselves in the same kind of circumstances. So, I'll try to show you how.

Even some guns with poor reputations for accuracy are capable of amazing long-range work if you learn to handle them properly. In this connection, I recall an incident more than a quarter of a century ago when as a young Lieutenant I was training troops in marksmanship. When some green recruits complained that their M-1 Carbines couldn't be made to stay on target at 200 yards, I bellied down with a sandbag rest and consistently stayed within the scoring rings (often in the black) at those ranges with a military-issue Colt M1911A1 .45

auto. This story has caused me to be called careless with the truth, and I won't be upset if some readers take the same attitude now. Nevertheless, such shooting *can* be done. It's all in learning how, and in burning up thousands of rounds of ammunition in practice.

There are a few basic rules in learning passable long-range shooting. Not necessarily in order of importance, they are as follows:

1. Use a gun/cartridge combination with the flattest trajectory possible within your ability to withstand blast and recoil.

2. Never shoot with one hand if you can use both, and never shoot from a standing position if any form of rest or more solid position is at all possible.

3. Tune your gun (or have it done) so that it offers the best possible trigger pull.

4. Use the longest-barreled gun practical, mainly for the long sight radius but also for the added velocity it will extract from any given load.

5. Use first-quality, finely adjustable target-type sights of the standard Patridge form.

6. Learn to handload (and do it well) because you will never otherwise be able to afford the large amount of practice ammunition needed to make you a first-class long-range handgun shot.

Selecting the proper gun and cartridge will get you off to a good start. Rifle-type pistols and pistol-type rifles are out, as far as I'm concerned, as are basically rifle-type cartridges sometimes used in these guns—the .221 Remington Fireball, .30–30, and the like. These are special-purpose pistol/cartridge combinations. Some of them excel in long-range varminting, and I'll deal with them in the chapter on that topic. But right now the goal is to learn long-range marksmanship with the same general kind of gun you'll use on most varieties of game—that is, with a gun that has a more or less conventional revolver or pistol configuration and feel. As a practical matter, I consider the .357 AMP Auto Mag pistol with eight-inch barrel the best long-range handgun of the hunting class. Its cartridge and barrel length produce the flattest trajectory; it has excellent sights, the longest sight radius of any production repeating handgun, an adjustable trigger, and a demonstrated mechanical accuracy (that is, its own precision, unaffected by human error) on the order of two minutes of angle—which means two-inch groups at 100 yards.

Second to the Auto Mag, the long-barreled Magnum revolvers are the best bet. And they cost only about half the price of an Auto Mag.

Among the Magnum calibers it's difficult to make a choice. I personally prefer the .41, but the .44 is far more popular and, provided the proper load is chosen, the .357 is just as accurate and holds up just as well as the other two. Therefore, unless you're going to take large game at long range—where the additional power is essential—the .357 Magnum is probably as good an all-around revolver choice as you can make. It has the advantages of lower ammunition cost in either factory or handloads and less recoil and blast.

With regard to makes and models, quality and inherent accuracy are more important than anything else. It makes no difference whether you use a double-action or single-action sixgun, and if you favor either the .41 or .44 Magnum, the only choice is between the S&W N-frame DA gun and the Ruger Blackhawk series in single-action persuasion. In other calibers, Colt SA and DA revolvers enter the picture, and are capable of doing work fully as good as the two makes already mentioned. Keep in mind, though, that some models and calibers are not available in barrel lengths greater than 6 or 6½ inches. Certainly, nothing shorter than this should be chosen; the 7½-inch barrel is better, and the 8⅜-inch tube of the S&W Magnums is better yet. Remember the rule about using the longest barrel practical in order to get a long sight radius and improvement in cartridge performance.

Below the performance level of the Magnum revolvers, there aren't any *really* first-class, long-range combinations readily available among today's *production* guns. This isn't to say that quite good long-range work can't be done with many gun/cartridge combinations but, other factors being equal, the lesser calibers do not come up to the standards of the Magnum revolvers or the Auto Mag quick-firer. Even so, let's take a look at what else is available. The various Colt, S&W, and Ruger DA and SA revolvers in .38 Special can be made to produce excellent results insofar as marksmanship is concerned, but the cartridge lacks the power for game big enough to be hit consistently at long ranges. Any of the better medium- or heavy-frame .38 Specials with six-inch or longer barrels and target sights can be paired with the proper load and you'll be able to do good work. Because of their relatively flat trajectory, the heaviest high-performance, jacketed-bullet factory loads in this caliber must be used for best results.

Beneath the medium-frame .38 Special revolvers, nothing currently available merits serious consideration for long-range work. However, should you run across one of the discontinued better-quality models chambered for the .32–20 Winchester cartridge, don't let it get away. For many years this cartridge in 6-inch and 7½-inch barrels was applauded by many as the best long-range number available. This isn't necessarily true today because only the low-velocity lead-bullet loading is still produced, but if you handload it to maximum performance within the capabilities of the individual gun, it is truly a finer performer out to 200 yards. A modern counterpart of the .32–20 Winchester is to be found in the .30 Carbine cartridge, for which only the Ruger Blackhawk is currently chambered. Unfortunately, the standard .30 Carbine load is formulated for 18-inch rifle barrels and does not perform its best in a handgun. Besides, its flash and blast are atrocious in the shorter barrels. When handloaded, though, it will match the handloaded .32–20.

Among conventional autoloading pistols, the .38 Colt Super Auto in the Colt Government Model (or the Spanish copies thereof) is by far the best combination after the Auto Mag. The old standard ball round in this caliber, with its 130-grain bullet at 1300 fps, long ago developed an excellent reputation for long-range accuracy. Today, though, it is inferior to the 112-grain JSP Super Vel loading. This not only produces a flatter trajectory but seems to be more accurate—other factors being equal—and it is suitable for hunting, whereas the old ball round is not.

When the 9mm Parabellum (Luger) cartridge is used in a gun comparable to the Colt .38 Super, then it follows a mere handful of percentage points behind the latter. Again, the standard ball round is inadequate for long-range work, but the Super Vel 112-grain JSP and similar high-performance loads do quite well, considering their approximately 100 fps velocity lag behind the .38 Super.

If you're curious why I have left out the .45 ACP, particularly after my early reference to it, consider that its trajectory height is simply too great for consistent long-range work. Its very stubby and blunt bullet sheds velocity at too great a rate, even when loaded to the hilt. When it hits, it does hit well, but the sharpest long-range pistolero will not normally be able to match his 9mm or .38 Super work with the big .45.

I would like to emphasize again that good long-range work with any gun in any caliber depends upon choosing the load that produces the flattest trajectory possible over the range at which you wish to shoot. Generally speaking, I consider 200 yards the maximum range at which anyone may expect to develop a high degree of pistol marksmanship. Therefore, pay no attention to 100-yard mid-range trajectory height or to what it might be out beyond the recommended distance. Use the 200-yard value in making your selection and you can't go wrong. If you'll be shooting handloads or a factory load for which this value cannot be obtained, then do a lot of shooting at 200 yards and 100 yards on paper targets, plotting the center of impact of your groups at both ranges. Then transfer them both to a single target and measure the vertical difference. That, for all practical purposes, *is* the mid-range trajectory height.

I've already mentioned that a long-range handgun must have first-class, finely adjustable target-type sights. That alone isn't enough, for you must have a front sight that extends uncluttered well above the barrel or its base. Generally speaking, I consider that sight protrusion must be ¼-inch or slightly more. Thus, the relatively low front sights found on quite a few revolvers and the even lower sights on some autos are not suitable. The reason is that the long-range handgun is not targeted or zeroed for any great range. It is targeted with the chosen load—and very carefully, too—at a comparatively short range, say 50 yards. For greater ranges you employ a variation of "Kentucky windage," using the front sight to compensate for bullet drop. The top of the front sight is placed on the point you wish your bullet to strike, then centered laterally in the rear-sight notch, and the two sights are aligned so that a specified amount of front sight protrudes *above* the top of the rear sight.

This form of sight alignment places the center line of the barrel at a greater upward angle in relation to the line of sight, and thus compensates for the drop of the bullet at the greater range. The effect is exactly the same as if the rear sight were mechanically elevated in the usual fashion and a conventional sight picture were taken. How do you know how much front sight to hold up? While a mathematically inclined pistolero could calculate it for any given range, the practical answer to that question is, *practice* (and practice and practice and practice) until you develop an instinctive *feel* that enables you to get it right.

There is, however, one front-sight improvement—I believe it was first used and mentioned by Elmer Keith—which will greatly facilitate learning the correct amount. This consists of placing a contrasting light-colored horizontal line(s) across the rear face of the front sight at the proper point for any given distance(s) beyond that of the zero range. Once you've selected your load and have targeted the gun initially, fire enough careful trial rounds at some greater range to get a *rough* idea of the amount of front sight that must be held up to get on target. Then, arbitrarily scribe or paint a horizontal line on the rear face of the front sight, even with the top of the rear sight when that amount of front sight is held up. Then go back to shooting and vary the position of that line until you have it exactly right for the chosen range. Once that has been done, the reference line can be made permanent, if you like, by having a jeweler inlay a piece of thin gold or platinum wire. Also, if you wish, you may then proceed to "shoot in" the proper location for one or two additional lines for other ranges. Personally, I prefer a single line, as it's too easy to get confused and choose the wrong one if several are present.

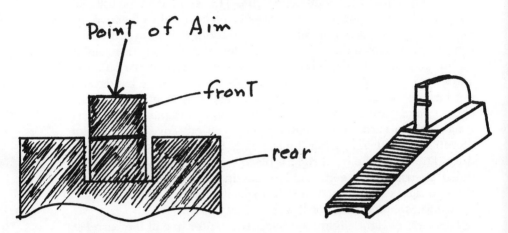

ABOVE LEFT This is the "up-front-sight" sight picture, described in the text, showing how you line up a horizontal marker on the front sight to get the needed elevation at a given range.

ABOVE RIGHT Here's how a long-range marker for the proper amount of up-front-sight can be made across the face of your front sight.

Okay, now you've got a good, long-barreled, far-reaching handgun, and have selected a high-performance cartridge and load—and you want to pair them up and learn how to make 200-yard shots. There are two ways to go about learning: either on a formal target range with paper targets or out in the field with makeshift targets such as rocks, stumps, five-gallon cans, etc. Personally, I much prefer the field method, but in a good many parts of the country the wide-open, uninhabited spaces needed for this simply aren't available. If you use a conventional range, keep in mind that even daily practice at paper targets at a *known* distance won't guarantee hits in the field where the target is invariably irregular in shape and size, drab in color, and blending in with its surroundings, and where you must quickly estimate the distance.

Regardless of the method you'll be using, begin by verifying the 50-yard zero of your gun and load. This *must* be a center-hold zero, with the top of the front sight exactly on point of impact with a conventional sight picture. A six o'clock hold on a crisply outlined circular bullseye may work well enough for some (and I've used it plenty) but tell me, where in the hell is six o'clock on a coyote, jackrabbit, or mule deer?

Assuming you're beginning on a formal range setup, put up a 100-yard target consisting of a plain buff or tan-colored background containing a 12-inch circular black aiming point. Don't worry about that bull being too big; you'll find soon enough that it isn't. Make certain the background extends a couple of feet below the bull to catch those low shots that are coming.

Don't, whatever you do, make the mistake of attempting your first shots from the classic one-hand target-shooter's stance, or even the two-hand standing position. Those are the most unsteady of all positions, and are guaranteed to produce results so disappointing in the beginning that you may give up the whole idea after the first session. After a few months and a few thousand rounds of practice, you'll be able to use the two-hand standing position when it's absolutely necessary, but the one-hand position is a waste of time.

Of the several positions available to the long-range handgunner, all of your early practice and training should be carried out from the steadiest. I consider this to be sitting at a bench rest, both hands on the gun, arms straight, with elbows resting on sandbags or padding, and the hands and gun butt solidly bedded on the sandbags. The height relationship of the bench and stool (chair) should be such that you sit up fairly straight, which means that the typical bench rest

The two-hand offhand stance is better than one-hand, but should never be used in the field except as a last resort.

Always use a rest if you can possibly find one. Any support is preferable to an unsupported shot. Here Paul Slavens forms a solid rest by planing one hand against a tree trunk, then resting the gun hand across it.

made for rifle shooting is too low. Hunching over the way rifle shooters do at a bench reduces the distance from your eye to the gun's sight, whereas sitting up straight maintains essentially the same sight-to-eye distance as you'll encounter in most good field positions. That doesn't mean you can't use the bench rests that are on the range—it just means you raise the level of the gun and your arms with extra sandbags. The position will be even better for some shooters if a back rest is available, but usually nothing suitable for this is incorporated in the typical rifle bench rest.

Lacking a bench from which to work, give consideration to making a portable shooting bench. Though perhaps technically not quite as stable as a massive concrete bench rest, it is still more stable than any other position that might be practical. The bench is cheap and simple to make, and takes down quite easily to stow in the trunk of your car. If you do go this route, don't forget to use exterior-grade or marine plywood, sand and seal the edges well, and give it two or three coats of good exterior paint to prevent it from deteriorating in the weather on those occasions when you'll certainly want to leave it out for a few days or overnight.

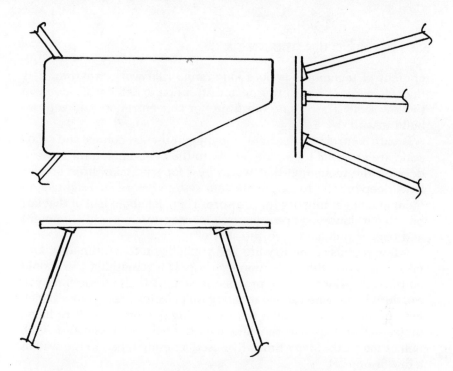

This drawing shows how to build a portable shooting bench. Make the top from 3/4-inch or thicker plywood; attach pipe flanges to the underside, canted outward by wood wedges; screw in one-inch pipe legs. The legs can be removed easily for transportation. Splayed legs make the bench stable in spite of light weight.

For shooting at paper targets, you'll need a good spotting scope with a magnification of 20X or more. Otherwise, you'll spend most of the time walking back and forth to check the strike of your bullet. Then, too, if other people are using the range they won't want to suspend firing every few minutes for you to walk down and check your target. I consider the spotting scope—and it need not be a costly one—essential, at least in the beginning. Of course, if you're shooting a .44 or .45, a good pair of 8X binoculars may enable you to see the big bullet holes, at least when they are in the white.

Now get down in position and align the sights on target. Don't settle for a position that is *almost* right. Raise or lower your stool, shift the sandbags around, do whatever is necessary to obtain a near-perfect position. Don't pick up the ammunition yet—dry-fire a few shots. Note carefully how the target looks over the sights, and psych yourself up with some very careful dry-snapping. This kind of hand-gun shooting takes the same high degree of concentration and development of technique as does long-range rifle work. Anything less than 100 percent concentration and attention to detail will cause you to blow shots. There is no substitute for concentration, and you can build it with dry fire.

Breath control and a certain amount of muscular control and relaxation are essential to precise let-off. In the beginning, until you can develop the technique that works best for you, take three or four long, deep breaths to oxygenate your system before final sight alignment and beginning trigger pressure. Then, let about half of that last breath out slowly, compose yourself, concentrate on sight alignment and trigger pull, and wish the shot off.

A few rounds of this dry fire and you'll begin to get the idea. Dry fire is not a one-time initiation exercise. It is something you should go through prior to every practice session. It is also something you can do at home when actual shooting isn't possible. Set up your bench in the garage or den, and fix a small aiming spot on the wall, reduced in size so that it appears the same over the sights as does your 12-inch bull at 100 yards. Many times I've used a penny taped to the wall as a dry-fire target.

Now it's time to progress to live ammunition. Load up; a single round is enough, regardless of whether you are using a sixgun, auto-loader, or single-shot. This isn't a game where you crank off as many shots as possible in a hurry. One at a time with careful concentration is what it takes. Make certain, if you're using a revolver, that the sandbags aren't crowded up around the barrel/cylinder gap where the high-velocity jet of escaping gases will cut it or blow up dust and grit to clog the gun.

This first shot will be exactly like your dry firing. Absolute concentration, breath control, muscular control—the whole bit. Hold dead-center on the bull with a conventional sight picture, and send the shot on its way.

No, it most likely won't hit the black, even if you do everything perfectly. A .44 Magnum with 8⅜-inch barrel, zeroed for 50 yards (as it should have been) will print several inches below point of aim at 100 yards. That far below the center of the black is where your shot should strike on the target.

If that first shot can't be seen through your spotting scope, don't get excited. Simply take a two- or three-minute breather, and fire again. Eventually, you'll have a cluster of shots on the paper somewhere below the center of the bull. If you're extremely fortunate or extremely skillful, that cluster may be five inches or less in diameter. Or it may be the size of a dinner plate or larger. Assuming that you are accustomed to shooting fairly tight groups at 50 yards, those 100-yard groups should not be much more than twice their size. Don't expect better than that.

At this point, you may elect to continue practice to reduce your group size, ignoring the fact that the shots are striking below point of aim. I think this is probably the best route to take. The more you can shrink your group before switching to up-front sighting, the more easily you'll be able to obtain hits when you do start compensating for bullet drop. If you're anxious, though, you can go ahead now and start trying to place your bullets on point of aim.

In either case, go down to the target and locate the center of impact of your group(s). Carry a small tape measure along for this purpose. If you're not especially good at mental arithmetic, use a scratch pad and a pencil. Measure from the left side of the target paper horizontally to each bullet hole, discounting any that are way out of the group; then add all those distances together and divide them by the number of shots to obtain the *average* distance of all shots from the left side of the paper. Draw a vertical line on the target face that distance in from the side. Repeat this operation, measuring vertically from the bottom of the target, and draw a horizontal line the average distance from the bottom. Where those two lines intersect is the center of impact of your group. Of course, if you have a nice circular 10-shot group that doesn't go over four or five inches, simply looking at it will locate the center of impact with adequate precision.

Measure from the center of impact to the center of your aiming point, and you have the amount of drop (from 50-yard zero) that your particular combination of gun/ammunition/shooter produces. This drop figure may well bear little resemblance to the drop values published in various ballistic charts. Most published drop values are calculated rather than developed on the range, and they are based on the industry-standard barrel length and test-barrel velocities. Not only is your particular gun unlikely to produce those same velocities, even if it is in the same barrel length, but your own shooting techniques and the manner in which you absorb recoil will affect the amount of drop actually produced in the field. Book figures are at best only a rough guide. Don't be surprised at the amount of drop your plotted center of impact shows. Depending on the various factors we've just mentioned, it might be hardly perceptible or as much as a foot or more. It can't be predicted so you must determine it for yourself by actual shooting.

Now, back to the bench to try and put your bullet on point of aim.

Try a few dry-fire cycles holding up just a tiny bit of front sight. If you have difficulty holding the same amount of blade above the rear sight from shot to shot, place a horizontal mark on the rear face of the front sight. This can be done with 1/64-inch white chart tape, a white pencil, or whatever suits your fancy. In any event, use something that's readily removable.

Once you've got the hang of holding up a consistent amount of front sight—with or without the guideline—switch back to live ammunition and shoot a slow, careful five-shot group. Spot the group through your scope, and most likely you'll find that you've held up either too much or too little front sight. If you're not certain, continue shooting with the same amount of front sight until you can be positive. Then, if your group was too high, repeat the exercise holding up a bit less sight; or if too low, hold up more. Repeat this, firing five-shot groups until you have determined the amount of front sight that must protrude above the rear sight to give you point-of-aim hits, or, rather, to place your calculated center of impact on point of aim.

Once you're getting 50 percent or more of your bullets into the aiming point at 100 yards, I suggest moving the target to 150 yards, and when you've achieved the same level of proficiency there, move it out to 200 yards. Depending upon your eyesight, you may find it desirable to increase the size of the aiming bull at the greater ranges. Using a larger bull will not necessarily reduce the accuracy you'll be able to obtain. In fact, if a larger bull produces less eyestrain, you'll probably shoot *smaller* groups on it than you will on the original bull. After all, the circular black bull is intended only to serve as an aiming point. It does not represent by its diameter a particular group size that you must obtain. If you need a two-foot bull in order to be able to aim accurately, by all means use it. Once you have the hang of things, your group sizes will likely be smaller than the bull itself.

Of course, all this doesn't mean you can't do some practicing at ranges *beyond* 200 yards, if the facilities are available and your curiosity prods you. You can employ exactly the same methods at even longer ranges, but the results will be of merely academic interest because the excessive bullet drop will require you to hold so high that guesswork and luck become significant. One doesn't use a pistol to do the job of a mortar. Remember, you won't be handgunning game at half the 200-yard distance you've now mastered, and beyond 200 yards the trajectory of the average handgun bullet becomes an ever-deepening curve. The difference in drop between 200 and 300 yards, for example, may be *several feet.* You will quickly reach a point where you need a target face several yards high in order to be sure

354-3

# VALUABLE BOOK REDEMPTION COUPON

You have been fully enrolled in your book club, and you'll begin to enjoy full benefits associated with membership immediately. Your billing, which accompanies this package, reflects the total introductory charge. This coupon will enable you to select another book replacing the title that we were unable to ship.

### HOW TO USE THIS VALUABLE BOOK REDEMPTION COUPON:

In order to complete your introductory package, simply choose any Alternate Selection you want having a publisher's edition price of $25 or less from your book club's Advance Announcement, which is enclosed with this mailing. This coupon may not be used to order the Featured Selection. Note your choice at the right, giving both Book Code Number and Title, and mail this postpaid card today. Your book will be shipped, at no additional charge to you, when we receive your completed coupon.

Please remember that if you are not completely satisfied with your Introductory Package, you may return all books within 10 days and your membership will be canceled; you'll owe nothing.

### MAKE YOUR CHOICE HERE

Book Code No. _____ Title (Do not use to order Featured Selection)

IMPORTANT: To avoid delay, please enter your current book club account number:

| 4 | 7 | 0 | 1 | 0 | 5 | 6 | 0 | 3 | 0 | 9 |
|---|---|---|---|---|---|---|---|---|---|---|

WILLIAM

Name _____ (please print)

Address _____ Apt. _____

City _____ State _____ Zip _____

## REDEEMABLE FOR ONE BOOK WORTH UP TO $25.00 IN PUBLISHER'S EDITION PRICE

A

# BUSINESS REPLY MAIL

FIRST CLASS    PERMIT NO. 1    GARDEN CITY, N.Y.

POSTAGE WILL BE PAID BY ADDRESSEE

## BOOK CLUB ASSOCIATES
## Customer Service Center
## Garden City New York  11535

of having the bullets strike where they can be seen. I recall that my good friend Colonel Charles Askins ran some tests of this sort a number of years ago with the .44 Magnum, and at 500 yards he was measuring bullet drop in yards instead of feet.

I may have made long-range paper punching sound simple. As a matter of fact, it *is* simple *in theory*. The essentials of solid position, breath control, muscular control, sight alignment, careful trigger let-off, concentration, etc., remain the same for *all* ranges. The difference is only in degree—as the range increases, a greater degree of concentration and practice is required to produce satisfactory groups.

Once you're putting a fair percentage of your bullets in the aiming points at 100 yards or more, don't get careless and forget about shorter-range shooting. I think the best results are obtained if you begin each practice session with at least one or two carefully fired 50-yard groups. By doing this, you will have established the level of your proficiency (as affected by light, what your wife said before you left home, money worries, etc.) for that particular day. These pace-setting groups will give you a pretty good idea of whether your long-range work will be hot or cold.

Field shooting is another matter. The basics remain the same, but the conditions are entirely different. Ideally, you need a long, fairly flat or ascending field or area whose surface is dry enough to emit a goodly puff of dust when the bullet strikes. For safety's sake, unless this open field of fire is so remarkably long that stray bullets can't possibly do any harm—for example, far out on a desert where there are no buildings, vehicles, people, or livestock in the direction of fire —you must have a backstop at the far end, such as a high hill, cliff, or other barrier. A dry plowed field with a high cliff behind is ideal, but will seldom be found.

Targets present no problem. Almost anything will do as long as it is large enough to offer reasonable certainty of hits. A rock will do; a clump of grass or bush; a patch of dark-colored earth; in fact, almost anything that stands out well enough from its background to be seen clearly. For the first few sessions, though, I would prefer an empty five-gallon can set out at about 200 yards. Its outline will be sharper than any natural object, and this will help in aligning the sights. You might even paint it yellow or white to contrast with the background.

This sort of shooting should begin at about 200 yards for several reasons. First is that you must learn to spot the bullet strike from the puff of dust it raises. This requires a bit of time between the firing of the shot and the strike of the bullet if you are to see it. The time of flight from shot to target of the .44 Magnum at 200 yards is just under one-half second. With a little practice, this is plenty of time for you to spot the bullet strike. Anything less would probably handicap you in the beginning. In addition, the greater drop of the bullet at 200 yards or so makes for bold changes from your 50-yard zero, and large changes are easier to make and control than the small ones that would be necessary at 100 yards.

Position is no less important in the field than on the range—and the most important aspect of it is its solidity. Obviously, your isolated pasture or field is not going to come fully equipped with a bench rest.

Here's a good position for shooting downhill when no rest is available. The heels are dug in solidly and the knees spread slightly, then the elbows are planted inside the knees and the gun grasped with both hands.

ABOVE LEFT There is no name for this position, but it's one often used by the author on open ground where no rest is available. It puts the gun and line of vision higher than the back position and is very nearly as stable.

ABOVE RIGHT This is a slight variation of the Keith back position; it's a good one for long-range shooting over open ground where no rest is available.

You can, if you like, carry a portable shooting bench to the field, and it might be wise to do so in the beginning. However, the modified back-rest sitting position is quite solid, if you learn to use it properly. It consists of sitting on the ground with your back firmly rested against a solid object (even a wheel of your car will do), with your knees drawn up sharply, and the wrists of both hands wedged between the knees to support the gun. It is a rather inflexible position, not suited for shooting moving game, but is ideal for learning the long-range bit. If you're accustomed to long-range rifle shooting, you may be tempted to try the prone position—but I advise against it. It's unnatural and strained with the handgun and is actually less steady than the modified sitting position. It's best to stick with this one position until you've developed a fair degree of skill at 200 yards; then you can vary positions to suit your taste.

Every effort should be made to avoid shooting into the sun, even slightly. Naturally, a northward line of fire is most desirable, and south is poorest. If you're stuck with shooting either east or west, simply shoot during the time of day when the sun will be mainly to your back. Just avoid very early or very late hours when the low angle of the sun throws a lot of long, hard shadows that interfere with target identification and spotting the bullet strike.

Once you have a target out there and have settled into the modified position, leave the ammunition aside and concentrate on dry fire as mentioned earlier in this chapter. Pay particular attention to breath control, muscular control, sight alignment, and trigger let-off. Work out the kinks with dry fire, calling your shots carefully, and you'll avoid disappointments when live ammunition is used.

Then it's time to load up and get serious. Begin shooting at yon distant target with a conventional sight picture and dead-center hold. Fire the first couple of shots without worrying about seeing the spurt of dust that the bullet will throw up when it strikes. If you begin thinking about making sure you see it while you're still trying to get the shot off, you're certain to screw things up. If you do see it without any effort, that's fine, but don't worry about it. Just get the feel of the gun and the load under those conditions. If you've never done this sort of thing before, you might do well to go 15 or 20 rounds without worrying where you hit.

After that, it's time to begin looking for the bullet strike. However, you must completely separate the act of getting the shot off from the act of watching for that puff. No one can shoot well if the two actions become mingled. Concentrate fully on the shot, then shift gears mentally as the gun starts back in recoil and switch your eyes to the impact area. Remember, as I've said, time of flight is nearly half a second, plenty of time to make the adjustment both in your mind and your eyes. It may be that the gun, your hands, or your knees blank out where the bullet strikes. If so, develop your own technique for countering this problem. With just a small amount of practice, you'll be able to twist your eyes to the right and the gun to the left (or vice versa) during recoil, and get a clear view of the impact area. Just make damn certain you don't try twitching the gun or your eyes *before* the gun starts moving back in recoil, signifying that the bullet has left the muzzle and nothing you do will have any further effect upon its flight.

Now it's time to work on getting the bullets into the target. Still with center hold and standard sight picture, fire five consecutive shots, noting each bullet strike. This is just to obtain a full picture of how much *below* the target the bullets are falling. Pay no attention whatever to the horizontal distance upon the apparent vertical distance the bullets strike below the target. Assuming your five shots were fairly close together, it's time to bring them up into the target. And, for the time being, pay no attention to any lateral deviation off target that might exist due to a crosswind. Let's first get the bullets up on a horizontal line passing through the target, then if any lateral correction is needed it can be made. You've got enough to do without trying to concentrate on two types of correction simultaneously.

Raise just a wee bit of front sight above the rear sight, and hold on the center of the target and fire again. Watch for the bullet strike, and if it is not on target, try a second or third shot, holding as nearly the same amount of up-front sight as possible. Here, as before, a reference line across the rear face of the front sight can be most helpful.

If your shots went over the target, repeat the operation holding up a little less front sight; if they were still under, hold up a bit more. Eventually, you'll get at least some of your bullets into the target, or at least on a horizontal line with it. When you've reached that point, it's time to make any lateral corrections that are necessary.

Assuming your shots are striking a bit to the left of the target due to a crosswind from the right, estimate the amount that the bullet struck to the target's left in *widths of the front sight.* This is fairly easy to visualize, and let's say your shots were striking about three sight-widths left. Hold three sight-widths to the right of the target, and if there happens to be any feature on the ground (clump of grass, rock, shadow, etc.), use it as an aiming point and fire again. Obviously, if you hit three widths left the first time and hold three widths right the second time, you should hit the target.

In a really strong wind, the width of the front sight becomes too small a unit of measure to use for correction; a stiff wind can push the bullet several feet sideward at 200 yards. Instead, estimate the distance to the left of the target that the bullet struck as accurately as you can, then pick out some aiming point the same distance to the right of the target. Again, this can be any feature on the ground that is identifiable enough to aim at. Keep in mind that the farther you must hold off laterally, the more important a secondary aiming point becomes. Seldom will an aiming point of this sort be situated exactly the correct distance from the target. Nevertheless, if it seems approximately correct, hold on it and fire one shot. Watch the bullet strike, and then make small corrections from the secondary aiming point, using the width of the front sight to gauge them. This may sound like a three-cushion shot, but it's not as tough as it sounds. The real difficulty arises in doing the practice (practice, practice, practice) necessary to become consistent in making the necessary corrections to plunk the bullet into the target.

The pronghorn shown in the foreground was taken by Lee Jurras at the phenomenal range of 217 yards. The arrow indicates the position from which he fired.

You may find that after only a couple of hundred rounds you have a feel for this type of shooting that enables you to sense the proper amount of correction on the first shot. Or you may be one of those less fortunate individuals who find it necessary to slowly *walk* consecutive shots into the target. "Walking the shot" (an old artillery term) is employed when the first shot lands well away from the target; relatively small corrections are then made in the direction of the target, each successive bullet landing a bit closer, with the third or fourth shot hitting it squarely.

Beyond 200 yards, it won't often be possible to estimate drop closely enough to make first-shot hits, so don't expect them. Instead, let the first shot be deliberately a bit low. Then you'll be able to see the amount of correction needed and can make it more easily. The same applies when shooting in a strong wind. Long-range handgun work can be most rewarding. It's really good for the ego when you can bust a target with your sixgun after a compadre has missed it with his rifle.

# 16

## Varmint Hunting

In most parts of this country, some form of varmint hunting is available when regular game seasons are closed. But what constitutes a "varmint" has become increasingly unclear. The word is derived from "vermin" and, according to the dictionary, is a synonym meaning "an objectionable or undesirable animal." Just about everyone used to agree that a varmint was an animal species that competed with man for food to an objectionable degree, usually by damaging or consuming crops or pasturage, or by preying on livestock or poultry. To hunters, a varmint was a bird or mammal that—because of its undesirability when present in abundance—was not protected by game laws. There are still no bag limits or closed seasons on some of the species we call varmints, but when you're dealing with anything nobler than rats on a garbage dump the definitions become fuzzy with the changing times.

The crow now receives federal protection as a migratory bird, and cannot legally be hunted during the peak nesting period. Like many other hunters from agricultural regions, I have a hard time trying to think of the crow as a game bird, at least in the usual sense. Crows take millions of bushels of grain annually; you won't persuade a farmer who's had crow problems that these birds are anything but a pest species requiring severe population control. They do, however, provide wonderful hunting; no argument there. Sportsmen (who have traditionally spearheaded reforms in conservation and game regulations) have succeeded in elevating such varmints as bobcats, cougars, and prairie dogs to game status in some regions where these species are no longer numerous enough to be pestiferous. All of us are for such reforms *where they're appropriate.*

In the East there has been a movement among some sportsmen to classify the woodchuck as a game animal so that the season can be closed until late June, by which time the young have usually been weaned; earlier in the spring, if a nursing female is killed her litter will starve. And now that the coyote has begun spreading its numbers into the East I'm told there's some sentiment in that part of the country for keeping it protected unless (or until) there's a population explosion of the little predators. I can't imagine that kind of sentiment in sheep country, and where I come from I don't think you could convince many people that the coyote needs any other protection than its own ability to survive and proliferate. Of course, some of the same folks who want to protect the coyote would like to see the fox or raccoon almost exterminated. I guess your viewpoint depends on what's doing the raiding in your part of the country. It's beyond the purpose of this book to get involved in such controversies; when I talk about varmints in this context I'm not implying that they're inherently undesirable animals; I'm merely talking about species that provide a great hunting bonus when the regular game seasons are closed.

Probably the best-known varmints are the marmots—that is, the woodchuck in the East and the rockchuck in the West—the crow

Not often thought of as a varmint, the armadillo is very plentiful in some areas of the Southwest. Fairly easy to bag, armadillos are excellent for sharpening your skill.

TOP Though Westerners sometimes encounter thick gatherings of rock chucks like this, nothing else offers the abundance of targets you'll find in a good dog town.

ABOVE Considered a furbearer in some regions rather than a varmint, the raccoon makes nice handgun game.

from coast to coast, the prairie dog in the Midwest and West, and the coyote wherever he is found. Many other species, both large and small, have been and are considered vermin in certain areas. Probably the largest animal ever to be classed as a varmint in North America is the big bear. During the last century, grizzlies were a menace

In the Southwest, jack rabbits are pests and make some of the finest handgun varminting to be had anywhere.

to both livestock and people on the Pacific Coast. And much more recently, the brown bears of Alaska were shot on sight because of their predilection for killing cattle. Though protected in most places now, the cougar was once considered a varmint, and in many areas his smaller cousin, the bobcat, is still so classified. Though often overlooked, the common house cats gone wild—feral cats—are vicious predators of small game and birds, and in some areas they are hunted. Another domestic animal gone wild and classified in some areas as a varmint (and in others as a game animal) is the feral hog. This species reverts very quickly to wild form once freed from man's influence, and multiplies rapidly in the swampy woods and brush it prefers.

Feral hogs not only provide superb hunting but most excellent eating. It seems appropriate at this point to say something of the food value of varmints. The more common varmints are essentially vegetarian and (if the meat is not destroyed by the shot) can make quite toothsome meals. Woodchuck has long been favored by many Eastern varmint hunters, some of whom tell me they prefer it to chicken or rabbit. Prairie dogs have long been common fare among the Southwestern Indians, and when properly prepared do as nicely on the table as squirrel and rabbit. The nutria, a varmint in some Gulf Coast states, is much like the muskrat, and any old-time trapper will tell you that it makes tasty fare. My own favorite is the tender young armadillo of the Texas plains, marinated overnight and slow-cooked in the oven. Superb eating! So, if you've looked upon varmints only as targets, you have missed many a good meal.

Many kinds of varmint shooting can be had at relatively short ranges, so a wide variety of guns and cartridges will be suitable if that's as far as you want to go with it; yet it is essentially a long-range sport. Obviously, long-range varminting requires highly specialized guns capable of delivering rifle-type accuracy, paired with cartridges that produce the flattest trajectory possible. In addition, varmints require lightly constructed bullets, which will produce explosive expansion in animals as small as the prairie dog. These characteristics are of sufficient importance so that we can afford to dispense with many usual handgun features in order to obtain them.

Since high velocity and flatness of trajectory require high chamber pressures, they are best obtained by abandoning the traditional revolver and autoloader for a more solidly breeched, single-shot pistol. By doing this, we can operate at rifle-type pressure levels and obtain vastly improved performance. This does not mean that *only* single-shot pistols can provide the performance desired. The Auto Mag can operate at chamber pressures in the 50,000 psi range. But the single-shots are more economical and, generally speaking, they're the most desirable for serious long-range handgun varminting.

Fortunately, today two very fine single-shot pistols are chambered for varmint cartridges. The older of the two is the Remington XP-100, introduced in 1962 along with its companion .221 Remington Fireball cartridge. It is essentially a rifle-type bolt-action fitted with a modernistic molded plastic handgun stock and a tapered 10½-inch barrel. It has repeatedly demonstrated its ability—with the .221 Fireball cartridge—to produce groups measuring only slightly over one inch at 100 yards. The .221 Fireball cartridge drives a 50-grain bullet at 2650 fps with a 200-yard mid-range trajectory height of only about four inches. This makes it by far the flattest-shooting of all handgun cartridges. It's unbeatable for the smaller species, although it cannot be considered ideal for the larger animals except under ideal conditions at shorter ranges. Chambered only for the .221 Fireball cartridge, the Remington XP-100 pistol can easily be fitted with a scope sight, and though its appearance and design defy tradition, you can't go wrong with it.

The other single-shot pistol available as a production item is the Thompson/Center Contender. This gun presents a more traditional appearance. It employs a hinged-barrel, exposed-hammer mechanism opened and closed by a finger lever formed by the trigger guard. Its most unique feature is that it allows interchange of barrels in a matter of moments. You simply pull off the small wood fore-end, punch out a barrel pin, lift out the barrel, insert a new barrel, and put the pin and fore-end back in position. To exploit this feature, Thompson/Center offers a wide variety of interchangeable barrels in over 30 calibers, and will also custom-chamber basic barrels for almost any cartridge the customer wants.

Due to its configuration, the Contender carries its sights on the barrel; different barrels may carry different sighting equipment, already zeroed to suit the gun to varying conditions. No re-zeroing is required when barrels are exchanged. The interchangeable-barrel feature and the wide variety of chamberings offered make the Contender the most versatile of all varmint-hunting handguns. One might obtain a basic Contender in .22 Hornet or .222 Remington caliber for small varmints at long range, then add a .44 Magnum or .30–30 Winchester barrel for larger animals.

One other single-shot pistol was manufactured in fair quantity, and though discontinued, it makes an excellent varminting piece if one can be found. This is the Ruger Hawkeye adaptation of the Ruger Blackhawk single-action revolver. It was chambered only for the .256 Winchester Magnum cartridge with its 60-grain bullet at 2350 fps. The 8½-inch-barreled Hawkeye is capable of very good accuracy, and you'll get excellent service from it.

Over the years, a number of other single-shot pistols have been made up mainly for varmint shooting. The only one to achieve series production has been the modern replica of the old Remington Rolling Block pistol, produced by Navy Arms in .357 Magnum and .22 LR caliber. The others, made in very small quantity, are now discontinued and may be regarded only as collector's items.

The Auto Mag pistol may be considered a superb varmint-shooting gun in the smallest of its calibers, .357 AMP. This gun is described in detail elsewhere in this volume. The .357 AMP drives a 125- to 137-grain bullet at nearly 2000 fps and, with judicious handloading, lighter bullets may be driven as fast as 2750–3000 fps. You can adapt any larger-caliber Auto Mag to varmint shooting by merely installing an interchangeable .357 AMP barrel unit, thus having a gun suitable for several kinds of hunting.

Of all revolver/cartridge combinations, only the S&W M53 in .22 Remington Jet delivers typical varmint-shooting performance. This combination has disadvantages outlined elsewhere in this book, but the careful user will find it produces flatter trajectory and higher velocity than any other production sixgun combination available.

Of course, virtually all of the Magnum revolvers and better autoloading pistols may provide a fair degree of varmint-hunting success at shorter ranges. Doubtless the majority of today's handgun varminters use just such guns, simply because they are immediately available. However, none of these guns and cartridges can equal the long-range performance of those just described.

Long-range handgunning for varmints differs not in the least from the same game played with a rifle. It requires the ultimate in accuracy, and therefore sighting equipment is of great importance. Personally, I do not often use scopes on my own handguns. And it *is* a matter of personal preference. For me, a scope spoils the traditional look and feel of a handgun, besides adding a lot of bulk and weight. Still, I readily admit that at long range I can shoot more accurately with a scope than with traditional open sights.

The scope sight offers the same advantages on a handgun as on a rifle. Magnification is probably the least of these advantages, while the most important is that a scope places the target image and the aiming device (the reticle) in the same focal plane. This eliminates the need for one's eye to rapidly shuttle back and forth between a rear sight, front sight, and target at vastly different distances. This is especially true for those of us whose eyes, with age, have lost some of their ability to "accommodate." When using a scope, you need only to look through it, align the reticle on the target, and squeeze off the shot. This is quite different from first aligning two sight elements, bringing them into alignment on the target, and then squinting to obtain satisfactorily sharp images of all three objects simultaneously.

The magnification offered by a scope sight is certainly an advantage, particularly in that it allows easier identification of the target and also allows better selection of aiming point upon the target. But very little magnification may be used on handguns as a practical matter. Extremely few are those individuals who can handle more than 1½ to 2½ diameters of magnification on a handgun unless the gun is firmly imbedded in sandbags on a bench rest. There is simply too much distracting tremor in the average shooting position, and since it is magnified along with the target, aiming problems arise.

Any scope intended for use on a handgun must have long eye relief. The typical rifle scope with only two to four inches of eye relief is in no way suitable. Several major manufacturers and a few small shops offer special scopes with 18 to 24 inches of eye relief so that the scope may be properly utilized with the gun held at arm's length. This long eye relief is obtained at the expense of field of view. The limitations of basic telescope design simply prevent having *both* long eye relief and a wide field of view. Either can be had, but only at the expense of the other.

The very narrow field of view makes the use of a scoped handgun somewhat difficult. It is not possible to simply point the scope in the general direction of the target and then expect to see the target in the instrument's field. Instead, the scope must be very accurately pointed at the target in order to encompass the target within its narrow field of view. Most people accomplish this by a form of "aiming" over the top of the scope, and some have even gone as far as to fabricate a rudimentary set of open sights on top of the scope tube for this purpose. In any event, those who take the time to learn to utilize the scope properly on a handgun will find that their long-range accuracy on varmints (and anything else, of course) will be substantially improved.

Installing a scope on a handgun introduces a few problems not normally encountered on rifles. Even though handguns generally fire cartridges of less recoil than those found in rifles, the much lighter weight of the gun causes recoil velocity and recoil acceleration of the gun to be greater. This places added strain not only upon the components of the scope but upon the mount. As a result, a scope and mount which will serve quite satisfactorily on the typical hunting rifle may be pounded to junk on a .44 Magnum revolver. The much sharper acceleration (which amounts to several hundred Gs) may overload the internal components of the scope and cause damage. It likewise overloads the screws holding the mount to the gun and can shear them.

For these reasons, you're far better off using only those scopes specifically designed for handguns, and you can reinforce the mount installation by additional screws or other load-transferring members. In addition, the usual smooth ring clamped around the tube may not always hold the scope permanently in position, even when tightened to the point of damaging the tube. This can be overcome by cleaning the ring and matching portion of the tube chemically, and then applying a thin coat of epoxy compound between the two and allowing it to cure *thoroughly* before shooting.

Varminting is one form of handgun hunting wherein the gun should be zeroed at a fairly long range. If you're shooting a high-velocity combination with a telescopic sight, I strongly recommend zeroing at 100 yards, followed by a goodly amount of shooting at 200 yards to become thoroughly familiar with the amount of drop produced at the longer range.

In the field, you'll need a good way to carry your gun. I'll have more to say about this in a later chapter, but right now let me state that for the unusually large and heavy guns often used in varmint hunting, I can think of nothing more suitable than a shoulder holster worn under a light jacket. Several different makes and styles are available. I've found the model offered by Safariland to perform extremely well. It holds the gun securely, yet allows it to be drawn with ease, and at the same time places the gun high enough so that even a very long barrel can be accommodated without difficulty.

The handgun varminter needs more than just a good gun and ammunition. He needs the highest degree of accuracy that can be attained—and as an economic matter, that demands handloading. Some of the cartridges involved cost as much as 37¢ each; much shooting at that price could play hell with the family budget. Cost can be held to 7¢ or 8¢ cents by handloading, making adequate practice economically practical. Handgun varminting requires careful stalking and a high degree of fieldcraft. Anything you can do to reduce your visibility will help. This includes the use of camouflage clothing and face paint, blinds, netting, and non-reflective finishes on gun and equipment.

I've found that two methods of handgun varminting are more productive than all the others. The first works well only out West where large concentrations of prairie dogs and rockchucks exist. It consists of simply driving a closed jeep up within range of a colony, then waiting silent and motionless until the animals come back out. Shooting is done right from the halted car (where not prohibited by law) with padded rests over the window frames. With care, several hours of intermittent shooting can be had this way in a well-populated chuck or dog colony.

The second method is calling, and it works beautifully on all the predatory species—fox, coyote, raccoon, the cats, etc. Mouth calls do nicely but, where legal, electronic calls are often more effective and are a lot less work. Calling should be done from a carefully camouflaged blind situated so animals must approach within your field of fire and within range. Generally, if calling doesn't produce results in 20 to 30 minutes, the area is dry, and you'd best move on to another location.

All the other traditional methods of hunting varmints will work well with handguns. The main differences are simply that you must get closer and shoot more carefully than with a rifle. Handgun varminting may lack some of the excitement and danger of big-game hunting but technically it is the most difficult and challenging of all shooting sports.

# 17

*Guns & Ammunition*
*Under Unusual Conditions*

If you're living in the Midwest and will be doing most of your hand-gun hunting there, you'll never encounter temperatures much below zero or above 100 degrees, and you'll not be concerned with desert conditions, blowing sand, arctic temperatures, or the oppressive heat and humidity of tropical jungle or rain forest. You need not concern yourself about unusual conditions producing any significant effect upon the durability, reliability, or efficiency of your gun and ammunition.

On the other hand, if you journey to the Great American Desert in midsummer to pistol jacks, coyotes, or prairie dogs; or if you expect to find yourself in the jungles of Central or South America, or the Pacific Northwest rain forest; or if you seek your sport in arctic Alaska or Canada, then the every-day care normally lavished upon your equipment may not be sufficient to keep it functioning properly.

Generally speaking, both gun and ammunition are designed and produced for optimum performance at a standard temperature of 70 degrees Fahrenheit, under relative humidity values of 50 to 80 percent or so, and are intended to be operated free of rain or excess moisture. In addition, they are intended to function best when at least moderately clean and free from foreign material, and when lightly lubricated with conventional oils and greases. There is nothing wrong in this—every product is designed to function its best under ordinary conditions. Probably the best example is your automobile. We all know the difficulties that begin to arise with a car when conditions stray too far from those of the temperate zone.

We can expect similar difficulties with handguns and ammunition under extreme conditions of temperature, moisture, dryness, dirt, etc. If we know the effects of these conditions and take steps to compensate for them, then we can ensure that both gun and ammunition will function reliably under the worst circumstances in which we might expect to use them.

Let's take a look at ammunition first. Modern nitrocellulose propellent powders vary in their energy output according to temperature. Ballistic tests and development are normally conducted at 70 degrees Fahrenheit, or the results are corrected to that temperature. As temperature increases from that point, the energy released by combustion also increases, and as the temperature drops, the reverse is true. The standard values we have for this change are based upon tests conducted with rifle cartridges approximating the characteristics of the .30–06; the effects on pistol cartridges are similar though less pronounced.

Each degree Fahrenheit of change from 70 degrees will produce a velocity change for the .30–06 of 1.7 fps in the direction of the temperature change. Thus, at 100 degrees Fahrenheit, we would have a velocity increase in the amount of 1.7 × 30, or 51 fps greater than the velocity produced under "standard" conditions. At zero

Arid, dusty areas such as this South African high veldt can cause plenty of functioning problems if guns are not properly prepared.

Careful preparation and maintenance is essential if handguns are to function reliably in hostile environments. This wolverine was killed a half-mile out at sea on snow-covered pack ice where the temperature was 35 below zero.

Fahrenheit we would have a velocity loss of 70 × 1.7 or 119 fps. Keep in mind, now, that these values have been calculated for rifle ammunition, and are probably substantially less for typical handgun loads.

Obviously, this influence on velocity is produced through a temperature effect on pressure, for which we have no precise value. As temperature goes up, chamber pressures increase, and vice versa. It must be made clear that this effect is brought about by the internal temperature of the *propellant*, which is not necessarily the ambient air temperature. In the case of extremely low temperatures, it is likely that propellant temperature will be nominally the same as air temperature. But in the case of very high temperatures, propellant temperature may be 20, 30, or even 40 degrees *higher* than air temperature. For example, ammunition left in the closed trunk of a dark-colored automobile might well achieve propellant temperatures of 120 degrees on a bright, sunny day with an air temperature of only 100 degrees. If that same ammunition is left exposed to the direct rays of the sun under the same conditions, its propellant temperature could conceivably rise as high as 130 or 140 degrees.

However, on a very cold day, say zero Fahrenheit, if ammunition is left exposed to the direct rays of bright sun, the propellant temperature could very well rise to 50 or 60 degrees, almost negating the effect of extreme cold.

While there are other effects, for all practical purposes temperature need concern us in only two areas. The first is that of excessive chamber pressure produced under high temperature; the second is gun malfunction produced by low temperature. If you are using ammunition loaded to the highest pressures compatible with gun design, then a propellant temperature of 130 or 140 degrees (and it could be higher under some conditions) might well produce pressures sufficiently excessive to produce blown primers, excessive impact on the gun, or even gun or case failure. At the other end of the scale, with autoloading pistols a load that is marginal or minimal in recoil energy for proper functioning of a particular gun will produce substantially less energy at zero Fahrenheit and may be incapable of activating the gun's operating parts.

Most factory loads suitable for hunting will not produce dangerous chamber pressures at propellant temperatures up to 140 degrees or a bit more; likewise, they will produce correct and reliable gun functioning down to zero Fahrenheit or slightly below. Handloads are another matter. I've encountered many in the hands of other shooters which produce obviously excessive pressures at high temperatures, as well as some that simply would not function the gun correctly at low temperatures. This occurs in spite of the fact that those loads exhibited normal pressures and behavior under *standard* temperatures.

Yet another temperature factor must be considered. As propellant temperature decreases, proper ignition becomes more difficult. This is particularly true of ball-type propellants with heavy deterrent coatings, and the larger the powder charge, the more likely that low-temperature ignition difficulties will be encountered. Even factory ammunition is by no means free of this problem, as became evident a few years ago when some high-performance revolver loadings produced low-temperature ignition problems in service.

When anticipated, low-temperature ignition problems can be countered by using "hot" or Magnum primers in handloads *intended* for use in extremely cold weather. Problems can also be avoided by selecting easily ignited propellants rather than those known for low-temperature ignition problems.

Abnormally low humidity dryness will have no measurable effect upon ammunition performance—except, perhaps, where prolonged periods of exposure might cause some drying-out of the propellant. This will produce some slight increase in chamber pressure and velocity, but for all practical purposes it may be ignored.

Excessive humidity, moisture, or heavy rain can produce profound effects upon ammunition exposed to it for any great period of time.

Brass-cased cartridges that are not protected by nickel or some other resistant coating will corrode very quickly when exposed to high humidity (and especially the high humidity/high salt conditions of sea and shore). Cases first begin to turn dark; if corrosion is not promptly removed, it will develop into a lumpy coating of thick, green verdigris which not only weakens the case but increases dimensions so that the cartridge may not enter the chamber. Copper bullet jackets are somewhat less subject to the same problem. Exposed lead will slowly oxidize into a powdery whitish coating which may look odd but seems to have no deleterious effect. The only certain corrosion prevention under those conditions is to have the ammunition packaged in air-tight containers, along with a desiccant, or moisture-absorbing material. British makers at one time supplied hunting ammunition sealed in airtight tin containers for this reason, and designated this as "tropical pack." Once ammunition is removed from its airtight container, only daily wiping and cleaning will keep it free of corrosion. Where possible, though, the use of nickel-plated cases keeps the hazard to a minimum. A light coating of paste wax applied over the entire cartridge will provide a substantial degree of protection as long as the film is not broken.

A very definite mistake is the practice of oiling or greasing cartridges to cut down corrosion. Sure, this will eliminate or limit corrosion, but it introduces the considerable possibility of primer or propellant contamination with the attendant hazard of misfires, hangfires, or squib shots. Though factory loads are generally considered oil-proof, they are by no means proof against modern spray-on lubricants and preservatives whose volatile vehicle is often a solvent for the lacquer sealer applied around primers. Handloads, of course, are not oil-proof (or moisture-proof, for that matter) unless intentionally sealed as described in the chapter on handloading. Oiling or greasing cartridges also increases thrust against the breech by reducing case adhesion to the chamber wall.

The best method I have found for protecting ammunition not only from moisture and the effects of high humidity but from dirt, grit, and all other hazards, is to use small heat-sealed polyethylene envelopes, each containing the number of rounds necessary for reloading my gun. If these packets are made up under conditions of relatively low humidity, they need not contain any desiccant, and a number of them may be placed in a small plastic or metal container which is tightly sealed with non-permeable plastic tape. Ammunition packaged in this fashion will remain bright and fresh until the envelopes are opened.

In any event, by careful selection and treatment of your ammunition, and by recognition of the effect of various abnormal conditions, it is possible to shoot, and shoot well, in almost any part of the world at almost any time of the year, even under conditions so bad that you find them personally intolerable. So much for the effect of unusual conditions on ammunition—now let's take a look at what cold, heat, damp, dry, and all of those other nasty conditions do to the gun.

Abnormally high temperatures—at least those you can stand—will cause your gun no problems whatever unless allied with other undesirable conditions. A gun normally clean and lubricated with conventional oils and greases will perform at temperatures far, far above 100 degrees Fahrenheit in a perfectly normal manner. In fact, the mere firing of a few rounds rapid-fire will heat the gun far beyond any temperature you are likely to encounter. Extremely cold temperatures, on the other hand, can present problems. Down around zero and below, springs begin to lose their power, and become less rapid in recovery; small, highly stressed parts become more brittle, and breakage can be a real hazard at 20 below and colder. Metals shrink somewhat, and, depending upon the design, working tolerances can change, causing greater friction, which can reduce functional reliability.

There is absolutely nothing you can do about the effect of cold upon metals and their physical properties other than attempt to keep the gun relatively warm, and that's not always a good idea. You can, of course, carry the gun in a shoulder holster underneath your outer clothing, where body heat alone will keep it from being "cold-soaked" to ambient air temperature. This has its hazards, though, for when the warm gun is exposed, it will become chilled very quickly, and if it is then returned to the warm, moist confines of your clothing, moisture will condense on it, and may freeze the gun into a solid non-functional lump when it is again exposed to cold. So, in the end, it is not a good idea to attempt to keep the gun warm—in fact, the reverse is true. It has long been the practice of men hunting regularly in arctic temperatures to let their guns thoroughly cold-soak to reach ambient air temperature before beginning the hunt, then leave them that way as long as there is any shooting to be done. Guns are not taken inside tents or other warm shelters, but are left outside both day and night to avoid any condensation which might freeze and jam the mechanism. (With scoped firearms, such condensation can also bring on sighting problems, another reason to leave the guns outside the tents.) So you must simply recognize the effect of cold upon a handgun, be it auto or revolver, and work within the limitations imposed thereby.

Actually, it isn't the metal of the gun that will most likely cause malfunctions in extremely cold temperatures; it's the lubricant greases on the metal. Conventional oils and greases commonly used to lubricate firearms and ensure their functional reliability simply thicken or freeze solid at temperatures of zero and below. Thus, if you clean and lubricate your gun conventionally in the temperate zone and then move directly to the Arctic, the gun's parts may become immovable when the oil freezes. In the old days, this was countered by thoroughly degreasing every bit and piece—every square millimeter—of the gun with acetone or a similar solvent. Dry powdered graphite was then applied sparingly to lubricate the more critical areas. With manually operated arms this generally worked quite well, but autoloaders often refused to function under these conditions until carefully prepared by meticulous polishing and smoothing of all high-friction areas.

An autoloader that requires fairly copious lubrication for functioning in normal temperatures will usually not respond well to the dry form of Arctic preparation. Unless it is thoroughly polished and tuned until it will function with perfect reliability at around 70 degrees without any lubrication whatever, it probably won't work dry-lubed in the cold. If you elect to go the dry route for extremely cold weather, it's best to check autoloaders out by thoroughly degreasing every part, then firing them in the coldest weather available at home without any lubricant at all. If they function okay under those conditions, they will probably function well below zero with the addition of powdered graphite lubricant. But, if they will not do so, then careful polishing is needed before you can expect that same gun to function well when dry at extremely low temperatures.

Since World War II, though, we have been supplied with low-temperature synthetic lubricants that maintain their fluidity and lubricating properties at temperatures far below anything in which you are likely to go hunting. These are special lubricants developed for aerospace use, and many function normally through a range of several hundred degrees Fahrenheit. Such lubricants make it possible for a handgun to be well lubricated with a non-freezing fluid material at the lowest temperatures. All too often, though, pistoleros assume that simply *adding* such a low-temperature lubricant to a gun will make it function well in the Arctic. Such is not the case; every trace of conventional oil or grease must be removed from the gun first, after which it is then completely re-lubricated with the low-temperature lubricant, closely following the manufacturer's instructions. Once this is done the gun should function reliably at even 60 or 70 degrees below zero if nothing else is wrong. The best method of preparing a handgun, particularly an autoloader, for extremely low temperatures is thorough degreasing, followed by application of one of the special low-temperature lubricants currently available, and it will certainly do no harm also to polish critical surfaces to reduce friction, in view of the lessened recoil impulse supplied by the cartridge under those conditions.

Extremely high humidity, rain, and the salt-laden atmosphere found at shore and sea have two deleterious effects upon handguns. The first is simply corrosive: rapid rusting. The second is that *direct* continued exposure to water or rain (with or without the presence of the other factors) will wash away conventional lubricant and greases and thereby may induce malfunctions, particularly in autoloaders, if functioning was marginal in the beginning.

Elimination of corrosion under these conditions no longer presents any great problem. Many guns are now available in special models fabricated entirely (or almost entirely) from stainless steel which will not corrode in any environment you might enter. In addition, there are several special plated metallic finishes that are highly resistant to all manner of corrosion, including Armoloy (a special application of chrome), chrome, nickel, and black chrome (another special application of chrome). Non-metallic protective coatings are also available.

Maximum corrosion resistance is obtained with finishes used in combinations. Nickel is impractical to coat the interior of bores and chambers, and Armoloy is not applied in this fashion, but bores can be coated with hard chrome (principally by Marker Machine Works) to provide almost total corrosion resistance and improve ballistic efficiency somewhat as well. Internal working parts may be coated with any of the aforementioned materials, but hard chrome is the most practical.

Unfortunately, both stainless-steel guns and the special finishes are rather costly. An alternative can be found in daily—sometimes even hourly—care and maintenance of a blued, conventional-steel gun with modern preservatives. After all, long before special finishes and stainless steels were common in firearms, soldiers and civilians all over the world managed to keep their guns in perfect condition under the worst of conditions. You have one advantage over the old-timers in that there are modern combination lubricant/preservative compounds which are vastly superior in corrosion resistance and lubricity to the mineral and animal fats and oils once used. Among the compounds now available are TSI 300 and Dri-Slide, both of which form a very thin but tough coating on metal when applied in accordance with the maker's instructions. They have lubricating value, and resist corrosion extremely well. Others as good doubtless exist, but these two brands are generally available at gun shops. The most important thing about application of such materials is that every vestige of other lubricants and preservatives be removed first with acetone or a similar solvent. Only then can these compounds form a thin and tough coating on the metal. It is worthy of mention that these materials were developed to meet the unusually severe conditions of humidity, rain, temperature, and abuse found in the jungle combat zones of Indochina.

There is yet another set of unusual conditions to which your hunting handgun might be subjected—dust and sand, both generally associated with hot desert country, but also encountered in cooler climes under some conditions. When dust and sand enter a handgun to any great extent, they act as an abrasive, producing scoring and accelerated wear on moving parts, and if a sufficient amount accumulates, friction will be increased to the point where the gun simply will not function. This is true not only of autoloaders with all their reciprocating parts, but to a lesser degree with revolvers where only the limited power of one's fingers is available to manipulate the mechanism. With prolonged exposure to wind-driven sand and dust, internal accumulations may be so great that it is impossible to cock and fire the gun.

Two approaches may be taken to reduce the effect of dust or sand. The first is to remove all fluid lubricant and preservative. Any fluid or any moisture of any sort will catch and hold the abrasive particles. This not only produces greater accumulation but forms an abrasive paste which literally grinds away critical surfaces and ruins trigger pulls. Obviously, then, the most effective way to prevent this is to remove all fluid lubricants and replace them with the dry type. The best I have found for this purpose is molybdenum disulphide under the trade name "Moly D," which is finely divided molybdenum disulphide in a volatile vehicle contained in an aerosol spray can. After Moly D is sprayed on, the vehicle evaporates, and only the dry powder remains. It has a high affinity for metals, so it clings tightly—it simply cannot be removed except by grinding or scraping away the metal to which it adheres. When this is used, the interior of the gun is completely dry, and there is nothing to trap and hold particles of sand and dust. This greatly reduces the accumulation and avoids that nasty abrasive paste.

Aside from that, the gun must be protected as well as possible from airborne particles. The traditional flap holster provides a good deal more protection than the open-top designs, but still allows a good deal of sand and dust to enter. And with any type of holster, abrasive particles quickly become imbedded in the leather (or any other material). Where they come in direct contact with the gun—as they must in any well-fitted holster—they literally grind away the finish. If a gun is carried long enough in such a holster, substantial amounts of metal will be cut away by abrasive action; many old guns that saw heavy service in desert country actually have their muzzles worn to oval shape, as well as other areas ground out of shape, all by the abrasive action of sand and grit imbedded in the holster.

To the best of my knowledge, there are no holsters which provide complete protection from sand and dust. There does exist the clamshell type, which could be modified to enclose the entire gun, then fitted with a soft rubber or plastic foam seal to provide maximum protection. Unfortunately, the few clamshell models that are available are open at the butt and possess no seal. Perhaps some day a clamshell maker will move in this direction.

In the meantime, the only certain method of providing maximum protection against sand and dust is to enclose the gun in a sealed plastic bag or wrapping. This certainly interferes with getting the weapon into action in a hurry, and therefore doesn't appeal to many people. My own solution to the problem is to keep the gun in a sealed plastic bag at all times except when I anticipate that a shot may be imminent. If a thin but tough bag, of minimum size that will accept the gun, is sealed off over the butt with a tight-fitting rubber band, the gun may still be carried in a holster. And, when action is impending, the gun may be drawn and the bag stripped off—usually being torn in the process—with only a second's delay. If under those conditions you anticipate much shooting, you'll need a fair supply of spare bags and rubber bands. But they cost little and are easily carried along.

Since there isn't any really first-class method of fending off sand and dust in the field, most pistoleros I know simply use a close-fitting flap holster or a shoulder holster covered well by a light jacket, and accept whatever amount of grit may enter the gun in a given day's hunting. Of course, beforehand they have prepared the gun with proper dry lubricant, and then the pistol is cleaned meticulously at the end of each day's hunting and sealed in a plastic bag until it's time to go out again. Normally, this will be sufficient care to prevent any malfunctions due to grit. After all, you aren't going to be hunting in a sandstorm or dust storm, and for jeep-riding cross-country, in a billowing cloud of wheel-thrown dirt, you simply slip the gun inside a bag and leave it there until you are going to hunt.

Users of autoloaders often take pains to keep dirt and grit out of the gun but forget completely about spare loaded magazines carried on their person. Sand and grit seeping inside a loaded magazine will probably cause a feeding malfunction sooner than grit in the gun. Again, sealed plastic bags are the best protection, but close-fitting leather pouches with tight flap closures do an excellent job if a wad of facial tissue is clamped between the flap and the exposed end of the magazine. It may not keep out *every* particle of grit, but it will stop 99 percent of it. And, of course, loaded magazines should get the same daily cleaning and attention as the gun proper.

I think I should mention—at the risk of being hung in effigy by sixgun aficionados—that autoloaders are generally less susceptible to sand and grit problems than revolvers. A loaded autoloader possesses far fewer openings through which wind-blown dirt can reach the interior. For all practical purposes, the muzzle is the only orifice of any size through which foreign material can enter—while revolvers are literally festooned with holes.

I think I've probably covered all the environmental hazards your gun and ammunition might encounter in the field. If you follow the procedures outlined here for the varying conditions, it's unlikely that you'll ever miss a record-book trophy because of such problems.

# 18

---

# *Handguns in South Africa*

When you've hunted with all manner of handguns for a wide variety of American, European, and Near Eastern game, your thoughts will naturally turn toward Africa. The Dark Continent possesses a mystique and allure all its own, and it's doubtful that any hunter has ever considered its profusion of game without at least some yearning.

I'd done those other things, but had never seriously considered an African handgun hunt until after Lee Jurras returned from his Botswana pistol safari in 1970. I'd thought about handgunning some African species (but not the *big* ones), and had even once looked for a likely lion while carrying a .357 Magnum in my belt. But that was while Val Forgett and I were hunting in Tanzania with muzzle-loading rifles, and the idea of using my .357 on a lion was at that time just a passing thought. Later, after seeing more of African hunting conditions, I became convinced that much game there was just as well within expert handgun capabilities as most North American species. In short, I agreed with Jurras that with a little modification of African hunting methods, it would be possible to take any species the continent had to offer except elephant, rhino, and possibly Cape buffalo and hippo. Assuming one worked as a *hunter* rather than just a *shooter,* and used proper guns and loads, the other species seemed no more difficult or dangerous than the bear, elk, and big cats of our own country.

So when Jurras proposed I join him on his second handgun safari to South Africa, I accepted with alacrity, disregarding the fact that my wallet couldn't really stand the price of a round-trip ticket to Port Elizabeth, R.S.A. After all, Lee had taken 13 head of African game with a sixgun on his 1970 trip, and I couldn't allow him to get too far ahead of me.

We planned to take a pair of the then-new Auto Mag pistols in .357 AMP and .44 AMP. Both combinations exceed by far the velocity and energy that can be safely obtained from contemporary revolvers, and the hunt was to be another field test for the guns and ammunition. After much experimentation we'd established standard loads for both guns. As insurance—more against mechanical failure than anything else—I also took along a pair of S&W Magnum revolvers with 8⅜-inch barrels—one M29 .44 Magnum and one M57 .41 Magnum. As it turned out, these guns proved invaluable to the early part of the hunt. The sixguns—and ammunition packed with them—arrived in R.S.A. promptly in good shape, right along with my other baggage. Not so the Auto Mags, which were misplaced by the airlines (along with Jurras' other baggage) and showed up several days late. Unfortunately, no ammunition was packed with them. It had been shipped separately and earlier, and didn't arrive until nearly 10 days after the hunt was to have started. Consequently, the Smith & Wesson Magnums received a good workout.

We were to be the guests of Wyn Goosen and Rory Reider, and they'd promised us all the plains game we wanted. And so it was that

A herd of blesbok runs full tilt past the hunter's "hide," but at too great a range for a certain kill.

we found ourselves afield in a new country, with arms and ammunition the local hunters considered more than passing strange. It wasn't that they doubted the ability of the big, heavy pistols to kill game but that they didn't really believe handguns could be shot with the necessary accuracy at ranges of more than a few yards. We were both able to show that the accuracy is there if you learn to use it. Checking guns (and our ability with them) before going after blesbok on C. T. Van Schalkwyk's holdings, Jurras placed his first .44 Magnum shot on a beer can at just under 100 yards. My showing wasn't that impressive but was adequate.

Blesbok gave us a runaround that day, and though shots were offered, they were all running flat-out, and we missed. Blesbok are faster than they seem until you've observed them a while. Hidden in brush and rock outcroppings on the rather barren high veldt, we could only take potluck on moving small herds that occasionally came within range (which we considered to be 100 yards at the outside). Eventually, though, after moving to a better hide, I gambled a bit on a slow-walking blesbok at about 125 yards, two-handed the gun over my raised knees, held a bit high, and touched off the long-barreled .41 Magnum—and beseeched the god of hunters a bit.

The "thwock" of a striking bullet drifted back, and the animal went down, hit just behind the diaphragm, then lurched to its feet

Lee Jurras (left) and I pose with two fine blesbok taken the same day on Bobby Miller's holdings in South Africa. That it's raining and uncomfortable is apparent by the water on the guns and the wet hides of the animals. Jurras used a .44 Auto Mag, while my buck was taken with a long-barreled S&W M57 .41 Magnum.

and stayed with the herd, which spooked and galloped full tilt directly toward my rocks and brush.

I tried a couple of shots when the wounded animal was running in the clear, to no avail, then decided to hold off so long as the herd came my way. At about 60 yards they crossed a dry wash, finally spotted me (I think) and veered sharply to my left. For a second or two the already-hit animal was broadside and in the clear, and the big gun thundered almost of its own volition. Neck broken, the blesbok somersaulted to earth. Not a very big one, but the first trophy I'd taken in Africa with a handgun.

Another day on Van Schalkwyk's holdings, we were spotted a bit differently. Jurras waited patiently most of the day, with lots of blesbok in sight, including some very nice heads. But he was never offered anything but impossibly long shots or running shots nearly as far. Had he been using a high-velocity rifle he could have taken a good 16-inch or better head within the first hour, and probably others as the day wore on. The difference between rifle and handgun hunting became very evident to all concerned. Limited to the shorter range of a shortgun, he had to wait the bucks out, since a stalk was impossible over the bare, rocky ground. Of course, the difficulties—including the range limitations—are what make handgun hunting such an exciting challenge, but there are times when those difficulties mount to the point of frustration and really test a hunter's patience and determination.

In the meantime, at one point I divested myself of gun and glasses and was photographing some out-of-range game. Suddenly, a small herd of light-footed blesbok came upon me from the rear, and halted stock-still. Much chagrined, I looked hungrily at the 16½-inch or better ram up front, a bare 25 yards away, while my gun lay out of reach a few paces off. When I moved, they moved, and were long gone before a shot could be taken. My tactical error was offset later, and I got the same (we think) animal.

By then, I'd moved a half-mile or so and was again well hidden in rocks and scrub near where a game trail crossed a small weedy bog. We'd seen five nice blesbok rams a mile away, apparently headed for that spot. Van and I had then moved to the new hide to await their arrival. Arrive they did, shortly, coming across the bog, passing into my sights only after reaching solid ground. Having crossed slowly, they then broke into a trot before I could get a shot. To have fired earlier would have meant moving and we'd have certainly been seen.

Anyway, at about 85 yards I put the sights on the biggest ram's nose and touched off a shot. He stumbled, hit too far back (not enough lead) and broke into a run. Frantically I fired again, missed clean (over his shoulders) and then tried again. At the third shot there was a hell of a "crack" instead of the dull "thwock" a bullet makes when it hits meat. The ram stumbled again, shook his head, and disappeared around a rock outcropping. I'd hit him in the *horns!* The .41 bullet punched straight through the near horn and chipped the other. We trailed him a few hundred yards to where he'd gone down, and the .41 Magnum finished him off.

Eventually Jurras shifted, hoping to take better advantage of the movements of the game, again half-hidden in a tiny, rocky copse. Here, too, a good rifle would have secured his trophy quickly, but the handgunner compensates for the limitations of his equipment with infinite patience and caution. Seemingly countless times he was tempted by acceptable heads beyond certain killing range. Knowing he had made clean kills back in the U.S. at ranges over 200 yards made it all the harder to hold back when similar opportunities were presented. But patience does sometimes have its reward, and eventually a fine ram drifted nearly within the 100-yard limit.

As Jurras prepared for the shot, easing the big gun into position, something—who knows what—spooked the ram. He launched himself full tilt diagonally across the line of fire, and when he passed the hide at about 80 yards, Jurras touched off a shot as the sights swung past the ram's nose. Nothing more was needed. The hollow-point bullet smashed through the neck to ricochet howling off the earth, and the ram slid to a halt on his nose, the ivory-like tips of his

This fine springbok fell to Jurras' Auto Mag at about 85 yards. Running flat out, the animal somersaulted to a low heart shot.

You can never be entirely certain what will happen in handgun hunting. The bushbok is essentially a nocturnal animal that hides in deep thickets, yet this one exploded from under Jurras' feet in an open field when he'd shed his gun. It was finally dispatched with a single neck shot while galloping at about 125 yards.

16½-inch horns gleaming in the South African sunlight. First success on a new hunt in new country is always a bit momentous, so it was time to put the guns away for the day, retire to the distant Toyota, and toast our hosts in amber Scotch from a bottle carefully packed for just such an occasion.

With Lee's fine kill and my second (accomplished less neatly with more shots), our several hosts became convinced that there is a place for handguns in the type of hunting they enjoy in the vast rolling veldt. Accustomed to the handgun as a point-and-shoot weapon for plinking and self-defense, they saw it now in a new light, as a precision arm within its range limitations. Consequently, they were ready to take us after more species and without so much concern.

And so they did. We covered hundreds of miles in a fan north and west of Port Elizabeth. We took impala, springbok, redbok, bushbok and numerous other species, from rock rabbit upward. There were good days and bad days, good shots and bad shots—but the best of all occurred on the last day, almost in the last hour, when Jurras jumped a fine brown bushbok in midday and neatly broke its neck with his .357 Auto Mag as it hurtled toward cover 125 yards away. What magnificent fireplace memories are made of shots like that, and places like South Africa!

# 19

---

# *Black Powder &*
# *Muzzle-Loaders*

Had this book been written 15 or 20 years ago, I doubt that one reader in a thousand would have cared if black powder and muzzle-loading handguns had been ignored completely. We've seen a renaissance of muzzle-loading, accompanied by the phoenix-like resurrection of many old Civil War gun designs, the factories to produce them, and companies to handle their sales and distribution.

It probably began in the late 1950s when Val Forgett, President of Navy Arms and Service Armament, made arrangements with an Italian tool and die company to produce very close copies of the 1851-vintage Colt .36 Navy revolver. Prior to that time there had been some modest interest in shooting such percussion guns, but since all the available specimens were century-old collector's items and most had deteriorated with age, shooting activity was severly limited. A few people had hunted, mainly small game, with the old guns—but among the influential shooting writers, I can recollect only Elmer Keith saying much about those experiences in print. Generally speaking, by the 1950s most really good muzzle-loading handguns had already been gathered in by collectors, and prices had been inflated to the point that it was economically impractical to use them for shooting even if more handgunners had known anything about using black-powder guns.

When the first of Navy Arms replica Colt Navy revolvers hit these shores in 1957, the scramble was on. These *new* guns looked exactly like the originals, both inside and out; they felt the same, functioned the same, and gave comparable shooting results. Equally important, they were produced from modern materials by modern methods and were therefore much stronger, more durable, and less likely to get out of order than originals; and, of course, even as brand-new guns they cost far, far less than an original Colt Navy in shooting condition.

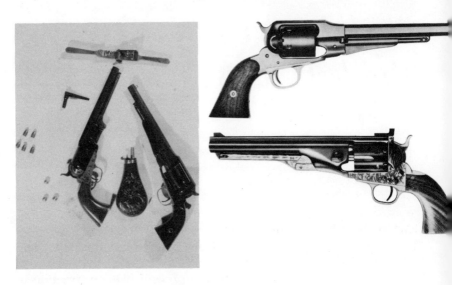

ABOVE LEFT Here are replicas of the Colt and Remington percussion revolvers, with implements and bullets.

RIGHT TOP The Remington-type revolver is the simplest, strongest, and most durable of the cap-and-ball sixguns. This makes it the best choice for hunting.

RIGHT BOTTOM This .44-caliber Navy Arms revolver is offered with target sights and is far better for hunting than the standard model with sights like those on the original Civil War guns.

The commercial success of the replica Colt Navy revolvers was instantaneous. To this day, production has never quite matched demand in spite of increasing manufacturing facilities. That success quickly prompted the rise of new companies producing and distributing copies of percussion revolvers—the Colt Army, Remington Army and Navy, Colt Dragoons, etc. The increasing availability of these guns spurred interest in shooting them, and this gave rise to a surge of interest in using muzzle-loaders to take game. Thus arose today's tribe of hunters who specialize in using such revolvers or other muzzle-loading handguns.

Let's take a look at how capable the various percussion revolvers are for taking different species of game. First of all, we must consider the fact that loading and reloading of the percussion revolver is slow and laborious. This argues against any type of hunting where a large number of shots might have to be fired rapidly, but in most situations you can reasonably expect to get by with the five shots that you can safely load in a six-shot cylinder, or four shots in a five-shot gun. More on this characteristic of percussion revolvers will be found in the loading instructions farther along.

The second limitation is the greater susceptibility (than cartridge handguns) of the percussion revolver to misfires brought about by poor cleaning and maintenance, damp weather, improper handling, etc. However, by very careful handling and attention to detail in loading and preparation for firing, these modern percussion revolvers can be made to provide reliability approaching that of the finest modern guns and cartridges.

We must also consider that these replicas of guns made nearly 140 years ago possess certain design defects of the originals. By today's standards, in spite of legend to the contrary, they are generally more susceptible to parts breakage and other mechanical malfunctions than modern guns, even though made of excellent materials.

Of course, all of the modern replicas are of single-action persuasion, and the double-action fans may find this objectionable, even though SA functioning presents no disadvantage for hunting.

There is also the very evident fact that most percussion revolvers were fitted with only the most rudimentary sights. The typical set consisted of a tiny brass cone, bead, or pin up near the muzzle, accompanied by a barely perceptible V-notch at the rear, with no adjustments whatever. This type is at its worst in the old Colt design, wherein the rear-sight notch is cut into the hammer nose, making its alignment and position dependent on the wear and condition of lockwork parts. It is also likely to be accompanied by considerable side-to-side wobble of the hammer. Obviously, then, the sights of today's true replicas are a severe handicap. They can be improved substantially, though, and we'll discuss that farther along.

For some hunting uses, the limited power of cap-lock revolvers presents no particular disadvantage. These guns are generally utilized with round balls cast or swaged from nearly pure lead, and bullet weights are generally limited to 50 grains in .31 caliber, 75 grains in .36, and 135 grains in .44/.45. Inasmuch as the balls must be seated entirely within the mouth of the chambers, chamber volume (space for powder) is limited. It is not possible to obtain more than a bit over 1000 fps with the maximum amount of powder that can be loaded even in the massive Colt Walker replica. It becomes apparent, then, that there is no way percussion revolvers can be loaded up to the performance levels of even medium-power metallic-cartridge revolvers of similar caliber.

Penetration of percussion revolver loads can be improved by substituting heavier conical bullets for round balls, but the longer bullet reduces the powder space within the chamber. Little real improvement in bullet energy can be obtained, though penetration may be increased.

Even the most powerful percussion revolvers, therefore, cannot be considered adequate for most big-game species. Our accompanying table of loads and velocities should make it clear that percussion revolvers are essentially small-game hunting arms except under ideal conditions and in the hands of a superior hunter and marksman. My personal list of game taken with percussion revolvers is probably representative of their capabilities. It includes ground squirrels, prairie dogs, woodchucks, foxes, coyotes, wild turkey, small whitetail deer, feral hogs weighing up to a bit over 200 pounds, and one small black bear that blundered too close and presented an irresistible temptation. Of the lot, the feral hogs presented the most difficulty. None of the hogs was killed cleanly with a single shot, even with the big Colt Walker loaded to the hilt. I don't doubt that some people have taken larger game with a percussion revolver, but I certainly wouldn't recommend it under ordinary circumstances.

Beware the smoke. After firing a black-powder gun, you may not see your target again until the wind blows.

For small game, though, the percussion revolver can be a real joy. Of the three calibers and gun sizes available, I consider the .36 to be the most practical. The smaller .31 presents more difficulty in obtaining satisfactory accuracy, and the guns chambered for it are really too small for good handling. The larger .44, though quite good from any other viewpoint, is more powerful than need be for small game. It also uses a lot more powder and lead than the .36, and if you do much shooting the economic factor rears its ugly head.

As far as gun choice is concerned, the selection really isn't very wide. In .36 caliber, we have only two basic types available from the various replica makers—the open-top Colt with the sights I've already complained about, and the solid-frame Remington design, which is superior not only in the sight department but in strength and durability. It is also less complex than the Colt. Therefore, in choosing a percussion revolver for small-game hunting and general shooting, the Remington .36 Navy wins. But in standard form it, too, carries lousy sights—a brass cone up front and a tiny V-notch in the rear. If you expect to bag many squirrels for the skillet, replace the front sight with a 1/10-inch-wide blade and recut the rear notch to square Patridge form to match. When doing this, it's best to make the front blade substantially higher, then carefully file it down so bullets print exactly on point of aim at 25 yards with the standard load that you eventually choose.

Fortunately for those who don't care to undertake such gunsmithing, replica Remington revolvers are available with adjustable, target-type sights. While of modern design, these sights are by no means as precise as those on current target revolvers and autoloaders, so some gunsmiths make a practice of fitting better sights. Personally, I like the micrometer-style rear sight from the Smith & Wesson K-series target revolvers. Its installation on a Remington frame requires careful machining, a job for a specialist. On the other hand, the flat-base Micro revolver target sight can be home-fitted at far less cost if you wish. Either of those rear sights will require a higher front sight, and both are equally accurate.

With regard to internal modifications, both the Colt and Remington designs can be improved considerably by tuning them as outlined for modern single-action revolvers elsewhere in this volume.

Loading of a percussion revolver is critical because performance depends on particular attention to detail. The slightest carelessness will bring misfires, lousy accuracy, or even malfunctions of the gun. The important thing is never to overlook any of the steps I'm about to describe and always perform them in the proper sequence.

First the revolver must have its chambers scrubbed completely free of grease or oil, using lighter fluid or some similar solvent for the purpose. If the gun is new, of course, preservative grease should be removed from the rest of its parts. Once the chambers are clean, blow through the nipples to remove solvent or residual grease. Then, place the cylinder back in the gun, and seat a cap on each nipple. Fire each cap in sequence, observing carefully whether smoke and/or flame comes out of the muzzle, as it should if there are no obstructions in the nipples or elsewhere. If you cannot be certain of this, place the muzzle near grass or dusty earth, and then the jet of gas from the exploding cap will be clearly visible. Don't make the mistake of holding your hand over the muzzle to feel the gas exit; people have been burned that way. If there is any doubt in your mind that the nipples are clear, seat a second series of caps and fire them also. The heat of the cap flame will evaporate any residual solvent, and the rushing gas will clear out any grease or oil. If this is not done, the cap may not ignite the powder charge. The nipple vent *must* be free and dry for maximum reliability and consistency of ignition.

Pick any bits of exploded cap off all the nipples, then check to make certain no pieces of cap have fallen down between the frame and hammer or between recoil shield and cylinder to possibly tie up the gun later. It's a good idea to carry a short piece of spring wire to pick out such bits, and thus avoid any disassembly of the gun. It's no problem on initial loading, but pieces of cap can become lodged in those places while you're shooting in the field, and that's no time to have to take the gun apart to remove them.

The first step in actual loading is to place the powder charge in the chamber. The most practical method of doing this is with a measuring powder flask of the type originally supplied with percussion revolvers and fitted with the proper spout for your particular caliber. See the load chart for charge weights. Holding the gun muzzle-up in your left hand, and with the flask in your right hand, drop the powder charge into the chamber nearest the rammer. For this you'll need the hammer drawn back to the loading notch, and it's a good idea to steady the cylinder with your thumb and forefinger. Then, drop the flask to dangle from its shoulder strap, and with thumb and finger place a ball in the mouth of that same chamber. If you're using cast balls, place the flattened sprue upwards and centered as accurately as possible. Thumb the ball as tightly into the chamber mouth as it will go.

Now carefully rotate the cylinder so that the ball lies directly under the cup end of the rammer, and with your right hand unlatch the rammer lever and pivot it downward until the rammer contacts the

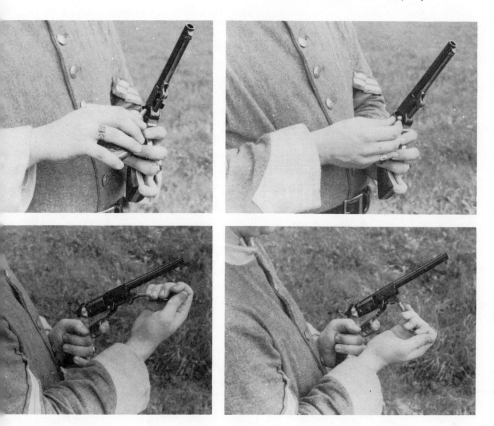

TOP LEFT After caps have been snapped to clear all the nipples, you're ready to load your cap-and-ball revolver. Set the hammer in the loading notch and pour the proper powder charge into a chamber. A measuring flask helps here.

TOP RIGHT Next, place the ball in the mouth of the charged chamber. If using a cast ball, its sprue should be aligned with the axis of the chamber.

ABOVE LEFT Rotate the chamber under the rammer, centering it carefully, then unlatch the rammer and pull down on the handle to make firm contact with the ball. Force the ball into the chamber mouth, noting if a thin ring of lead is sheared off. This indicates proper fit, for the ball should be slightly oversized.

ABOVE RIGHT Continue the rearward levering with a single smooth motion of the rammer to seat the ball snugly against the powder.

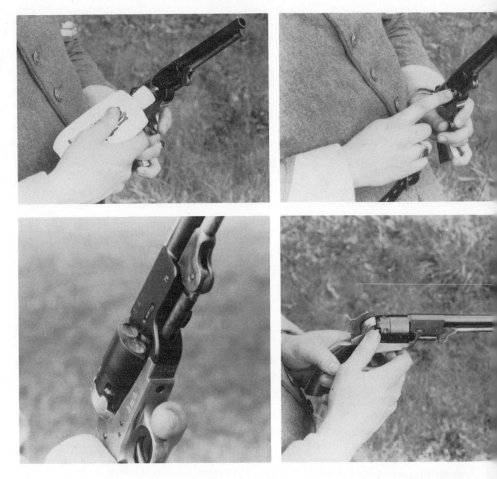

TOP LEFT To prevent multiple discharges, to lubricate the ball's passage through the bore, and to keep the powder residue soft, fill the chamber mouth over the ball with some form of grease, as suggested in the text.

TOP RIGHT Make certain the chamber is filled flush to the front. Here, the shooter's forefinger points to a gap in the grease at the chamber mouth.

ABOVE LEFT Properly filled with powder charge, ball, and grease, the loaded cylinder will look like this. Don't pile grease beyond the chamber mouths, as the excess will be blown in all directions when the gun is fired.

ABOVE RIGHT The last step is capping the nipples. The caps can be seated with thumb or finger, though the job is easier with a magazine capper.

For carrying a gun loaded in the field, it's extremely important that the caps fit smoothly but snugly over the nipples of the cylinder.

ball. At this point you may have to move the cylinder very slightly to obtain precise alignment. Then bring the rammer lever on down in a single, smooth but forceful movement, seating the ball solidly against the powder charge. Don't use *too* much pressure; stop when you feel the ball contact the powder solidly. With a standard full charge of powder, this should leave the ball seated about 1/16-inch below the chamber mouth. As the ball is seated, the sharp edge of the chamber mouth will shear off a thin ring of lead. If this does not occur, the ball is too small and will neither stay in place properly during firing nor shoot accurately. On the other hand, if a large amount of lead is sheared off and unusual force is required to seat the ball, then the ball is too large.

Repeat these operations until all but one chamber are filled with powder and ball. Leave the remaining chamber empty, so that the gun may be carried with the hammer down upon that particular nipple without any chance of inadvertent firing. Even though there are safety pins or notches which, in theory, allow the gun to be carried safely with all chambers loaded, history is replete with acci-dental firings when this was done. Play it safe and keep one chamber empty with the hammer resting on its nipple.

Now to lubricate each ball. There are special muzzle-loading lubri-cants for this purpose, but Vaseline or a vegetable shortening such as Crisco is less costly, more easily obtained, and works just as well. Place a dab of lubricant in the mouth of each chamber, and force it down with a knife blade or small wood paddle to completely fill the chamber over the ball.

This lubricant serves two purposes. First, it prevents multiple discharges which occur when the flash from the firing of one chamber is communicated to adjacent chambers, igniting their powder and causing them to fire almost simultaneously. Even though the ball is tight in the chamber mouth, there are often fine particles of powder and minute gaps which allow this to happen. Filling the chamber mouth with grease flame-proofs it and prevents multiple discharges. Second, the lubricant prevents leading of the barrel and ensures sustained accuracy. As a side effect, it also keeps the black-powder fouling moist, especially in dry weather, and makes subsequent cleaning easier. This also causes the major portion of the fouling to be blown out by subsequent shots, rather than accumulating in a thick, hard layer which can destroy accuracy even if leading does not occur.

Once all the desired chambers are charged with powder, ball, and lubricant, it remains only to place caps on the nipples, and the gun is ready to fire. For hunting, it is essential that the caps fit the nipples snugly so that they won't work loose or back off during a day's carrying and thus bind against the recoil shield during cylinder rotation. Though nipples and caps are both fairly well standardized, there are still manufacturing tolerances to contend with. It's essential that you try different makes and sizes of caps until you find the one that can be seated *completely* by thumb pressure and yet will cling tightly enough to the nipple not to jar off during handling or firing. A cap that is just a shade loose can be tightened sufficiently (most of the time) by simply pinching its open end together somewhat, thus causing it to grip the nipple more snugly. It will also happen sometimes that the tops of the nipples will be a bit square-shouldered, with a sharp rim that digs into the inner surface of the cap, preventing the cap from being fully pressed home. When this is encountered, you may either replace the nipples or simply polish the sharp edge to a smooth radius with a bit of abrasive cloth. This is seldom encountered in the better makes of guns or replacement nipples, but it crops up occasionally in cheaper merchandise.

With the hammer still in the loading notch, align each nipple successively with the capping groove in the right side of the recoil shield, and press a fresh cap home. When all of the loaded chambers have been capped, rotate the cylinder a couple of revolutions to make certain the caps are not rubbing against the recoil shield. Now carefully thumb the hammer back so that the trigger may be drawn out of the loading notch, at the same time rotating the *uncharged* chamber under the hammer; then let the hammer down all the way on the uncapped nipple. In this condition, the gun will be entirely safe for all normal carrying and handling. Yet, when you want to fire, simply thumbing the hammer to full-cock brings a loaded chamber into position and you're ready to go. All other manipulation of the percussion revolver is the same as with any other single-action six-gun.

When in the field, you may have occasion to fire several rounds but not the full cylinder, and thus want to reload without discharging those unfired chambers. Reloading can be perfectly safe under those conditions, provided that you *always* remove the caps from the nipples of the loaded chambers before proceeding. This isn't always as easy as you might think—once pressed home, properly-fitted caps cling tightly, and may defy all efforts to remove them, short of prying them off with the tip of your knife blade. This can be hazardous, for if the knife slips and cuts through the thin copper of the cap, it's conceivable that the priming pellet can be detonated, firing the charge. If this occurs, the odds are about even that you'll receive the ball in some portion of your anatomy, or that the flash will remove your eyebrows and moustache. By far the best bet under those circumstances is to simply go ahead and fire the one or two rounds remaining in the cylinder and then reload all chambers.

Generally considered a fair-weather mechanism, the percussion revolver can be water-proofed sufficiently to function reliably in anything short of a torrential downpour. The first step in achieving this is to seat a tight-fitting felt wad, which has been thoroughly soaked in melted beeswax/Vaseline mixture, over the powder charge and beneath the ball. In some instances, this may require a slight reduction of the powder charge. Then, when the ball is properly seated, it must still be lubricated with whatever grease you fancy. This takes care of waterproofing the mouth of the chamber, but there is still a chance that water will seep up between the nipple and cap, and either contaminate the cap or seep on into the powder charge and do damage there. If you're loading a clean gun under shelter, a drop or two of clear lacquer may be applied at the bottom of the cap after loading is completed. The lacquer will run into the minute gaps between nipple and cap, harden in a few moments, and effectively seal out all moisture.

Unfortunately, this method doesn't work too well when you're loading out in the field. Under those conditions, carry along a small pill box of beeswax softened with Vaseline, and smear it around the nipple just below the nipple face. Make certain you get a ring of it completely around the nipple, so that when the cap is pressed home the grease will not contact the priming pellet. Then, when the cap is seated properly, the gap between its mouth and the nipple will be filled with the grease mixture, effectively sealing out moisture.

Some individuals recommend obtaining a spare cylinder which can be loaded and waterproofed ahead of time and carried along on the hunt. This sounds great, but unless some sort of rigid container is made for the cylinder to absolutely prevent any impact from reaching the capped nipple, there is always the danger—though it may be slight—of one or more chambers being accidentally discharged. An unprotected capped and loaded cylinder in your coat pocket could easily be set off by banging against a rock or tree trunk, and thus plant one or several bullets in your body. Carry extra loaded cylinders afield if you wish, but make absolutely certain the caps are properly protected to prevent accidental discharge by some random impact. While light loads can be great fun for plinking or practice, I don't consider anything less than the full charge loads given in our table for hunting. Certainly, a light load will kill a grouse or squirrel if you are close enough and hit him solidly, but considering all the conditions under which you might take a shot, you need the maximum velocity, power, and flatness of trajectory that the full-charge load produces.

If you decide you would rather use the heavier conical bullets, loading procedures remain the same, and separate powder-charge weights are listed for them in the table. Particular care must be taken in seating conical bullets. Unless seated in the chamber mouth with their longitudinal axis parallel with that of the chamber, they will enter the barrel in a skewed attitude, and accuracy will be very poor. Obtaining accurate alignment during seating is considerably more difficult than with round balls, and some guns may even require slight modification of the cup end of the rammer to fit the bullet nose closely and avoid tipping. Of course, you must keep in mind that a percussion revolver will not shoot round balls and conical bullets to the same point of aim with a given sight setting.

While revolvers are certainly the most fun and do provide rapidity of fire, they're not the only muzzle-loading guns you may use for hunting. In fact, if you wish to load a great deal of power for really big game, you'll be forced to switch to the conventional single-shot muzzle-loading pistol. Such guns are generally available in the same calibers as revolvers, but may also be had in .50, .54, and even .58 caliber. By virtue of having a one-piece barrel, they place no practical limitations upon the amount of powder that may be used. Therefore, when maximum power is desired, a single-shot pistol may be loaded with two or even three times as much powder as can be accommodated by a revolver of like caliber. This allows much higher velocity to be obtained with both round balls and conical bullets.

Loading a percussion single-shot pistol differs substantially from loading the revolver. After the preliminary cleaning, drying, and clearing the nipple, the powder charge is poured down the barrel from the muzzle. Then a ball of the proper diameter (normally about .005-inch less than the bore diameter of the barrel) is encased in a thin, greased, cloth patch and rammed solidly down the bore against the powder. The gun is then capped and is ready to fire.

When conical bullets are desired, generally the "Minie" type with its hollow base and peripheral grease grooves is utilized. This bullet is *not* used with a patch, and is sufficiently undersized to be thrust easily down the bore against the powder. The lubricant upon its surface and its fairly close fit in the bore serve to keep it snugly against the powder until fired. Then the action of the powder gases inside the hollow base expands the bullet to fill the rifling grooves and thus seal off powder gases and be rotated by the rifling as it is driven down the bore. At normal handgun ranges, the Minie-type bullet is equal in accuracy to the patched round ball. At the same time, it is of much greater weight and even though it cannot be driven as rapidly its velocity is great enough to exceed the energy obtained from a round ball in the same gun.

Though I do not know of its having been done, it is conceivable that with .54 or larger-caliber pistols that are currently available, one could safely take on any non-dangerous North American game with proper loads. Unfortunately, such guns offer only a single shot, and reloading is both slow and laborious. For this reason there has been relatively little interest in using such guns for big game. They are often seen in use on small game and for plinking, but that's about it. This is unfortunate, for the single-shot percussion pistol offers far greater energy and thus far greater game-getting potential than the revolver.

Considering the revolver's limitations, if I were in need of the ideal muzzle-loading handgun for taking big game, I would endeavor to have made a double-barreled percussion pistol in .50 or .54 caliber, barrels about 10 inches long, and loaded with maximum charges and heavy conical bullets. I'm certain such a gun would be entirely adequate for most North American non-dangerous game if one stalked in close and chose his shots with extreme care. Certainly a gun of this description would deliver greater power than many of the so-called Kentucky percussion rifles which are regularly used on such game.

Assuming you choose the best gun and load available, hunting with a muzzle-loading handgun differs very little from the use of modern handguns. The limitations of muzzle-loaders are essentially those of modern handguns, but somewhat exaggerated. It remains only for the individual to evaluate the limitations of his equipment and to work within them.

# PERCUSSION REVOLVER LOAD DATA

*31 caliber, 5¾" bbl., Gearhart-Owen black powder*

*round ball (.319")—13 grains G-O FFFg—700 fps*

*.36 caliber, 7½" bbl., Gearhart-Owen black powder*

*round ball (.375")—26 grains G-O FFFg—1075 fps*
*round ball (.375")—20 grains G-O FFFg—970 fps*
*round ball (.375")—17 grains G-O FFFg—880 fps*
*conical ball (150 gr.)—15 grains G-O FFFg—670 fps*
*conical ball (150 gr.)—12 grains G-O FFFg—560 fps*

*.44/.45 caliber, 8" bbl., Gearhart-Owen black powder*

*round ball (.451")—35 grains G-O FFFg—1000 fps*
*round ball (.451")—31 grains G-O FFFg—930 fps*
*round ball (.451")—25 grains G-O FFFg—800 fps*
*conical ball (185 gr.)—28 grains G-O FFFg—860 fps*
*conical ball (185 gr.)—25 grains G-O FFFg—880 fps*
*conical ball (185 gr.)—20 grains G-O FFFg—710 fps*

*(Note: Other black powders generally produce less velocity than Gearhart-Owen used above; larger granulation will also produce a bit less velocity. Lighter charges may be more accurate, but not necessarily.)*

# 20

## *Palmetto Hogs &*
## *Black Powder*

Several years ago, my good friend and shooting companion, Dick Eades of Bedford, Texas, decided that in conjunction with attending the National Police Pistol Matches, we should drum up some sort of an unusual handgun hunt in the Deep South. After talking to a lot of people and looking around a bit, we settled on going out for wild (feral) hogs in central Florida. Probably no other state in the Union has as large a population of wild hogs as Florida. The climate, terrain, and flora indigenous to that steamy state appear to be ideal for wild hogs, and they thrive there better than Durocs in a feed lot. In any event, central Florida—once you get away from the big towns—is crawling with wild hogs; at night you see them on the roads there just as we see deer in Illinois.

Those Florida hogs aren't usually large, so to make things a bit more interesting we elected to use modern replicas of percussion revolvers dating originally from the 1840s. We figured that with the chambers crammed with FFFg black powder and a .44-caliber round ball we'd match our armament and ammunition fairly well to those fast-stepping razorbacks. We arrived at River Ranch Acres equipped with a suitcase full of assorted Navy Arms cap-lock revolvers. Dick allowed as how he would prefer the lighter Dragoon, while I settled for the five-pound Walker with its greater powder capacity and thus greater power.

I chose this Navy Arms replica Walker revolver because it will accept a larger charge of powder than any other percussion revolver available. Obviously, more powder means more power.

Having long since been thoroughly confused by the mass of legend and ill-supported writings about the "knockdown" power of the old .44 cap-lock sixguns, we prepared for the hunt with a fairly extensive series of tests. We didn't doubt that the guns had plenty of energy to take care of the hogs, but on the other hand we didn't believe the old stories about a Walker shooting end-to-end through a charging calvaryman's horse.

First it was determined that both guns required a .452-inch-diameter round ball, and that when this projectile was seated just below the chamber mouth (without any over-powder wad to steal space), the Walker would hold 55 grains of FFFg, while the Dragoon, with its quarter-inch shorter cylinder, held 40 grains in the same fashion. If anyone questions the use of FFFg black-powder granulation, keep in mind that we wanted to make certain all of the propelling charge would be burned in the relatively short sixgun. The Walker carried an eight-inch barrel, while the Dragoon carried a seven-inch barrel. Having had good experience in the past with Curtis and Harvey powder, we chose it for both the test and the Florida shooting, even though we did eventually discover that the Walker blew a bit of unconsumed powder out of the muzzle at each shot. The seven-inch Dragoon did not exhibit this tendency with its 40-grain charge, so apparently it was operating at nearly maximum efficiency, while the Walker was loaded slightly beyond the powder-consuming capability of its eight-inch barrel.

Both guns produced excellent accuracy with those loads, so long as the space over the seated ball was completely filled with Crisco to eliminate leading and keep fouling soft. Just for kicks, we had decided to stick with the original sights on both guns—and anyone who has used them knows them for the abomination they are. Had we anticipated any long-range shooting, certainly better (and adjustable) sights would have been fitted. However, we didn't anticipate shooting those Florida hogs at any great range, and figured we could hit fairly well with the notched-hammer and brass-cone sights Sam Colt put on the original guns in 1847 and 1848. Be that as it may, after a little practice and a bit of work on the triggers, we were able to get fairly consistent five-inch, five-shot groups at 50 yards, shooting two-handed from the standing position. That's plenty for close-in hogs.

With all of that ironed out, we set up an Oehler Model 20 Digital Chronograph with Model 50 electronic screens and checked both guns for velocity. The big Walker, with its massive powder charge and long barrel, produced 1037 fps instrumental at 10 feet from the muzzle. A quick calculation showed this to produce 392 foot-pounds of energy. This is more than ample for the purpose, especially since soft-lead round balls have poor penetration capabilities and therefore could be expected to transmit all or nearly all of their energy to a tough-muscled hog. The Dragoon, on the other hand, with its shorter barrel and lighter charge, developed only 774 fps and about 215 foot-pounds of energy. We were slightly disappointed in the Dragoon's showing, but Pistolero Eades wasn't about to be deterred, and allowed he'd kill any hog just as well with that load as I could with the thunder-clapping Walker. As it turned out, he was right.

I've heard the accusation that hunting writers don't say much in print about their misses (any more than fishing writers do about the ones that get away). But in my account of this hog hunt I'm going to admit to some poor shooting that resulted in failure to make a quick, humane kill. Since we can learn from mistakes, I think it's essential to include such incidents. This particular episode proved once again the need for good sights and the importance of concentrating and taking the time to place every shot precisely. I'm sure you'll see the point as you read on—and maybe you'll enjoy reading how the so-called "experts" can sometimes goof as embarrassingly as anyone else.

In Tampa, Florida, we met Vince Smith and he drove us 80 miles to River Ranch Acres, near Lake Wales. This put us about 55 miles almost due south of Orlando, deep in the palmetto scrub country, noted not only for its quail and hog population, but for its plentiful and aggressive crop of rattlesnakes. Rattlers aren't my favorite people, and Dick isn't overly fond of them either. But we figured if those .44-caliber round balls couldn't eliminate them, the yard-long muzzle flame from all that black powder would barbeque any snake that got in our way. That's the only way I really care for rattlesnakes, barbequed—or possibly fricasseed, for they're right tasty either way.

The land there is barely above sea level, mostly sand, generally open and thickly dotted with head-high palmetto thickets and small live-oak groves. If a fellow uses his eyes, he'll see not only quail and hogs, but plenty of doves, along with the small Florida whitetail deer (usually under 100 pounds, live weight), and strutting but spooky wild turkey. What you won't see are the cats that thrive on this game population; and, of course, those pestiferous rattlers in the palmetto clumps. My friend Bev Mann, an old Florida bird shooter, always says you don't need to worry about rattlers you see, and we began to hope there weren't too many unseen ones in the palmetto thickets.

Our first day was spent mainly in getting acquainted with our guide-driver-dog handler, Sam Elder, and cruising the vast expanse of River Ranch Acres in a jeep equipped with a built-up "high seat" which allows one to spot game by virtue of being above the head-high grass and palmetto scrub that covers so much of the land. It was the rainiest, soggiest September of many a year, and we were alternately soaked and baked dry as showers and sun played peek-a-boo in the Florida sky.

Having been forewarned about the frequent if not enduring showers, we were prepared with the wherewithal to waterproof our muzzle-loading sixguns. Provided such a gun is loaded with a tight-fitting ball of the proper diameter, rammed solidly in a clean, smooth chamber and then well covered with water-resistant grease, the muzzle of the chamber is well sealed. No water or moisture can penetrate to dampen the powder charge and produce a misfire or blooper shot. However, normal loading procedures do not seal the nipple. Though the percussion cap clings tightly to the nipple when properly seated, there is still plenty of room for water to be sucked up by capillary attraction and work its way down through the nipple vent into the powder charge. Very little dampening of the charge is required to produce a misfire, for any water coming through the nipple will wet the portion of the charge most vital to ignition.

To prevent this, first off, we used "waterproof" caps which we knew to withstand moisture well. Then, when loading for the day's shoot, we completely degreased the nipples, then coated them with beeswax, pressed the cap down over the wax (forming a pretty good seal in itself), and then dripped melted wax around the lower end of

Reloading at Jeepside is simple enough in dry weather, but during the frequent Florida showers it can become vexing. Proper greasing is especially important in such situations.

the cap to seal it tightly to the nipple. When a properly loaded chamber is sealed in this fashion, the powder and cap will remain completely dry even if the gun is submerged in water for several minutes. The grease up front is required for ball lubrication anyway, and when the beeswax is applied correctly on the cap and nipple, it does not interfere at all with gun functioning, cap detonation, or proper ignition.

Prepared in this fashion, we weren't worried about the periodic rain that pelted our holstered cap-lock sixshooters. Other people who observed our guns felt differently and questioned their ability to fire when the time came. Later we were vindicated, for at the end of the first wet day several doubters were invited to spectate as we fired the loads that had been in the guns all day. As has long been my favored practice with any muzzle-loader, we fired the guns to empty them at the end of each day, cleaned them thoroughly by the traditional hot, soapy-water method, then reloaded afresh the next morning before sallying forth. The Doubting Thomases heard and saw every loaded chamber thunder into the dusk, spitting yard-long tongues of yellow-orange flame and billows of white smoke.

It was late that night (actually in the small hours of the next morning) that I made a tremendous discovery that may yet be the salvation of many a hunter forced to trample through long chigger-ridden grass. The beastly little red devils I had collected during the day had me in an itching, scratching agony by about three A.M. Soap and water, hot shower, cold shower, everything from the first-aid kit— nothing did any good. Most of the treatments seemed to accelerate their digging and nibbling. Finally, in desperation, I grabbed the only thing in the room I hadn't tried—a still-sealed bottle of first-class vodka which our host had thoughtfully provided, along with other potable goods more pleasing to our taste. In a frenzy, I uncorked the vodka and began splashing it all over my itching naked body.

It worked! The cool, soothing vodka stopped the itching. I don't know to this day whether it killed the chiggers, anesthetized them, got them so drunk they fell off, or simply kept their digging and biting from irritating me. After observing this admittedly ridiculous exhibition of a naked man dancing in the middle of a hotel room while slathering himself with vodka, Dick made the profound observation, "I'm glad somebody has finally found a use for vodka."

Having finally gotten rid of my pestiferous parasites, we were ready to go when Sam rolled up with jeep and dogs the next morning. Sam knows Florida hogs well, including where to find them, so it wasn't long before he was showing us shoats and sows with this year's pigs. We'd heard about his legendary hog catching—bare-handed yet —and were waiting for him to give us an exhibition. Soon he braked the jeep, turned the dogs loose, and put them after a young 100-pound boar a couple of hundred yards away. They sight-trailed

Snap-shooting running hogs isn't always productive. In this case, it resulted in a clean miss—note that the loading lever is dropping down under recoil; this is a disadvantage of the big Walker sixgun because it can prevent a quick follow-up shot.

the boar until he thought he was safe deep inside a hyacinth clump that clogged one of the many canals. We followed along for a good look, and erupting water hyacinths soon showed us where the dogs had the boar, one hanging onto his ear while the other distracted him with flashing teeth and strident yelps.

Sam dove headlong into the fray, ducking down to grab one hog leg while the dogs kept the rest of the animal occupied. Kicking a dog clear, Sam grabbed the other hind leg, and dragged the boar backwards, clear of the weeds. With the dogs worrying at his head, the boar couldn't do much, so Sam threw him and got a knee on his neck to keep his immature but sharp tusks out of play. Dick and I then helped to hold the boar while Sam castrated him in the classic manner, "so he'll keep his mind off sows and concentrate on eating and growing into a good trophy." Sounded a bit rough on the hog, but it made sense on a ranch operating for commercial hunting.

As Sam had already pointed out, it's easier to catch a hog than to let him go. It's like sitting on a safety valve—you gotta get away before it blows, and it'll blow as soon as you let it go.

Sam's technique was to get everyone clear of the area, then get a good hold on both hind legs and "wheelbarrow" the hog so he couldn't whip open a leg with his tusks. After that, a healthy shove to off-balance the hog in a safe direction allowed Sam to make a flying mount into the jeep. Naturally, the hog was upset by what had taken place, and if he could have turned around and identified his tormentor, he might have dealt harshly with that individual. He was in the mood to take on anything live that got in his way—and I know one handgun hunter who found himself the object of such a boar's attention. The hunter jumped straight up and shot straight down, hitting the boar in the spine between the shoulders as he passed beneath. Neither my shooting nor my jumping is that good so I stayed in the jeep.

We continued cruising and saw plenty of hogs, though nothing we really cared to shoot. Yesterday's alternating showers and sun were repeated, with nothing more than minor discomfort in that balmy clime. Eventually Sam announced: "We're goin' out and shoot some hogs." It didn't take very long, and I suspect he had known all along where to find worthwhile shooting but wanted first to show us around a bit. Nothing wrong with that—we enjoyed it tremendously, including the rains and ducking oak limbs and Spanish moss as the jeep cruised through the thickets.

In fairly short order, we spotted a good boar in shoulder-high grass and weeds, along with his current lady love and her (if not necessarily his) litter of skittish feral piglets. Circling downwind on foot, we finally were able to pick the boar out in a thinner patch of high grass and weeds. The range was a mere 25 or 30 yards, ideal for the big Walker, and I swung it up two-handed to squint over the sight at the hog's shoulder.

The hammer had come to full-cock almost reflexively, and as I tickled the trigger, weeds and hog alike disappeared behind a billowing cloud of white smoke that hung in the moist air. The report echoed and the ball's violent passage through the weeds was followed by a distorted "whap" as it smacked into the boar. Hurt, but not down, the boar took off to the right, while his consort and family headed otherwise. Again the hammer was back without conscious effort on my part, and the sights were on his fast-traveling nose as the Walker thundered and white smoke blotted everything out again. And again, and again, and the hog was still on his feet and moving, though I was *certain* of at least a couple of good solid hits.

The hog disappeared in the grass and weeds as Sam went back and brought up the jeep so we could have the advantage of the high seat for spotting him in the failing light. We soon located him about 30 yards away, still moving, though not very fast. I got off the two rounds remaining in the Walker, again certain I'd hit him, and then Dick took over with the Dragoon. As the smoke drifted away, we saw that the boar was finally down, all 160 pounds of him, and it seemed safe to reload.

Loading a cap-lock revolver in a drizzle (which had commenced about the time I fired my first shot) can be a bit of a chore if it's to be accomplished without getting the powder wet, but all went well.

Here is my first Florida hog just where he finally collapsed in the weeds after absorbing a handful of .44 balls. By this point I wasn't sure what might happen, so I kept the reloaded and cocked Walker at ready.

We eased up within 25 yards. The boar grunted and attempted to lurch to his feet—and the big Walker thundered again, knocking the hog down for keeps. The "armour-plated hog," as Dick was now calling him, was finished.

We were both embarrassed—and Sam was puzzled, having seen us perform much better on the range with those guns—by the amount of shooting needed to put the hog down. We began looking closely for evidence of hits. As it turned out, our shooting hadn't been quite as miserable as a bystander might have thought. There was a high shoulder hit (too high to do the job), a high lung shot, a ball through the flanks under the spine, a nick on one ham, a couple of other surface wounds, one broken front leg, and a hole through the other. The last-named may have been caused by the bullet that broke the opposite leg. Any one of the first three hits should have put the hog down; penetration was good, but he just wasn't ready to quit. The other hits were simply the result of hurrying and those abominable sights.

Anyway, the Walker had killed quite a nice hog, even if the action was a bit more spirited and prolonged than we had anticipated. Pleased with the results thus far, and with the hog in the jeep, we started racing a thunderhead and the heavy showers we knew were coming to the lodge.

Fortunately, Dick had reloaded his Dragoon while Sam and I gutted and loaded the hog, so when we suddenly came upon a smaller but well-tusked boar who resented our appearance, Dick was ready in spite of the rain. The hog stood head-on, clashing his choppers at our intrusion, and when the Dragoon crashed, the .452-inch ball took him at the base of the throat, ranging through and slightly upwards

This is Dick's hog, not terribly long of tusk but a classic example of the type. A single, .44 ball from a Navy Arms Dragoon dispatched him.

to break his spine. Certainly a one-shot kill, but Dick wasn't taking any chances and slammed another round into the near shoulder as the hog turned in collapsing.

None of the balls that hit my hog had been recovered, so in spite of the rain, we conducted an impromptu post-mortem on Dick's target. The first ball was recovered just under the skin behind the left shoulder, badly deformed but not greatly enlarged in area. The second ball had punched through the shoulder bones, broken the spine, and gone nearly through the heavy muscles of the off shoulder. Both had released *all* of their 215 foot-pounds of energy within the target. Not bad for a gun and ammunition that first saw service in 1848.

So, after appropriate celebration, we departed Florida with a goodly supply of wild pork chops and ham. Not the first taken with cap-lock revolvers, but the biggest animals we had killed up to that time with such armament.

The question arises, of course, as to whether the guns and loads we were using were, in fact, adequate for the game at hand. There's only one way to answer that question—I've killed animals bigger and just as mean with carefully placed shots from .32–20 and .38 Special modern revolvers, both of which are less powerful than the guns we were using. The key to the whole thing is in *carefully placed* shots. With the kind of shooting I did on the first hog, probably nothing less than a .44 Magnum would have laid him low any sooner. Yet the less-powerful load from Dick's gun did instant execution on his hog. The circumstances for the two animals were different. Mine was a running shot, partially concealed by weeds and brush, and I simply didn't take the time to place my shots as carefully as I should have —with the result that the animal was not killed quickly and humanely. Dick's shot was a "sitter," and he *did* place his shot precisely, with the result that *either* ball would have been instantly fatal; both struck the spine. So those .44-caliber cap-lock revolvers *are* adequate for wild hogs, provided one places his shots carefully; on the other hand, as with any other gun, if a hunter shoots hurriedly and without proper precision, neither the gun nor the load is adequate. As I've emphasized elsewhere, the final result is more dependent upon the shooter than upon the gun and ammunition.

Since that memorable Florida hog hunt, I've taken a good bit more game with cap-lock revolvers, and have never failed to kill or anchor with the first shot. I have become more accustomed to the gun's behavior in the field, have used better sights, and have been more cautious about my shooting. The result has been a very satisfactory track record on everything from cottontails and jackrabbits through

The unfired .44 lead ball at top is shown for comparison with two
identical projectiles recovered from hogs and showing massive
deformation.

wild turkey to deer and black bear. I'm certain your experience in
hunting big game with muzzle-loading revolvers will parallel mine
—get careless and both you and the gun will do a lousy job; be
cautious and precise, and you'll have plenty of one-shot kills.

# 21

---

# *Holsters, Belts, &*
# *Carrying Cases*

One of the major advantages of hunting with a handgun is that you don't have to spend all your time with both hands full of gun. With your favorite sixgun or auto safely tucked away, both hands are free for using binoculars or camera, fighting brush away from your face, or simply enjoying an unburdened freedom that the rifle hunter seldom knows.

A good leather holster is the traditional way of carrying a handgun, and the conventional type is hung over your hip from a heavy leather gunbelt. For many purposes, the belt rig is best, though for some types of hunting and some specific guns, a special shoulder rig will do the job better.

The holster's first job is simply to carry the gun securely and comfortably; its second function is to protect the gun from dirt, water, and damage. The traditional material for holsters is good leather, and for both of the foregoing purposes no other natural or man-made material has ever been able to do the job any better. Metals, plastics, and cloth have been used, but the average pistolero always seems to come back to leather after he's tried the off-beat materials.

Not just any leather will do. The best leather makes the best holsters, and that means the back portion of the hide which is, of course, the most costly. Probably no more than a quarter or a third of the total area of a good hide is really suitable for making holsters. Cowhide is the traditional leather, and over many years it has proved to be extremely suitable for the purpose. Yet top-grade horsehide is even better. Unfortunately, the supply of horsehide is extremely limited, in great demand, and therefore very costly. I don't have current market prices for the two types of leather to make a comparison, but a pretty good idea can be had from the fact that one specialty holster maker charges at least 50 percent extra for any model made of horsehide.

The principal advantages of leather are that it is easily worked, durable, can be made adequately water-resistant, and by boning or blocking it can be made to conform precisely with the contours of any particular gun. It also has a pleasing appearance and aroma, and lends itself well to certain types of decoration. No plastic, metal, cloth, or combination thereof combines all of these pleasing and functional characteristics half so well as leather.

The best holsters don't employ fancy gadgetry. They are simply closely-fitted pouches, usually formed of one piece of leather folded over at the front and hand-sewn at the rear. Seams are spaced to provide proper clearance by narrow strips of leather—called welts—placed between the main parts. Some models, intended for extremely hard service, have metal rivets at points of greatest stress. A portion of the holster is folded over and sewn down to form a loop that slips over the belt. In some instances, this loop and the shank portion running down into the body of the holster may be reinforced with a plate of thin, malleable metal which the individual may shape to suit himself and provide the desired gun angle and position.

Aside from that, the functional holster carries no frills—no straps or buckles, no springs or rubber bands, no tiedown thongs, just a simple, secure safety strap which may be engaged when desired to ensure that the gun cannot fall out if you take a tumble.

Too many shooters think of the gun belt as simply a necessary evil, just something on which to hang the holster, and so settle for any old piece of leather long enough to reach around their middle. The requirements for a good gun belt are no less demanding than those for the holster. It must be made of the best leather, and fitted with the finest hardware (buckle) securely attached by strong stitching and rivets. It must be matched to the holster so that the belt fits very tightly in the belt loop in order to prevent the holstered gun from slithering about as one moves in the field.

Hunting does not normally involve quick-draw shooting. Nevertheless, the gun must be positioned to suit the individual, and when he does reach for it, it must be where he is reaching—not around in the small of his back or dangling across his belly as is shown in so many old-time photographs of cowpunchers and lawmen. Further, the hunting gun belt should be at least two inches wide in order to distribute the weight of the gun (and any other items hung from it) evenly and comfortably around the wearer's body. Anyone who questions how important this can be need only talk to a working cop who carries 10 to 12 pounds of assorted equipment on his gun belt. The belt should also be several inches longer than one's pants belt so that it can be worn comfortably over heavy clothing. This length requires an extra keeper, or loop, or two to secure the tongue when it is worn over light clothing.

The gun belt should be worn snugly around the waist. The television gunslinger's notion of a loose belt angling down across the hip is entirely unsuitable for hunting. It distributes the weight of the gun poorly and leaves it bouncing and flapping about every time you move. A wide belt drawn up snugly around the waist is not only the most comfortable, but positions the gun securely and unobtrusively.

The gun belt serves not only to support the gun but often a knife and spare ammunition. The knife scabbard can be slipped over the belt at almost any point, and spare cartridges are best carried in a separate slide which also fits over the belt. Sewed-on cartridge loops usually interfere with the placement of other equipment, and it is often difficult to remove ammunition from them. A separate slide is best.

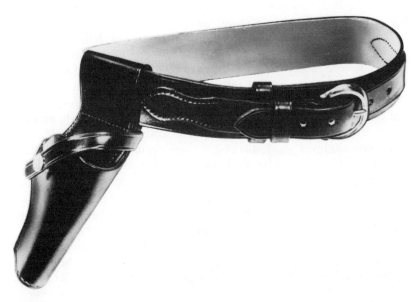

ABOVE An open-top belt rig such as this Hume "River" outfit is the most common type for hunting.

BELOW This Berns-Martin split-front design gives good mechanical protection, though it will not keep out dirt and debris.

When all of this is considered, the typical first-class belt/holster rig will consist of a heavy 2- to 2½-inch belt, from which is hung on the right side a heavy conventional holster with safety strap, with a knife sheath and slide for spare cartridges on the opposite side. If you will also be carrying a lunch, rope for hanging your deer, meat bags, compass, and perhaps a small bottle of water, it can all be placed in a small belt pack of the type sold for day hiking, attached to the gun belt across your back.

Unusually large and heavy guns, scoped guns, and those fitted with barrels longer than about six inches are difficult to carry in a hip holster. The underarm shoulder holster is ideal for such guns inasmuch as it places the load where it may be carried more comfortably and also places the bulk of the gun where it is less likely to interfere in getting through thick brush and tight spaces. The shoulder holster offers another advantage that you're not likely to notice until the time comes when you have to get down on your belly and make like a snake to get close enough for a clean shot. When you're down like that, crawling through snow or mud or brambles, a belt-holstered gun may well get clogged with dirt or snow, and is sure to impede your progress. In addition, such abusive treatment is certain to ruin at least the appearance of the belt and holster, and may well scar the gun up badly as well. A single belly-crawling stalk across rocky ground can easily ruin both gun and leather; it's happened to me.

Under those conditions, a shoulder holster worn under a jacket provides far more protection to the gun and will not impede the progress of your stalk in the least.

The plain pouch shoulder holster often used to conceal short-barreled guns is not at all suitable for carrying a much larger hunting gun. Too much time and effort is involved in getting the gun into action. But the spring-clip shoulder holster may not always provide adequate security for a large and heavy gun. Violent movement can dislodge the gun from this type of holster unless some added security is provided in the way of a Velcro strip or safety strap. In carrying guns as large as the eight-inch-barreled Auto Mag and 8⅜-inch-barreled S&W Magnum revolvers, I have found the Safariland spring-clip holster fitted with either a snap-fastened safety strap or a Velcro closing strip to be ideal.

Thus far I haven't dwelt much upon the protection a holster must provide for your hunting handgun. It must keep the gun as free from dust, dirt, snow, rain, and the like as possible. The shoulder holster is ideal in this respect, not so much for the protection it provides of itself, but simply because it places the gun in a protected position under your arm where it may also be shielded almost completely by a light jacket. No practical belt holster can provide so high a degree of protection from the elements, impact, and brush.

The typical open-topped belt holster offers virtually no protection for the rear portion of the gun. Some degree of protection can be obtained by wearing a jacket long enough to cover the butt of the gun, but unless it is so closely fitted as to present difficulty in drawing the gun, that protection is rather chancy. The traditional military-style flap holster provides a good deal of protection, but is still substantially open at the rear and to a lesser degree at the front. Under severe conditions, more protection is desirable. This can be provided by simply stuffing a wad of cloth into the two openings. It may look odd, but it won't interfere with getting the gun into action—when the flap is opened, the cloth will either fall away or will be pulled out with the gun and then drop clear.

Probably the ideal form of protective belt holster is the design made for many years for the Luger/Parabellum pistol in military use. It is equipped with a hinged flap closure which has been formed into a sort of cup or overlapping lid that completely encloses the butt of the gun and literally seals the top of the holster. To the best of my knowledge, no holster of this type is manufactured for any of the guns normally used for hunting. However, it is an idea worth pursuing, and if you're prepared to spend the money for a custom-made holster this would be a good design to choose for maximum protection. A clamshell design enclosing the butt entirely would do as well, but those I've seen leave the butt protruding, and are not offered for long, hunting-type guns.

Holsters alone do not meet the handgun hunter's needs for gun protection. At best, they're suitable only for those times when you're afoot in the field and actually hunting. On a typical hunting trip, this will consist of less than a quarter of the time, so better protection should be provided in camp and while traveling. Nothing is superior for this purpose to the rigid plastic, foam-lined cases. Given proper care and chosen to fit the particular gun(s), they'll provide adequate protection even under the abusive handling normally given luggage by airline baggage handlers. Though the closures of these cases are not water tight or entirely dust-proof, they will keep the gun clean and dry through anything less than a severe dust storm or complete submersion. If those hazards worry you, then you can spend a good deal more money for waterproof aluminum Halliburton carrying cases and fit them with foam padding. I know of no finer cases than those bearing the Halliburton name, and with gasketed closures they provide the absolute maximum in protection. However, you can accomplish the same end at far less expense by simply sealing guns inside plastic envelopes and then placing them in conventional rigid padded cases. A bit of moisture or dust may then get into the case, but cannot reach the gun.

# 22

## Tuning Your Own Hunting Handguns for Top Performance

There was a time when one could purchase a new handgun and expect it to give the designed degree of accuracy and reliability. That was probably more true during the 1930s than at any other time within recollection, but it continued to be true to a fair degree until recent years. Personally, I don't recall encountering any particular difficulty with factory-fresh guns until about the late 1950s. Problems began then more or less as a trickle, and by the late '60s and early '70s, one might say that they had become a flood.

The fact is, quality control today is a far cry from what it once was. In any mass-produced item there is certain to be some small percentage of defective parts and assemblies that are not detected until they encounter the hands of the user. It may be that I'm a bit old-fashioned but I believe this percentage should be minute. Very rarely should a new handgun fail to function correctly.

When the success of a hunt that may cost from several hundred to several thousand dollars hangs upon the gun's ability to deliver the goods in a split second, functional reliability and precise accuracy become exceedingly important. You might hunt for two weeks in the mountains of Alaska (at $250 a day) and finally obtain a single shot at a trophy—and if the gun lets you down then, you may not have another chance. Obviously, then, it behooves you to take whatever steps are appropriate to ensure that any hunting handgun will give the degree of reliability and accuracy (especially under field conditions) needed to ensure the success of your hunt.

There are several things you may do to a new gun to achieve this end. The first, and it applies equally to all makes, models, and types of handguns (and, incidentally, to all other firearms as well) is to thoroughly check and "break-in" the gun before taking it afield where a failure might be important. Inspect the gun visually. Are all parts put together the way they should be? Is assembly correct? Do all the controls function correctly—safety, slide stop, cylinder latch, extractor rod, etc.? Are the sights set squarely and in the correct relationship, and are the adjustments on target sights firm and positive, with a minimum of slop and backlash? Can you see roughness or tool marks at critical areas such as the chamber, ratchet, recoil shield, etc.? Next, the gun should be function-fired. This need not be done on a formal range, nor do you even require a target. I usually conduct this type of testing in the back room at my office, firing into a bullet-recovery medium or a bullet trap.

The object of function-firing is to break-in the gun, particularly an autoloader, with the dual purpose of discovering malfunctions that might occur and of eliminating minor malfunctions by the wearing-in process that occurs during the first couple of hundred rounds. It seems strange that individuals who readily recognize the necessity of breaking-in an automobile slowly and methodically while watching for malfunctions will feel that such a process is not necessary for

Extensive break-in shooting will eliminate many malfunctions without any other effort.

handguns. Actually, there are many minor malfunctions that may occur at the beginning of a gun's life which will resolve themselves with a modest amount of shooting. Minor roughness on a part which creates excessive friction, poor seating of rubbing parts, and burrs on the edges of parts will be quickly worn down to an acceptable level by repeated firing. On many occasions, I have taken handguns which contained one or more minor malfunctions and corrected those conditions by doing nothing more than firing 100 to 200 rounds of full-charged cartridges.

The ammunition for this functional testing is not terribly important except that it should be full-charged. Ideally, this testing should include *all* of the different loads (either factory or hand) that will be used in the gun later. Often, though, this can be costly, and many shooters prefer to use the *cheapest* full-charged ammunition available. In many instances, this means military surplus or a discount-store product. Use of this sort of ammunition is acceptable for the first 100 to 150 rounds of test-firing, but the balance should be conducted with the load the gun will be asked to handle in the field. It is not at all uncommon for either a revolver or auto to function perfectly with one make or load and not with another. Consequently, you might very well conclude a perfectly satisfactory functioning test with ball ammunition and then find in the field that the gun malfunctions with the high-performance load you use for hunting. All this can be avoided by proper function-firing beforehand.

If, after firing 200 full-charged cartridges, the gun still produces malfunctions, probably your wisest course of action is to return it to the factory for repair and/or adjustment. Admittedly, this often means the gun will be out of your hands for many months due to the backlog of service and warranty work. You might think it would be simpler in the end either to do the work yourself or have a local gunsmith take over. If you're a competent enough gunsmith to do this work, you can certainly save time—but if your efforts don't cure the problem, they will void the manufacturer's warranty, and it will probably cost you a bundle to correct not only the original defect but any others that your work has introduced.

Your local gunsmith may produce exactly the same problems unless he is *thoroughly competent* in handgun work. Unfortunately, many "gunsmiths" who do adequate or acceptable work with rifles and shotguns simply lack the training and experience to deal with the entirely different mechanisms found in handguns. Probably your best bet for prompt and proper corrections of new-gun malfunction is the nearest authorized *warranty station* of the manufacturer involved. There may or may not be one nearby, but almost inevitably there will be a warranty station much closer than the factory, and warranty stations generally provide much faster service. If you don't know the location and name of the nearest warranty station, any reputable dealer for that make can probably supply the information.

While we are on this subject, the effect of GCA68 (the gun-control law) on repair of your guns should probably be mentioned. Contrary to many stories that are told, you, as the owner of a handgun, may ship that gun intrastate or interstate to any licensed dealer, (holder of a Federal Firearms Dealer's License) gunsmith, or repair shop for legitimate repairs, modifications, or customizing. That shop may then return the gun to you, quite within the law. The law prohibits you from *buying* a gun by mail in interstate commerce, but it does allow you to *ship* a gun for repair (and to receive it back).

Out of pure cussedness, necessity, or convenience, you may elect to rid your own guns of minor malfunctions, and even to improve their functional reliability in the field. To do this requires little in the way of tools, just properly fitted screwdrivers, Arkansas stones and needle files, some punches and a small hammer and perhaps a small bench vise and a place to work. Patience and attention to detail are far more important to success than fancy tools. Even more important is the understanding of the inner complexities of the functional cycle of the gun in question. These capabilities can be obtained by studying exploded-parts views of the gun and at the same time studying the gun right alongside the drawing. If you examine the drawing closely, then relate it to the same parts on the gun, you will soon be able to determine exactly what happens and why. Until you reach that state of familiarity with the gun, don't even think about laying a screwdriver, file, or stone on any part of it.

From here on, there will be various operations put into two categories—revolvers and autoloaders. Since autoloaders are simpler to work on and offer the most potential for improvement, let's look at them first.

AUTOLOADER: Feeding and chambering malfunctions are by far the most common troubles and are almost invariably caused by bent, burred, or otherwise damaged magazine lips. Other magazine problems may also contribute. First, make certain that the follower and spring move throughout their full travel in the magazine body without interference. Do this simply by pressing the follower through its full travel with a pencil or dowel. If it binds at any point, locate that point, and polish or file away the interfering bump or burr. Also make

TOP The two high-performance hunting loads at left are less likely to feed perfectly in autos than the standard ball load at right.

ABOVE A few small Arkansas stones of various shapes are invaluable for smoothing surfaces where no real amount of metal needs to be removed.

certain the full complement of cartridges can pass through the magazine without interference. Follow that by removing all burrs and sharp edges on the feed lips and polishing them smooth. It is best to

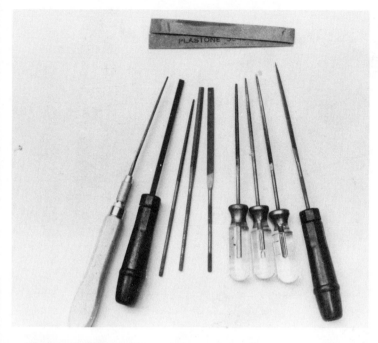

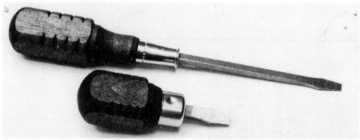

TOP Needle files such as these are the type needed to clean up burrs and rough surfaces.

ABOVE In working on your guns, use short-billed screw drivers that fit just right. Longer ones can slip easily and mar the gun.

do this with a new, unused, and unaltered magazine at hand as a pattern so as to avoid changing the shape and angle of the lips.

If feeding problems persist, and particularly if the cartridge jams

TOP This sophisticated target ramp by Bo-Mar for the GM incorporates an adjustable block that improves accuracy by functioning as a barrel stop.

ABOVE The single-column magazine at left shows how cartridges ride straight into feed lips; the double-column at right shows how cartridges are squeezed inward into a single column for feeding. Note in the double-column magazine that the feed lips have sharp edges, while the edges of the other are smoothly radiused. Sharp edges decrease feeding reliability.

TOP The surface of the breech face should be smooth and free from burrs, and it should provide ample clearance around the case head.

ABOVE The slide, breech face, and extractor hook must be smooth and free enough so that a cartridge may be pressed upward under the extractor without undue force and be held there.

with its nose up and its head down and halfway into the chamber, examine the feed ramp and chamber mouth carefully. You will prob- ably find a sharp edge where the ramp breaks into the lower chamber wall. Very gently polish and radius the area to remove the sharp edge. Don't remove any more metal than is absolutely necessary; just rake over the sharp edge. Also determine whether there is unusual roughness or any overlapping between two parts in the feed ramp. If so, polish smooth and eliminate any ledges or shoulders. At the same time, it's a good idea to very slightly break the sharp edge around the chamber mouth and polish it smooth. Very sharp edges here can—though not often—catch the mouth of an uncrimped case and prevent proper chambering.

If feeding problems still persist, and it appears that the case head is not rising as far as it should into the breech face of the slide, examine that area closely. It may contain burrs, deep tool marks, or a bulge around the firing pin hole. Or the recess into which the case head must enter may be undersized. There may also be a sharp edge or burr on the underside of the extractor claw which is digging into the case rim. If any of those defects are found, very carefully remove them with needle files and Arkansas stones. The face of the breech and of the extractor claw must not present any interference to the smooth movement upward of the case head.

Sometimes feeding malfunctions are the fault of the ammunition rather than the gun. If cartridges tend to bind in the magazine, check carefully to make certain that the cartridges are not excessive in length; this is particularly likely to happen with handloads. If certain case heads appear to be binding at the slide's breech face while other cartridges do not produce this problem, it may be that the case rims are oversized.

Autoloading pistols sometimes experience a malfunction called "short recoil." This occurs when the slide does not travel far enough rearward to throw the fired case from the gun or to pick up a fresh

All undersurfaces of the slide in any auto need to be polished smooth to reduce friction when riding over cartridges in the magazine; note the large number of tool marks still slightly visible, even after extensive polishing.

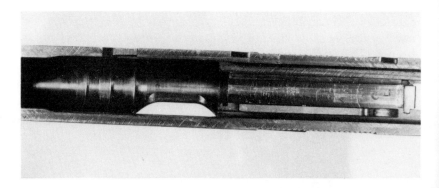

Home accurizing of a .45 auto can produce target results like this.

round from the magazine. Usually the fired case gets caught between the breech face and the barrel breech or gets shoved back into the chamber. Interference or excessive friction will cause this if the gun's at fault, or a too-lightly-loaded cartridge may cause the same problem. Check the fit of the slide to the frame and remove any burrs or excessive roughness. Examine the recoil spring also to make certain that it is not kinking and placing excessive friction on the slide. (A too-strong recoil spring would also cause this problem but is unlikely to be encountered.) Too-tight locking lugs or barrel link or barrel cam may also cause this trouble, jamming the slide in battery and causing too much of the recoil impulse to be utilized to unlock the breech. This will usually be indicated by peening or burrs on the locking surface.

If this occurs, lightly stoning or filing the offending surfaces will eliminate the problem. Short-recoil malfunctions may also be caused by roughness or dirt and fouling in the chamber. These things cause the case to cling more tightly in the chamber; therefore, a greater portion than normal of the recoil impulse is required to extract the case, leaving too little energy to drive the slide fully rearward. When this occurs, polishing the chamber is in order but this is a job not to be undertaken lightly. Without some experience or friendly guidance, it is very easy to make the chamber eccentric or oversized. Polishing can be done with a very fine abrasive cloth wrapped around a dowel and rotated in the chamber at low speed. Do not attempt this with a fast power drill. A less hazardous method of polishing the chamber is to twist a wad of fine, fresh steel wool into an oversized brass-bristle bore brush, to fit tight in the chamber, and spin it in the chamber at low speeds with a portable electric drill. This will take a lot longer but it will usually smooth up the chamber enough to provide reliable functioning without the hazard of spoiling the barrel. Incidentally, this is also an excellent method for cleaning out the very hard powder fouling that sometimes accumulates in the forward part of the chamber with extensive firing. This fouling alone can increase extraction loads to the point that short-recoil malfunctions occur, and at times it is virtually impervious to the usual cleaning methods.

The foregoing will generally ensure functional reliability in most autoloading pistols, but will have no effect on accuracy. If the accuracy of your gun seems to be inadequate, make certain first that both your shooting and ammunition are up to the task. More often than not, complaints of poor accuracy can be traced to one or both of those factors. If you are certain that *gun* accuracy is not up to par there are a few steps you may take to improve it, but to obtain *maximum* accuracy, you will be far better off to have the gun accurized by a specialist.

Obviously, poor sights mean poor accuracy with any gun, regardless of type—a truism demonstrated forcefully by my hog-hunting experience in the Florida palmettos, related in Chapter 20. There's no need to dwell on the subject here, because in earlier chapters I've already stressed that inadequate sights can and should be replaced with high-quality adjustable sights. Assuming you've taken care of that, let's concentrate here on other mechanical parts.

If your autoloader is of the basic Colt/Browning type, as it probably is, accuracy generally will be improved by tightening up the clearances between slide, barrel, and frame. As a first step, I would recommend installation of a "Match Grade" barrel bushing, carefully hand-fitted to minimum clearance in accordance with the manufacturer's instructions. Both Pachmayr and Micro Sight supply this item, as do some other makers.

A second step would be to install a device known as the "Group Gripper," manufactured by Dan Dwyer. This unit replaces the original recoil-spring guide and is equipped with a heavy spring finger acting on a special barrel link which aids in proper vertical positioning of the barrel when the slide is in battery. In addition, it also functions as a recoil buffer. Alternatively, a "long link" may be fitted on Colt guns, replacing the original barrel link with a slightly longer unit which forces the barrel more tightly into the roof of the slide and therefore ensures more consistent vertical positioning. Another device which aids in proper positioning of the barrel breech is the "Accuracy Block" or "Barrel Tuner" offered by Bo-Mar. It attaches to the upper rear surface of the slide by two screws and functions as an adjustable stop to ensure consistent vertical positioning of the barrel. Those constitute the basic add-on accessories that may be installed by the shooter to improve the mechanical accuracy of the gun.

Further accuracy improvements are obtained by tightening the fit of a slide to the frame. This can be accomplished only by very careful hand-fitting and requires some experience and a great deal of care. Essentially, it is accomplished by peening the slide guide ribs on the frame and by squeezing the lower edges of the slide slightly inward. Done *only* to the proper degree, these two operations greatly reduce the play between slide and frame. But if done excessively, they will cause the slide and the frame to bind and can even prevent firing or normal functioning. A great deal of care must be exercised. If you wish to enter this sort of work, it is strongly recommended that you obtain a detailed reference book on the subject. (My own book, *Pistolsmithing*, covers the subject in considerable detail.)

A higher degree of practical accuracy will be obtained if the gun possesses a first-class trigger pull. If it does not, significant improvement is generally beyond the average shooter. It is too easy to ruin the parts in question if you don't have a considerable amount of experience in the field. You'll be well advised to leave trigger-pull improvement to a competent pistolsmith.

Depending on the degree of accuracy your autoloader gives as it comes from the box, the foregoing operations can produce a significant improvement. However, it is difficult to predict the overall effect—one gun may show a 50 percent reduction in group size after this treatment, while another doesn't do nearly as well. You will never be certain of the results until the work is done.

REVOLVERS: Sixguns offer fewer possibilities for tuning than auto-loaders, but this doesn't mean they are any less subject to malfunctions, either when new or during service. Inherently, they are no more reliable than autoloaders. The fewer possibilities for improvement are due to the fact that most revolver malfunctions require the services of a trained gunsmith. They simply are not the easy operations that an untrained individual can apply to an autoloader.

Home remedies can, however, take care of certain cylinder problems. Hard cylinder rotation is usually due to burrs or roughness on the recoil shield, interfering with cartridge-head movement. This can usually be seen in drag marks on the case heads and often occurs only when cylinder rotation is attempted with the muzzle of the gun elevated. Careful stoning of the offending portion of the recoil shield will eliminate the problem. Difficult rotation may also be due to burrs thrown up around the firing-pin hole after extensive firing—and the

The closely fitted and highly stressed internal parts of a revolver aren't meant for home gunsmithing.

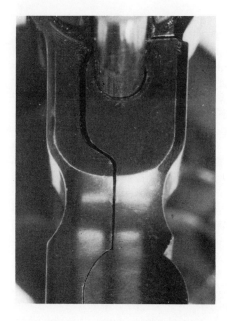

Dirt or burrs can prevent a revolver's crane from seating fully into the frame.

same corrective action is appropriate. In a new gun, difficult rotation may also be due to an incorrect barrel/cylinder gap. Either the gap may be too narrow, causing the front of the cylinder to bind on the barrel breech, or the final filing operation at the factory may have left burrs that drag on the cylinder. In either event, careful filing on the barrel breech is in order (usually with a fine-cut file), regulating the barrel/cylinder gap to a *uniform* width of .006–.008 inch.

Difficulty may be encountered in opening and closing the cylinder. This is generally due to burrs or improper polishing on the center pin of Smith & Wesson revolvers or the locking plunger on a Colt (and, of course, the corresponding parts on other makes). In either case, examine these parts very carefully for roughness that causes interference and remove it by careful polishing. Take care to avoid removing any more metal than is absolutely necessary.

If excessive pressure on the cylinder is required to force it into the frame far enough for the locking system to engage fully, there may be burrs on either the crane or frame which prevent the two from meeting smoothly at the area beneath the barrel. When this occurs, examine the crane seat in the frame and the corresponding surface of the crane very carefully for burrs or ridges which tend to hold the two apart. Sometimes the trouble may even be ridges raised by the stamping of serial numbers in this area. If so, care should be exercised in removing the offending bulges to ensure that the serial number itself is not made illegible. The same problem may also be caused if a piece of foreign material falls between crane and frame during assembly or packaging. In use, any foreign material lodged in this area can cause difficulty in closing and locking the cylinder.

Misfires in S&W revolvers may be due to loosening of the mainspring strain screw at the lower end of the front strap; simply tightening the screw by turning it into the frame will usually cure the problem.

If a revolver "spits lead"—that is, throws off lead particles from the barrel/cylinder gap, it is "out of time" and this should be corrected only by a competent gunsmith.

Difficult extraction is often encountered in new revolvers with high-performance ammunition. While this may sometimes be due to soft cartridge cases, it is more often the result of rough or improperly polished chambers. This can be corrected as described above for the chamber of an autoloader but again you are cautioned to be extremely careful to avoid damaging the chambers. For that matter, care is the key to success in all of the operations I've covered here, and it will pay off by giving you a better-shooting gun, whether your sidearm is a revolver or an autoloader.

Now let me stress one last time that more complex improvements or repairs should be left to a professional gunsmith who has the best equipment and experience to handle sophisticated problems. I've noticed that some gunsmiths become irritable with age, treating all but their most respected customers with the tenderness of a somewhat antagonized grizzly, and I wonder if the problem isn't a sense of frustration after years of repairing customers' mistakes.

But if you work slowly and carefully and with the proper tools, you can accomplish the kind of basic tuning I've described here without committing any gunsmith-enraging blunders. Apart from saving a little money by doing these things yourself instead of paying to have them done, there's a special satisfaction to be sought. It's the satisfaction you feel when your gun has performed well because *you've* performed well—in your home workshop, on the range, and finally in the field where it really counts when the sights come up against your game after a long, hard hunt.

# Appendix

## APPENDIX 1

### Case Capacity

Case capacities in a given cartridge vary slightly from manufacturer to manufacturer. Sometimes it is even possible to detect differences between lots from a single manufacturer. Assuming the cases are new, undamaged, unaltered in any way, and without defects, the differences are too small to be significant. The following listing shows average capacities, calculated from several lots of ammunition supplied by Winchester, Remington, and other manufacturers.

| CALIBER | Average net capacity (grs., water) to base of case neck |
|---|---|
| .22 Rem.-Jet | 16.9 |
| .221 Rem. Fireball | 20.8 |
| .256 Win. | 19.0 |

| CALIBER | Average net capacity (grs., water) to base of case neck |
|---|---|
| .32 S&W | 3.3 |
| .32 S&W Long | 9.5 |
| .32–20 Win. | 15.3 |
| .38 S&W | 7.0 |
| .380 Auto | 6.0 |
| 9mm Luger | 8.7 |
| .38 Super Auto | 10.7 |
| .38 Special | 11.7 |
| .357 Magnum | 15.2 |
| .41 Rem. Magnum | 21.0 |
| .44 S&W Russian | 18.8 |
| .44 S&W Special | 20.5 |
| .44 Rem. Magnum | 25.2 |
| .45 Auto Rim | 13.3 |
| .45 ACP | 13.9 |
| .45 Colt | 30.3 |

# APPENDIX 2

## Energy/Velocity Table

The following is a table for determining the kinetic energy of any bullet at any practical velocity. All you need to know is the bullet's weight and its velocity. Finding the energy then takes only a few seconds and should eliminate arguments about which cartridge or load "shoots the hardest."

Refer to the left-hand column and locate the velocity; then move to the immediate right and locate the energy value per grain of bullet weight. This is the energy possessed by each grain of weight of any bullet traveling at that velocity. Then, simply multiply the energy value by the weight of your bullet in grains to obtain the total kinetic energy of the bullet moving at that velocity.

# ENERGIES OF BULLETS

| Velocity in fps | Energy | Velocity in fps | Energy | Velocity in fps | Energy | Velocity in fps | Energy |
|---|---|---|---|---|---|---|---|
| 600 | .80 | 1010 | 2.26 | 1420 | 4.47 | 1830 | 7.43 |
| 610 | .82 | 1020 | 2.31 | 1430 | 4.54 | 1840 | 7.51 |
| 620 | .85 | 1030 | 2.35 | 1440 | 4.60 | 1850 | 7.60 |
| 630 | .88 | 1040 | 2.40 | 1450 | 4.66 | 1860 | 7.68 |
| 640 | .91 | 1050 | 2.45 | 1460 | 4.73 | 1870 | 7.76 |
| 650 | .94 | 1060 | 2.49 | 1470 | 4.79 | 1880 | 7.84 |
| 660 | .96 | 1070 | 2.54 | 1480 | 4.86 | 1890 | 7.94 |
| 670 | .99 | 1080 | 2.59 | 1490 | 4.93 | 1900 | 8.01 |
| 680 | 1.02 | 1090 | 2.63 | 1500 | 5.00 | 1910 | 8.10 |
| 690 | 1.05 | 1100 | 2.68 | 1510 | 5.06 | 1920 | 8.18 |
| 700 | 1.08 | 1110 | 2.73 | 1520 | 5.13 | 1930 | 8.37 |
| 710 | 1.11 | 1120 | 2.78 | 1530 | 5.19 | 1940 | 8.35 |
| 720 | 1.15 | 1130 | 2.83 | 1540 | 5.26 | 1950 | 8.44 |
| 730 | 1.18 | 1140 | 2.88 | 1550 | 5.33 | 1960 | 8.53 |
| 740 | 1.21 | 1150 | 2.93 | 1560 | 5.40 | 1970 | 8.61 |
| 750 | 1.24 | 1160 | 2.99 | 1570 | 5.47 | 1980 | 8.70 |
| 760 | 1.28 | 1170 | 3.04 | 1580 | 5.54 | 1990 | 8.79 |
| 770 | 1.31 | 1180 | 3.09 | 1590 | 5.61 | 2000 | 8.88 |
| 780 | 1.34 | 1190 | 3.14 | 1600 | 5.68 | 2010 | 8.97 |
| 790 | 1.38 | 1200 | 3.19 | 1610 | 5.75 | 2020 | 9.06 |
| 800 | 1.42 | 1210 | 3.25 | 1620 | 5.82 | 2030 | 9.15 |
| 810 | 1.45 | 1220 | 3.30 | 1630 | 5.90 | 2040 | 9.24 |
| 820 | 1.49 | 1230 | 3.36 | 1640 | 5.97 | 2050 | 9.33 |
| 830 | 1.53 | 1240 | 3.41 | 1650 | 6.04 | 2060 | 9.42 |
| 840 | 1.56 | 1250 | 3.47 | 1660 | 6.12 | 2070 | 9.50 |
| 850 | 1.60 | 1260 | 3.52 | 1670 | 6.19 | 2080 | 9.60 |
| 860 | 1.64 | 1270 | 3.58 | 1680 | 6.26 | 2090 | 9.70 |
| 870 | 1.68 | 1280 | 3.63 | 1690 | 6.34 | 2100 | 9.80 |
| 880 | 1.72 | 1290 | 3.69 | 1700 | 6.41 | | |
| 890 | 1.76 | 1300 | 3.75 | 1710 | 6.49 | | |
| 900 | 1.79 | 1310 | 3.81 | 1720 | 6.57 | | |
| 910 | 1.83 | 1320 | 3.86 | 1730 | 6.64 | | |
| 920 | 1.87 | 1330 | 3.92 | 1740 | 6.72 | | |
| 930 | 1.92 | 1340 | 3.98 | 1750 | 6.80 | | |
| 940 | 1.96 | 1350 | 4.04 | 1760 | 6.88 | | |
| 950 | 2.00 | 1360 | 4.10 | 1770 | 6.95 | | |
| 960 | 2.04 | 1370 | 4.16 | 1780 | 7.03 | | |
| 970 | 2.08 | 1380 | 4.22 | 1790 | 7.11 | | |
| 980 | 2.13 | 1390 | 4.29 | 1800 | 7.19 | | |
| 990 | 2.17 | 1400 | 4.35 | 1810 | 7.27 | | |
| 1000 | 2.22 | 1410 | 4.41 | 1820 | 7.35 | | |

X bullet weight in grains

# APPENDIX 3

## Cartridge Interchangeability Table

Cartridge interchangeability is limited. Among rimfires, for example, .22 CB and BB Caps, .22 Shorts, or .22 Longs can be used in Long Rifle Chambers, but they will not cycle an auto designed for the .22 LR.

More important in terms of safety as well as functioning, there is often only "one-way" interchangeability. That is, a chamber made for "Caliber A" (let's say the .44 Magnum) can be used with cartridges of "Caliber B" (let's say the .44 Special) but "Caliber A" *cartridges* must not be used in a "Caliber B" *chamber.* In the listing below, the calibers listed at the left represent chamberings that will also handle the cartridges listed at the right, but *the reverse is not always true.* In some instances, a listing at the right is merely an alternative designation of the very same cartridge listed at the left. In other instances, the cartridges differ in dimensions and/or power, and a chamber for a caliber listed at the right may not accommodate a cartridge in the caliber listed at the left, or may be unsafe with such a cartridge. Another example: A .357 Magnum chamber will handle the .38 Long Colt or .38 Special, but a .357 Magnum cartridge must *not* be used in a gun chambered only for the .38 Long Colt or .38 Special. (As a rule, it wouldn't go into the chamber; some of the older .38 Long Colt guns will accept a .357 Magnum cartridge but would be very dangerous to fire with such a load.)

.22 LR—.22 CB & BB Cap, .22 Short & Long
.22 WRFM—.22 WRF (.22 Special)
.25 ACP—6.35mm Auto Pistol
.30 Luger—7.65mm Parabellum
.30 Mauser—7.63mm Mauser
.32 ACP—7.65mm Auto Pistol
.32 S&W Long—.32 S&W Short, .32 Colt Short & Long
.357 Magnum—.38 Long Colt, .38 Special
.38 S&W—.38 Colt, .38 New Police
.38 Special—.38 Long Colt
9mm Luger—9mm Parabellum
.44 Special—.44 Russian
.44 Magnum—.44 Russian, .44 Special
.45 Colt—.45 S&W

# APPENDIX 4

## *Useful Reading*

### BOOKS

*Pistolsmithing,* G. C. Nonte (Stackpole)
*Pistol & Revolver Guide,* G. C. Nonte (Stoeger)
*Gunsmith Kinks,* Bob Brownell (Brownell's)
*Hobby Gunsmithing,* Ralph Walker (Digest Books)
*Modern Handloading,* G. C. Nonte (Winchester Press)
*NRA Handgun Assembly* (National Rifle Association)
*Small Arms of the World,* W. H. B. Smith & Joseph E. Smith (Stackpole)
*Sixguns,* Elmer Keith (out of print)
*Book of Pistols & Revolvers,* W. H. B. Smith (Stackpole)
*Pistols, A Modern Encyclopedia,* Henry H. Stebbins (Stackpole)
*Firearms & Ammunition Factbook* (National Rifle Association)
*North American Big Game Hunting,* Byron W. Dalrymple (Winchester Press)
*Hunting America's Game Animals & Birds,* edited by Robert Elman & George Peper (Winchester Press)
*Cartridges of the World,* Frank C. Barnes, edited by John T. Amber (Digest Books)
*Centerfire Pistol & Revolver Cartridges,* H. P. White & B. D. Munhall (A. S. Barnes)

### PERIODICALS

*Gun Digest,* annual (Digest Books)
*Shooter's Bible,* annual (Stoeger)
*American Hunter,* monthly (NRA)
*American Rifleman,* monthly (NRA)
*Guns,* monthly
*Guns & Ammo,* monthly
*Gun World,* monthly
*Shooting Times,* monthly
*Handloader,* bi-monthly

# APPENDIX 5

## Directory of Supplies & Services

### AMMUNITION (Commercial)

Federal Cartridge Co., 2700 Foshay Tower, Minneapolis, Minn. 55402
Micro Shooter's Supply, Box 213, Las Cruces, N.M. 88001
Peters Cartridge Div., Bridgeport, Conn. 06602
Remington Arms Co., Bridgeport, Conn. 06602
Weatherby's, 2781 E. Firestone Blvd., South Gate, Calif. 90280
Winchester-Western, East Alton, Ill. 62024

### AMMUNITION (Custom)

Andy's Reloading Service, Box 115, Wilmot, Wis. 53192
Blackhawk Small Arms Ammo, 616 Kingsley Dr., Rockford, Ill. 61111
Russell Campbell, 219 Leisure Dr., San Antonio, Tex. 78201
Drumm's Handloads, 410 Belden Ave., San Antonio, Tex. 78214
J&J Ammo, Box 2202, Memphis, Tenn. 38102
Maryland Reloading Service, 6835 Beaver Dam Rd., Beltsville, Md. 20705
Merrill Reloading Service, Box 249, Libertyville, Ill. 60048
Moody's Reloading Service, 2108 Broadway, Helena, Mont. 59601
Robert Pomeroy, Morison Ave., Corinth, Me. 04427
Reloading Service, Midland Ave., Washington, N.J. 07882
Shooting Assoc., Inc., 63 Parkwood Blvd., Poughkeepsie, N.Y.
Tri-Test Munitions Co., 075 Oak St., Mundelein, Ill. 60060

### AMMUNITION (Foreign)

Abercrombie & Fitch, Madison at 45th St., New York, N.Y. 10017
Canadian Ind. Ltd. (C.I.L.), Box 10, Montreal, Que., Canada Jov 140
Marshall Hyde, Inc., Port Huron, Mich. 48060
S. E. Laszlo, 200 Tillary, Brooklyn, N.Y. 11201
NORMA-Precision, South Lansing, N.Y. 14882
Oregon Ammo Service, Box 19341, Portland, Ore. 97219

Stoeger Arms Corp., 55 Ruta Ct., So. Hackensack, N.J. 07606
James C. Tillinghast, Box 565, Marlow, N.H. 03456

## CLEANING & REFINISHING SUPPLIES

Clenzoil Co., Box 1226, Sta. C., Canton, Ohio 44708
Forty-Five Ranch Enterpr., 119 S. Main St., Miami, Okla. 74354
Gun-All Products, Box 244, Dowagiac, Mich. 49047
Frank C. Hoppe, P.O. Box 97, Parkersburg, Pa. 19365
Jet-Aer Corp., 100 Sixth Ave., Paterson, N.J. 07524
Lehigh Chem. Co., Box 5197, Chestertown, Md. 21620
Mint Luster Cleaners, 602 W. Atlantic St., Appleton, Wis. 54912
Outers Laboratories, Box 37, Onalaska, Wis. 54650
Stoeger Arms Corp., 55 Ruta Court, So. Hackensack, N.J. 07606

## COMPONENTS—BULLETS, POWDER, PRIMERS

Accuracy Bullet Co., 2443 41st St., San Francisco, Calif. 94116
DuPont, Explosives Dept., Wilmington, Del. 19898
Green Bay Bullets, 223 No. Ashland, Green Bay, Wis. 54303
Frank A. Hensted, 7272 Valaho Dr., Tajunga, Calif. 91042
Hercules Powder Co., 910 Market St., Wilmington, Del. 19899
Herter's Inc., RR1, Waseca, Minn. 56093
B. E. Hodgdon, Inc., 7710 W. 50th Hwy., Shawnee Mission, Kans. 66202
Hornady Mfg. Co., Box 906, Grand Island, Neb. 68801
D. B. Hufnail, Town Line Rd., Rutland, Vt. 05701
Lyman Gun Sight Corp., Middlefield, Conn. 06455
Markell, Inc., 4115 Judah St., San Francisco, Calif. 94112
NORMA-Precision, So. Lansing, N.Y. 14882
Northridge Bullet Co., 9025 Parthenia, Northridge, Calif. 91324
Oregon Ammo Service, Box 7031, Portland, Ore. 97219
Robert Pomeroy, Morison Ave., Corinth, Me. 04427
Remington-Peters, Bridgeport, Conn. 06602
Shur-X-Bullet Co., 1493 Dewey Ave., Rochester, N.Y. 14615
Speer Products, Inc., Box 244, Lewiston, Ida. 83501
Winchester-Western, New Haven, Conn. 06504

## GUN CASES, CABINETS, AND RACKS

Amer. Safety Gun Case Co., Holland, Mich. 49424
Browning Arms, Rt. 4, Box 624-B, Arnold, Mo. 63010

Coladonato Bros., Box 156, Hazleton, Pa. 18201
Protecto Plastics, Inc., 201 Alpha Rd., Wind Gap, Pa. 18091
SAF-T-CASE, 2610 Overland Dr., Dallas, Tex. 75234


## HANDGUN PARTS, ANTIQUE

Philip R. Crouthamel, 817 E. Baltimore, E. Lansdowne, Pa. 19050
Dixie Gun Works, Inc., Hwy 51, South, Union City, Tenn. 38261
Greeley Arms Co., Inc., 448 Pompton, Cedar Grove, N.J. 07009
Hudson Sporting Goods Co., 52 Warren St., New York, N.Y. 10007
Bob Lovell, Box 401, Elmhurst, Ill. 60128
Numrich Arms Co., West Hurley, N.Y. 12491
Sarco, Inc., 192 Central, Stirling, N.J. 07980
N. F. Strebe, 4926 Marlboro Pike, S.E., Washington, D.C. 20027
Tilden Mfg. Co., 607 Santa Fe Dr., Denver, Colo. 80204
C. H. Weisz, Box 311-D, Arlington, Va. 22210


## HANDGUNS (Foreign)

Browning Arms Co., Rt. 4, Box 624-B, Arnold, Mo. 63010
Centennial Arms Corp., 3318 W. Devon, Chicago, Ill. 60645
Century Arms Co., 3–5 Federal St., St. Albans, Vt. 05478
Continental Arms Corp., 697 Fifth Ave., New York, N.Y. 10022
Dixie Gun Works, Inc., Hwy 51, South, Tenn. 38261
Firearms Intl. Corp., 515 Kerby Hill Rd., Washington, D.C. 20022
J. L. Galef & Son, Inc., 85 Chambers, New York, N.Y. 10007
H. F. Grieder, Box 487, Knoxville, Ill. 61448
Intercontinental Arms, 2222 Barry Ave., Los Angeles, Calif. 90064
International Firearms Co., Ltd., Montreal 1, Que., Canada
Mars Equipment Corp., 3318 W. Devon, Chicago, Ill. 60645
Replica Arms Co., Box 640, Marietta, Ohio 45740
Stoeger Arms Corp., 55 Ruta Ct., So. Hackensack, N.J. 07606


## HANDGUNS, (U.S.-made)

Charter Arms Corp., 430 Sniffens Ln., Stratford, Conn. 06477
Chicago Derringer Corp., Box 54, Bensenville, Ill. 60106
Colt, 150 Huyshope Ave., Hartford, Conn. 06106
Firearms Intl. Corp., 515 Kerby Hill Rd., Washington, D.C. 20022
Harrington & Richardson, Industrial Row, Gardner, Mass. 01440
High Standard Mfg. Co., 1811 Dixwell Ave., Hamden, Conn. 06514

Iver Johnson Arms & Cycle Works, Fitchburg, Mass. 01420
Numrich Arms Corp., W. Hurley, N.Y. 12491
Remington Arms Co., Bridgeport, Conn. 06602
Savage Arms Corp., Westfield, Mass. 01085
Smith & Wesson, Inc., 2100 Roosevelt Ave., Springfield, Mass. 01101
Sturm, Ruger & Co., Southport, Conn. 06490
Tingle, 1125 Smithland Pike, Shelbyville, Ind. 46176
Universal Firearms Corp., 3746 E. 10th Ct., Hialeah, Fla. 33013


## GUNSMITH SUPPLIES, TOOLS, SERVICES

Atlas Arms, Inc., 2704 N. Central, Chicago, Ill. 60639
Bob Brownell's, Main & Third, Montezuma, Iowa 50171
B-Square Co., Box 11281, Ft. Worth, Tex. 76110
Christy Gun Works, 875–57th St., Sacramento, Calif. 95831
Clymer Grinding Co., 14241 W. 11 Mile Rd., Oak Park, Mich. 48237
Dremel Mfg. Co., 4915-21 St., Racine, Wis. 53406
F. K. Elliott, Box 785, Ramona, Calif. 92056
Forster Products, Inc., 82 E. Lanark Ave., Lanark, Ill. 61046
Keith Francis, 8515 Wagner Creek Rd., Talent, Ore. 97540
Grace Metal Prod., 115 Ames St., Elk Rapids, Mich. 49629
H. & M., 24062 Orchard Lake Rd., Farmington, Mich. 48024
Palmgren, 8383 South Chicago Ave., Chicago, Ill. 60167
Redford Reamer Co., Box 40604, Detroit, Mich. 48240
Twin City Steel Treating Co., Inc., 1114 S. 3rd, Minneapolis, Minn. 55415
Wilson Arms Co., 63 Leetes Island Rd., Branford, Conn. 06405


## HANDGUN ACCESSORIES

Arm-A-Lok, 2884 Colorado Ave., Santa Monica, Calif. 95004
B. L. Broadway, Rte. 1, Box 381, Alpine, Calif. 92001
Case Master, 4675 E. 10 Ave., Maimi, Fla. 33013
Central Specialties Co., 6030 Northwest Hwy., Chicago, Ill. 60631
John Dangelzer, 3056 Frontier Pl., N.E., Albuquerque, N.M. 87106
R. S. Frielich, 396 Broome St., New York, N.Y. 10013
Joe F. Frye, Box 2202, Memphis, Tenn. 38102
Hunt Eng., 264 Coronado, Long Beach, Calif. 90803
R. G. Jensen, 16153½ Parthenia, Sepulveda, Calif. 91343
Pachmayr, 1220 S. Grand, Los Angeles, Calif. 90015
Jules Reiver, 4104 Market St., Wilmington, Del. 19899
Sportsmen's Equipment Co., 415 W. Washington, San Diego, Calif. 92103
M. Tyler, 1326 W. Britton, Oklahoma City, Okla. 73114

## HANDGUN STOCKS

Fitz, Box 49697, Los Angeles, Calif. 90049
Herret's, Box 741, Twin Falls, Ida. 83301
Marty Lihl, 760 Ravenhill Pl., Ridgefield, N.J. 07657
Mershon Co., Inc., 1230 S. Grand Ave., Los Angeles, Calif. 90015
Mustang Grips, 28030 Del Rio Rd., Temecula, Calif. 92390
Safety Grip Corp., Box 456, Riverside Sta., Miami, Fla. 33135
Sanderson Custom Pistol Stocks, 17695 Fenton, Detroit, Mich. 42819
Jay Scott, 81 Sherman Pl., Garfield, N.J. 07026

## HOLSTERS & LEATHER GOODS

Berns-Martin, Box 250, Elberton, Ga. 30635
Bianchi Holster Co., 100 Calle Cortez, Temecula, Calif. 92390
Edward H. Bohlin, 931 N. Highland Ave., Hollywood, Calif. 90038
Boyt Co., Box 1108, Iowa Falls, Iowa 50126
Brauer Bros. Mfg. Co., 817 N. 17th, St. Louis, Mo. 63106
Browning, Rt. 4, Box 624-B, Arnold, Mo. 63010
J. M. Bucheimer Co., Frederick, Md. 21701
Colt's, 150 Huyshope Ave., Hartford, Conn. 06106
Don Hume, Box 351, Miami, Okla. 74354
Kolpin Bros. Co., Inc., 121 S. Pearl St., Berlin, Wis. 54923
George Lawrence Co., 306 S.W. First Ave., Portland, Ore. 97204
Lewis Police Equip. Co., 1321 Sunset Blvd., Los Angeles, Calif. 90026
W. T. Moyers, 1510 Carlisle, N.E., Albuquerque, N.M. 87110
S. D. Myres Saddle Co., Box 9776, El Paso, Tex. 79988
Safariland Leather Products, 1941 Walker Ave., Monrovia, Calif. 91016

## SIGHTS

Bo-Mar Tool & Mfg. Co., Box 168, Carthage, Tex. 79633
Christy Gun Works, 875-57th St., Sacramento, Calif. 95831
George Elliason, 2109 Carroll Pl., Tampa, Fla. 33618
Firearms Dev. Lab., 360 Mt. Ida Rd., Oroville, Calif. 95965
Micro Sight Co., 242 Harbor Blvd., Belmont, Calif. 94002
Original Sight Exchange Co., Box J, Paoli, Pa. 19301

## MISCELLANEOUS

Bore Collimator, Alley Supply Co., Box 458, Sonora, Calif. 95370
Bore Lamp, Spacetron, Inc., Box 84, Broadview, Ill. 60155
Borescope, Eder Inst. Co, 2293 N. Clybourn, Chicago, Ill. 60614
Breech Plug Wrench, Swaine Machine, 195 O'Connell, Providence, R.I. 02905
Bullet Trap, Sterling-Fleischman, Inc., Penna. Ave., Malvern, Pa. 19355
Cartridge Box Labels, Milton Brynin, Box 162, Fleetwood, Mt. Vernon, N.Y. 10552
Chronograph, Avtron, 10409 Meech, Cleveland, Ohio 44105
Chronograph, Chrondek Electronics, Inc., 2125 D. St., La Verne, Calif., 91750
Chronograph, Hollywood Gun Shop, 6116 Hollywood Blvd., Hollywood, Calif. 90028
Chronograph, ITCC, 4117 Sherman, Riverside, Calif. 92503
Color Hardening, L.D. Machamer, 1903 Sherman, Coeur d'Alene, Ida. 83814
Custom Bluing, Stoeger Arms Corp., 55 Ruta Court, So. Hackensack N.J. 07606
Dry Firing Aid, Pitman Industries, Box 325, Pitman, N.J. 08071
Ear-Valv, Sigma Eng. Co., 11320 Burbank Ave., N. Hollywood, Calif. 91601
Firearm Ident. Service, H. P. White Co., Box 331, Bel Air, Md. 21014
Gas Pistol, Penguin Ind., Inc., Box 97, Parkesburg, Pa., 19365
Handgun Cartridge Holder, Arma, Inc., 300 High St., Hartford, Conn. 06103
Hearing Protector, American Optical Co., Southbridge, Mass. 01550
Hearing Protector, David Clark Co., 3600 Franklin St., Worcester, Mass. 01604
Miniature Guns, C. H. Stoppler, 1426 Walton Ave., N.Y., N.Y. 10452
Nipple Wrenches, Chopie Tool & Die Co., 531 Copeland Ave., La Crosse, Wis. 54601
NRA Targets, Stoeger Arms Corp., 55 Ruta Court, So. Hackensack, N.J. 07606
Optical Attach., Three V Prod., 3007 Rochester St., Arlington, Va. 22213
Powder Flasks, Jewell Powder Flask Co., Central Ave., E. Bangor, Pa. 18013
Shooting Glasses, M. B. Dinsmore, Box 21, Wyomissing, Reading, Pa. 19610
Shooting Glasses, Mitchell's, Box 539, Waynesville, Mo. 65583
Target Holder, Product Masters Mfg. Co., 5013 Aldrich Ave., Minneapolis, Minn. 55430
Target Patches, Time Products Co., 355 Burlington Rd., Riverside, Ill. 60546
Trigger Shoe, Pacific Gun Sight Co., Box 4495, Lincoln, Neb. 68504
Trigger Shoe, Melvin Tyler, 1324 W. Britton, Oklahoma City, Okla. 73114

## PISTOLSMITHS

Alamo Heat Treating, Box 55345, Houston, Tex. 77018
Behlert & Freed, Inc., 33 Herning Ave., Cranford, N.J. 07016
F. Bob Chow, Gun Shop, 3185 Mission, San Francisco, Calif. 94110
J. E. Clark, Rte. 2, Box 22A, Keithville, La. 71047
Custom Gunshop, 33 Herning Ave., Cranford, N.J. 07016
Alton S. Dinan, Jr., P.O. Box 6674, Canaan, Conn. 06018
DyBro Products, 5 W. Webster, Marshalltown, Iowa 50158
George Elliason, 2109 Carroll Pl., Tampa, Fla. 33618
Giles' 45 Shop, Rt. 1, Box 47, Odessa, Fla. 33556
Gil Hebard Guns, Box 1, Knoxville, Ill. 61448
Larry S. Krause, 5628 Winchester, Chicago, Ill. 60635
Rudy Marent, 9711 Tiltree, Houston, Tex. 77034
Modern Gun Craft, 18 Charles St., E. Norwalk, Conn. 06855
Pachmayr Gun Works, 1220 S. Grand Ave., Los Angeles, Calif. 90015
R. L. Shockey, 1614 S. Choctaw, E. Reno, Okla. 73036

## RELOADING TOOLS AND ACCESSORIES

Bonanza Sports, Inc., 412 Western Ave., Faribault, Minn. 55021
C-H Die Co., Box L, Owen, Wis. 54460
Division Lead Co., 7742 W. 61st Pl., Summit, Ill. 60502
Flambeau Plastics, 801 Lynn, Baraboo, Wis. 53913
Forster Products, Inc., 82 E. Lanark Ave., Lanark, Ill. 61046
H & H Sealants, Box 448, Saugerties, N.Y. 12477
Frank A. Hensted, 7272 Valaho Dr., Tajunga, Calif. 91042
Hensley & Gibbs, Box 10, Murphy, Ore. 97533
Herter's, Inc., RR1, Waseca, Minn. 56093
Lachmiller Eng. Co., 11273 Goss St., Sun Valley, Calif. 91352
Lee Engineering, 46 E. Jackson, Hartford, Wis. 53027
Lyman Gun Sight Corp., Middlefield, Conn. 06455
Micro-Precision, Box 1422, Omaha, Neb. 68101
Potter Eng. Co., 1410 Santa Ana Dr., Dunedin, Fla. 33528
RCBS, Inc., Box 1919, Oroville, Calif. 95965
Redco, Box 15523, Salt Lake City, Utah 84115
Redding-Hunter, Inc., 114 Starr Rd., Cortland, N.Y. 13045
Rotex Mfg. Co., P.O. Box 5355, Dallas, Tex. 75222
SAECO, P.O. Box 778, Carpinteria, Calif. 93013
Savage Arms Co., Westfield, Mass. 01085

# Index